Word for Windows® 95 Clear & Simple™

Clear & Simple™ *Computer Books*

● easy to follow ● jargon free ● practical ● task based ● easy steps

Thousands of people have already discovered that the **Clear & Simple** series gives them what they want ***fast!*** These are the books for you if you want to **learn quickly what's essential** and **how** to do things with a particular piece of software. If you:

- Need to produce letters, memos, reports, and other documents
- Want to get the job done quickly and efficiently
- Need a self-teaching approach
- Want results fast

for **clarity** and **simplicity**, **Clear & Simple** Computer Books stand above all others.

This **best selling** series is in your **local bookstore now**, or in case of difficulty, contact:

> Manager of Special Sales, Butterworth–Heinemann, 313 Washington Street, Newton, MA 02158-1626 Tel: (617) 928-2500

Series titles:

Excel for Windows 95	**Stephen Morris**	**0 7506 9802 0**
Word for Windows 95	**Keith Brindley**	**0 7506 9803 9**
The Internet for Windows® 95	**P.K McBride**	**0 7506 9801 2**
Windows 95	**P.K McBride**	**0 7506 9800 4**

Word for Windows® 95 Clear & Simple™

Keith Brindley

Butterworth-Heinemann
Boston • Oxford • Johannesburg • Melbourne • New Delhi • Singapore

Butterworth-Heinemann is a member of the Reed Elsevier group.

Recognizing the importance of preserving what has been written, Butterworth-Heinemann prints its books on acid-free paper whenever possible.

Library of Congress Catalog Card Number: 96–83476

ISBN: 0–7506–9803–9

The publisher offers special discounts on bulk orders of this book.
For information, please contact:
Manager of Special Sales
Butterworth–Heinemann
313 Washington Street
Newton, MA 02158–1626
Tel: 617-928-2500
Fax: 617-928-2620

For information on all Clear & Simple publications available, contact our World Wide Web home page at: http://www.bh.com/bh/

10 9 8 7 6 5 4 3 2 1

Printed in the United States of America

Designed and typeset by Co-publications
Archetype, Bash Casual, Cotswold, and Gravity fonts from Advanced Graphics Limited
All screenshots taken with Screen Thief for Windows from Nildram Software
(info@nildram.co.uk)
Icons designed by Sara Ward © 1994

Contents

Preface ix

1 The basics

Starting up 2
Word menus 4
Help me, I'm drowning! 6
Help – I'm not so Perfect! 11
Toolbars 12
Buttons 15
Normal view 16
Page layout view 17
Outline view 18
Full screen view 19
Zooming 20
Saving a document 21
Opening documents 22
Creating new documents 23
Good-bye – or just au revoir? 25
Summary for Section 1 26

2 Text essentials

Entering text 28
Editing text 30

Contents (contd)

Selecting text 32
Ooops – a mistake! 36
Cut, copy, and paste 38
Drag-and-drop editing 40
Entering symbols 42
Summary for Section 2 44

3 Formatting text

About formatting 46
Character formats 48
Painting a format 53
Paragraph formats 54
Tabs 60
Simple tables 62
More about tabs 64
Borders and shading 66
Summary for Section 3 72

4 Sections and pages

About sections 74
Setting up a document 76
Margins 77

Headers and footers 80
Line numbers 84
Columns 86
Summary for Section 4 90

5 Text control

Finding text 92
Replacing 94
Spelling 96
AutoCorrect 100
AutoText 102
Outlining 104
Tables 108
Table conversions 111
Table formatting 112
Counting your words 113
Graphics 114
Summary for Section 5 116

6 Automatic formatting

Styles 118
Character and paragraph styles 121

Contents (contd)

Creating styles 122
More about styles 128
About templates 132
Creating a template 134
Summary for Section 6 136

7 Technical thingamajigs

Print preview 138
Printing 140
Print options 141
Starting Word at turn-on 142
Shortcut keys 144
Toolbars 146
Summary for Section 7 148

Index 149

Preface

The computer is about as simple as a spacecraft, and who ever let an untrained spaceman loose? You pick up a manual that weighs more than your birth-weight, open it and find it's written in computerspeak. You see messages on the screen resembling some strange spy code and the thing even makes noises. No wonder you feel it's your lucky day if everything goes right. What do you do if everything goes wrong? Give up.

Training helps. Being able to type helps. Experience helps. This book helps, by providing training and assisting with experience. It can't help you if you always manage to hit the wrong keys, but it *can* tell you which are the right ones and what to do when you hit the wrong ones. After some time, even the dreaded manual will start to make sense, just because you at last know what the writers are wittering on about.

Computing is not black magic. You don't need luck or charms, just a bit of understanding. The problem is that the programs used nowadays *look* simple — but simply aren't. Most are crammed with features you don't need — but how do you know what you don't need? This book shows you what is essential and guides you through it. You will know how to make an action work and why. Less essential bits can wait — and once you start to use a program with confidence you can tackle those bits for yourself.

The writers of this series have all been through it. We know time is valuable, and you don't want to waste it. You don't buy books on computer topics to read jokes or be told you are a dummy. You want to find what you need — and be shown how to do it. Here, at last, you can.

1 The basics

Starting up 2
Word menus 4
Help me, I'm drowning! 6
Help – I'm not so Perfect! 11
Toolbars 12
Buttons 15
Normal view 16
Page layout view 17
Outline view 18
Full screen view 19
Zooming 20
Saving a document 21
Opening documents 22
Creating new documents 23
Good-bye – or just au revoir? 25
Summary for Section 1 26

Starting up

The first operation you ever do when using Word is to start it up. The easiest method of doing this, of course, is from the Windows 95 **Start** button. Click the **Start** button, then access the sub-menu you need (probably the **Programs** sub-menu, or the **MSOffice** sub-menu within it — depending on how your computer is set up, and Word has been installed) to locate and click the **Microsoft Word** program.

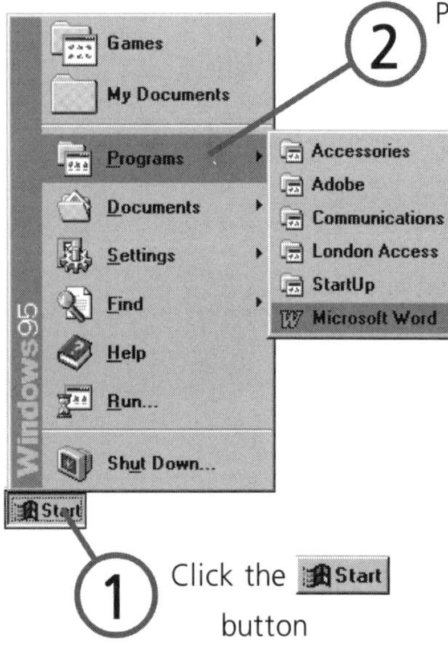
Games
My Documents
Programs
Documents
Settings
Find
Help
Run...
Shut Down...
Windows95
Start
Accessories
Adobe
Communications
London Access
StartUp
Microsoft Word
1
2
3

Point to the **Programs** menu entry (you don't need to click)

Point to and click **Microsoft Word**

Click the **Start** button

Basic steps:

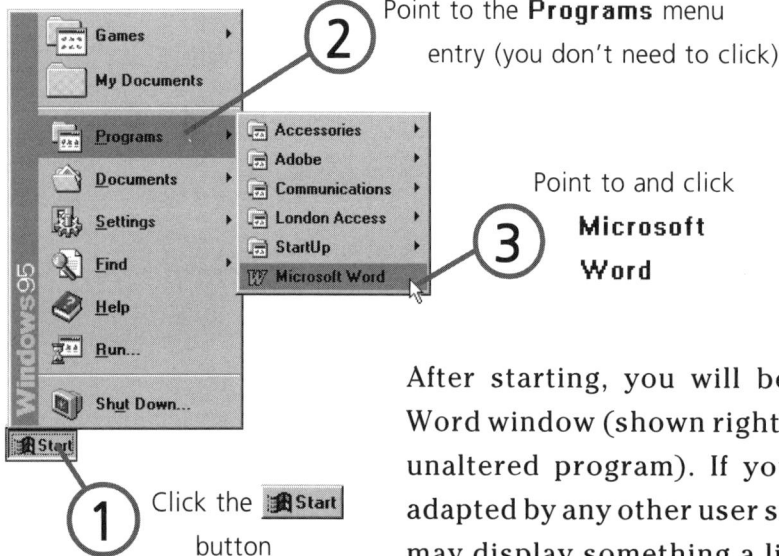

1. Click the **Start** button.
2. Point to the **Programs** menu entry — a sub-menu entry pops out.
3. Point to then click the **Microsoft Word** sub-menu entry (if you have Microsoft Office installed on your computer, you'll first have to point to the **MSOffice** sub-menu entry — which will create a further pop-out menu to locate the **Microsoft Word** sub-menu entry).

After starting, you will be presented with the main Word window (shown right — for a completely new and unaltered program). If your copy of Word has been adapted by any other user since installation your screen may display something a little different.

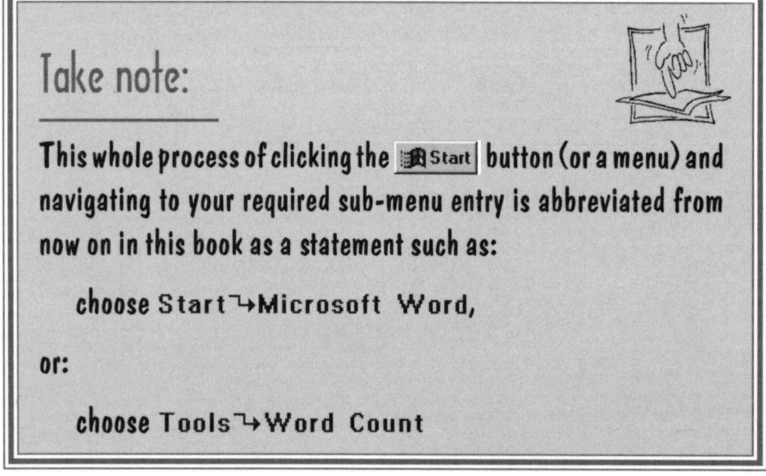

Take note:

This whole process of clicking the **Start** button (or a menu) and navigating to your required sub-menu entry is abbreviated from now on in this book as a statement such as:

choose Start→Microsoft Word,

or:

choose Tools→Word Count

Tip:

If you use your computer only for word processing, you can set up to run Word each time you turn on your machine – see page 142 for details.

Main features of a Word document window are shown below, but don't panic — they'll be looked at shortly. Soon you'll think Word is one of the easiest computer programs to get the hang of — and you'll be right.

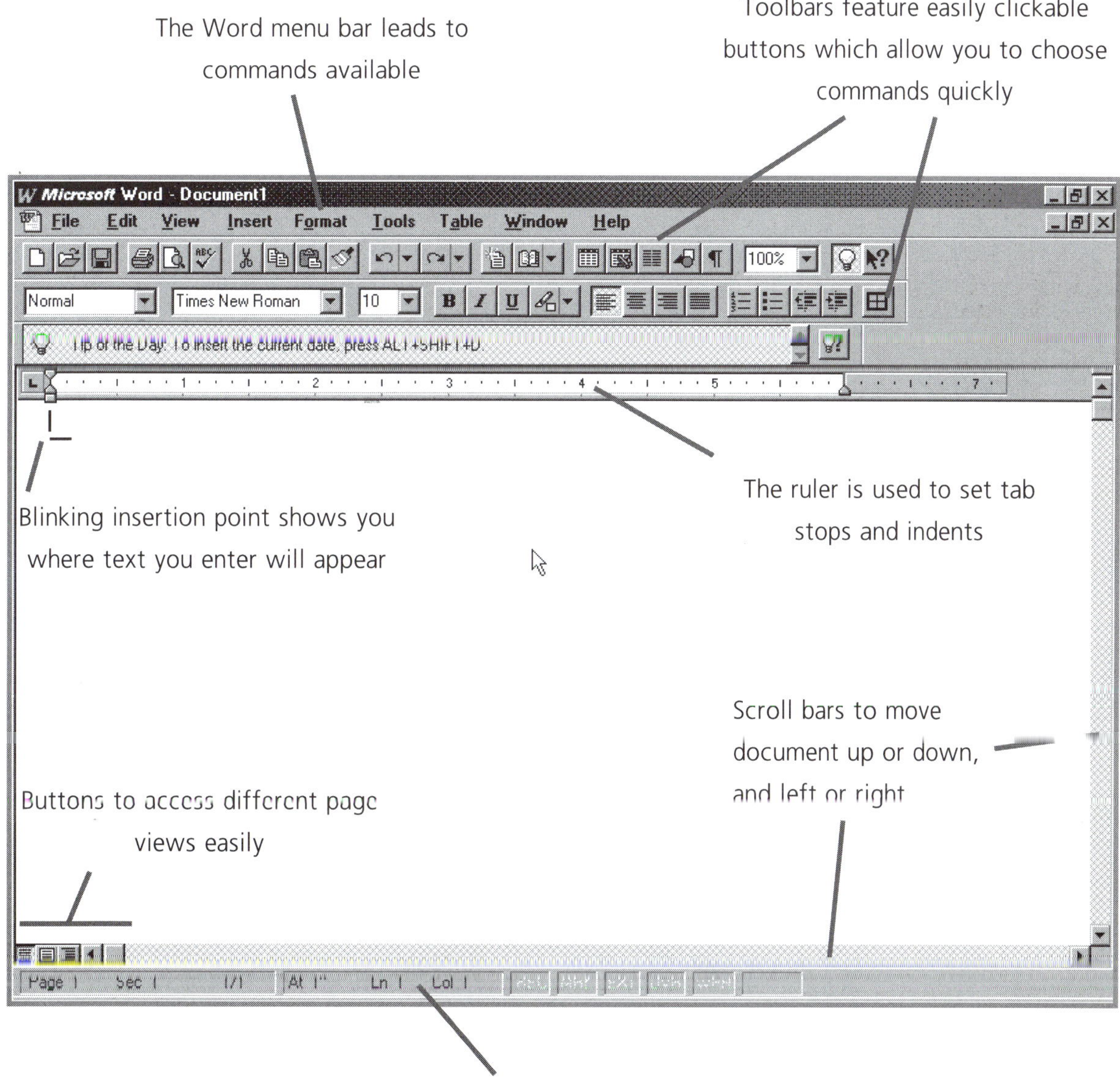

The Word menu bar leads to commands available
Toolbars feature easily clickable buttons which allow you to choose commands quickly
Microsoft Word - Document1
File Edit View Insert Format Tools Table Window Help
100%
Normal
Times New Roman
10
Blinking insertion point shows you where text you enter will appear
The ruler is used to set tab stops and indents
Scroll bars to move document up or down, and left or right
Buttons to access different page views easily
Page 1 Sec 1 1/1 At 1" Ln 1 Col 1

The status bar along the bottom gives details about the document in the window (see page 6, and pages 28–29 for more details)

Word menus

Word has nine menus in its menu bar. They hold all the commands and tools available to any user of Word. While you don't (and that's just as well!) need to know what all these commands and tools are to get good results from Word, it's worth looking at all the menus to get an overall feel for what they are about — use this page as a reference.

The menu bar itself looks like this:

Basic steps:

1. To display a menu, click on its name in the menu bar.
2. Alternatively, enter [Alt] + the menu's underlined letter.
3. To remove a displayed menu, click anywhere else in the window.

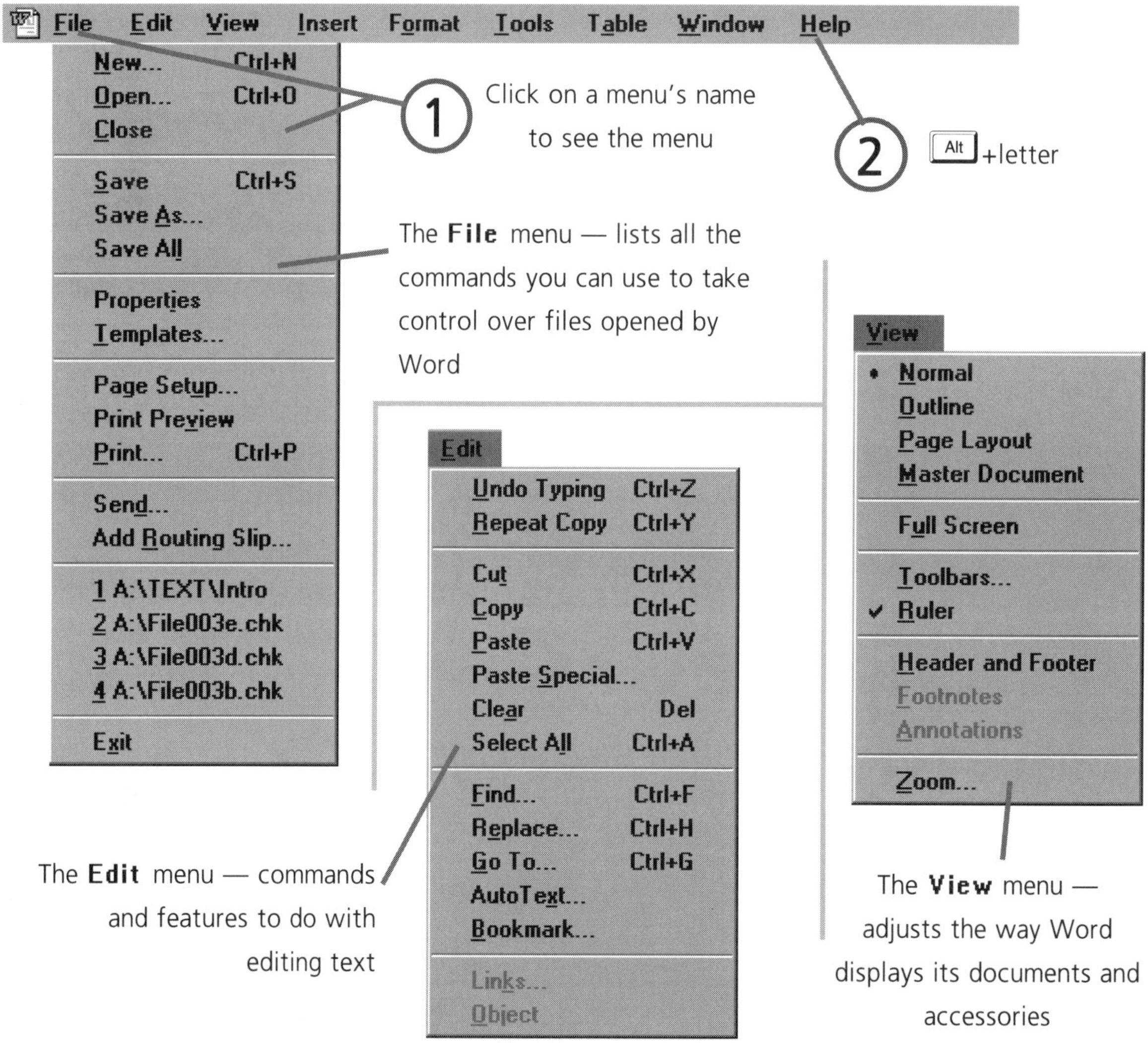

File Edit View Insert Format Tools Table Window Help

① Click on a menu's name to see the menu

② [Alt]+letter

File	
New...	Ctrl+N
Open...	Ctrl+O
Close	
Save	Ctrl+S
Save As...	
Save All	
Properties	
Templates...	
Page Setup...	
Print Preview	
Print...	Ctrl+P
Send...	
Add Routing Slip...	
1 A:\TEXT\Intro	
2 A:\File003e.chk	
3 A:\File003d.chk	
4 A:\File003b.chk	
Exit	

The **File** menu — lists all the commands you can use to take control over files opened by Word

Edit	
Undo Typing	Ctrl+Z
Repeat Copy	Ctrl+Y
Cut	Ctrl+X
Copy	Ctrl+C
Paste	Ctrl+V
Paste Special...	
Clear	Del
Select All	Ctrl+A
Find...	Ctrl+F
Replace...	Ctrl+H
Go To...	Ctrl+G
AutoText...	
Bookmark...	
Links...	
Object	

The **Edit** menu — commands and features to do with editing text

View
• Normal
Outline
Page Layout
Master Document
Full Screen
Toolbars...
✓ Ruler
Header and Footer
Footnotes
Annotations
Zoom...

The **View** menu — adjusts the way Word displays its documents and accessories

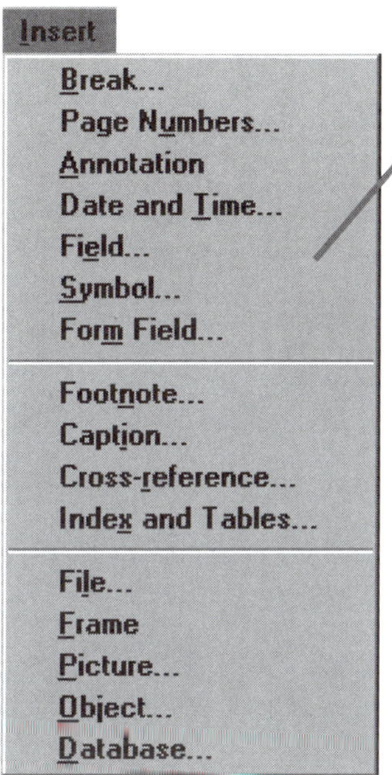
Insert
Break...
Page Numbers...
Annotation
Date and Time...
Field...
Symbol...
Form Field...
Footnote...
Caption...
Cross-reference...
Index and Tables...
File...
Frame
Picture...
Object...
Database...

The **Insert** menu — used to place certain features other than ordinary text into a document

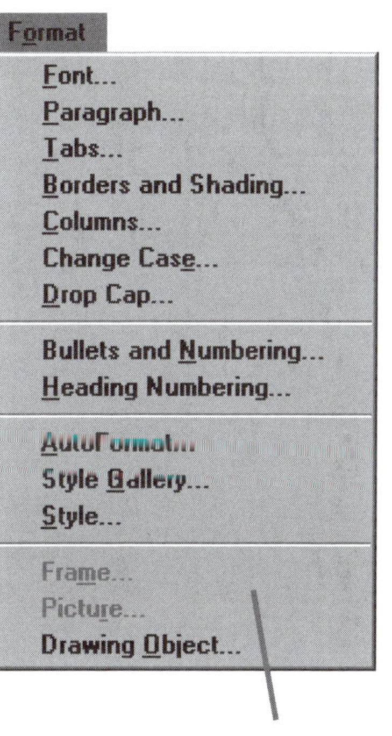
Format
Font...
Paragraph...
Tabs...
Borders and Shading...
Columns...
Change Case...
Drop Cap...
Bullets and Numbering...
Heading Numbering...
AutoFormat...
Style Gallery...
Style...
Frame...
Picture...
Drawing Object...

The **Format** menu — the menu you use to apply styles and so on to your document

The **Tools** menu — special features and controls

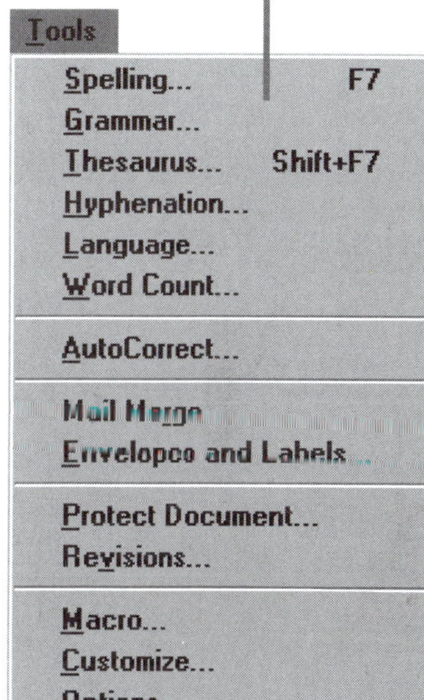
Tools
Spelling... F7
Grammar...
Thesaurus... Shift+F7
Hyphenation...
Language...
Word Count...
AutoCorrect...
Mail Merge
Envelopes and Labels...
Protect Document...
Revisions...
Macro...
Customize...
Options...

The **Table** menu — controls aspects of tables within a document

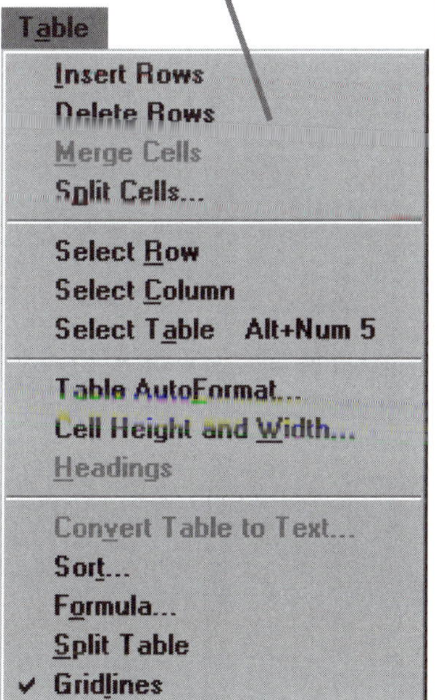
Table
Insert Rows
Delete Rows
Merge Cells
Split Cells...
Select Row
Select Column
Select Table Alt+Num 5
Table AutoFormat...
Cell Height and Width...
Headings
Convert Table to Text...
Sort...
Formula...
Split Table
✓ Gridlines

The **Window** menu — choose between documents and control how they are displayed

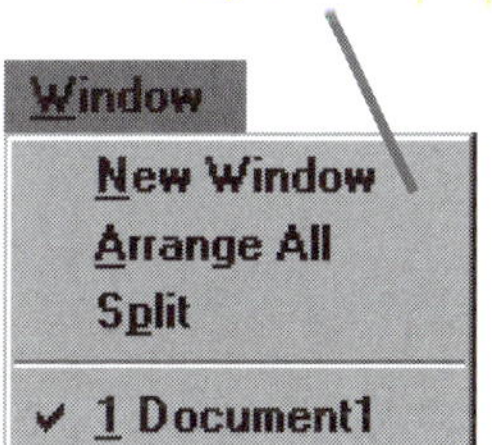
Window
New Window
Arrange All
Split
✓ 1 Document1

The **Help** menu — how to

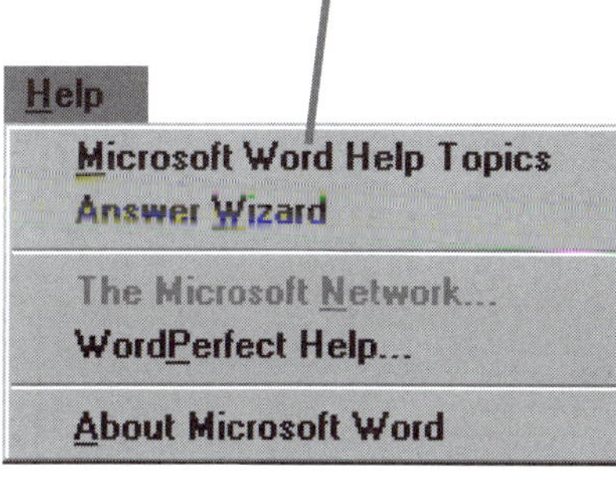
Help
Microsoft Word Help Topics
Answer Wizard
The Microsoft Network...
WordPerfect Help...
About Microsoft Word

Help me, I'm drowning!

Inevitably you will find there are times you don't know what you are doing. This happens whenever you are new (and, sometimes not-so-new) to a complex program like Word. Fortunately, Word has an incredibly useful — and even-more-incredibly comprehensive — on-line help system built in to it. This comes in four parts:

- first there are ToolTips — little labels which show up when you point over any of the myriads of buttons Word has in its many toolbars
- second is the status bar, whose contents change to display helpful notes about buttons and so on
- third is Help — an easily accessible system in which you can locate help about any feature, command, or topic in Word. There are many ways you can use the system to get help
- fourth are ScreenTips — descriptive labels you can access.

ToolTips name each button as the pointer passes over it

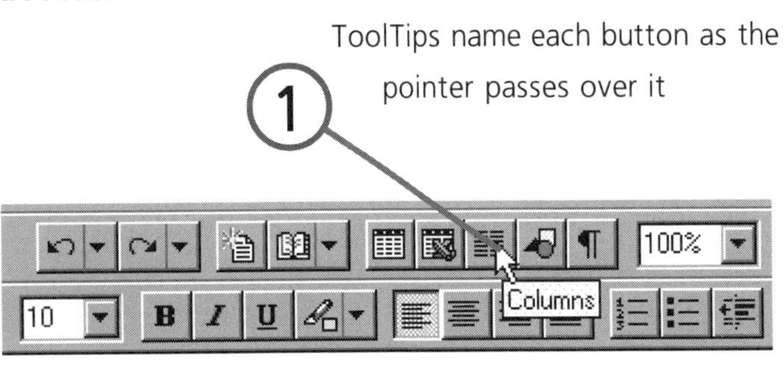
1
100%
10
Columns
1
Changes the column format of the selected sections

The status bar displays relevant information about the button your pointer is over

Basic steps:

TOOLTIPS

1 Simply position your pointer over any button in any toolbar to see the button's name as a label.

STATUS BAR HELP

1 As you position the pointer over a button, the status bar display changes to give you relevant information.

HELP BY TOPIC

1 Choose **Help→Microsoft Word Help Topics** to call up the **Help Topics: Microsoft Word** window.

2 Click the **Contents** tab.

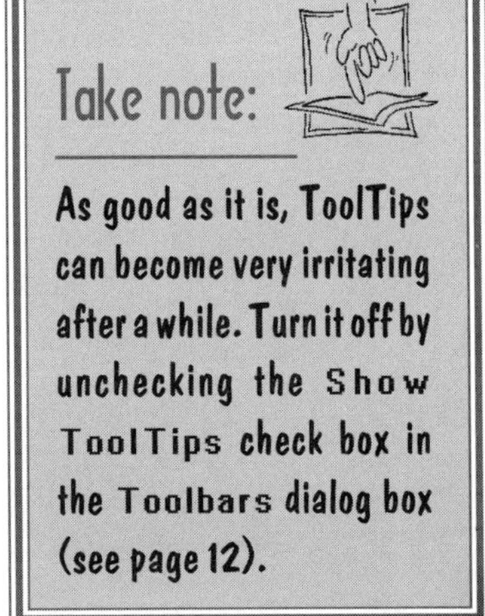

Take note:

As good as it is, ToolTips can become very irritating after a while. Turn it off by unchecking the Show ToolTips check box in the Toolbars dialog box (see page 12).

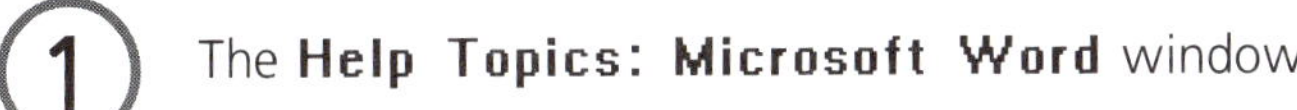

1 The **Help Topics: Microsoft Word** window

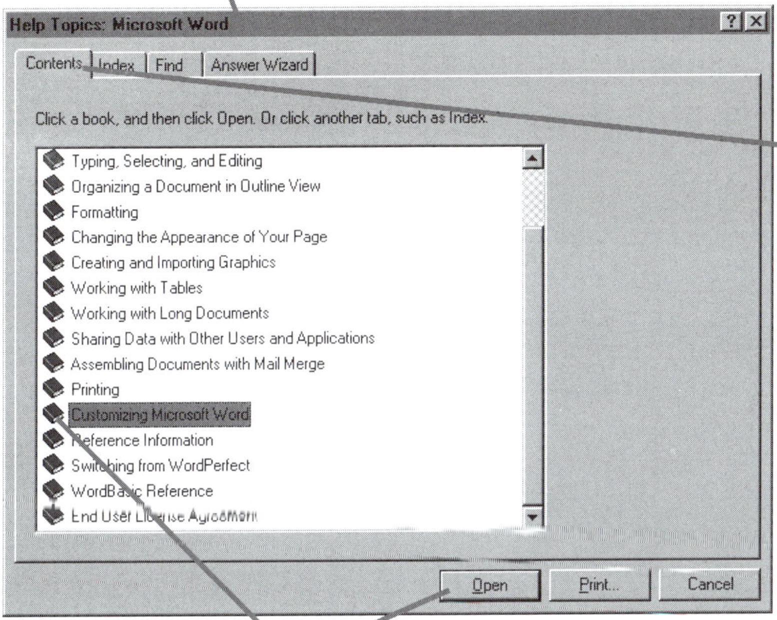

Click the **Contents** tab to bring the **Contents** sheet to the front

3 Click a topic and click **Open**

Basic steps (contd):

3 Click on any of the topics and click **Open** (or simply double-click the topic) to get help.

4 Further sub-topics can be opened in the same topic to give and locate further help.

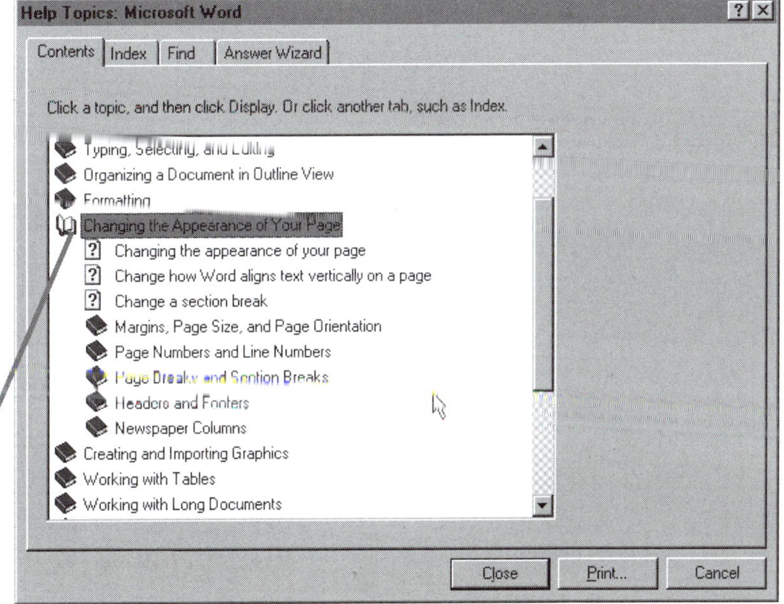
Help Topics: Microsoft Word
Contents
Index
Find
Answer Wizard
Click a topic, and then click Display. Or click another tab, such as Index.
Organizing a Document in Outline View
Changing the Appearance of Your Page
Changing the appearance of your page
Change how Word aligns text vertically on a page
Change a section break
Margins, Page Size, and Page Orientation
Page Numbers and Line Numbers
Newspaper Columns
Creating and Importing Graphics
Working with Tables
Working with Long Documents
Close
Print...
Cancel

4 Click further topics to locate the help you need

...drowning (contd)!

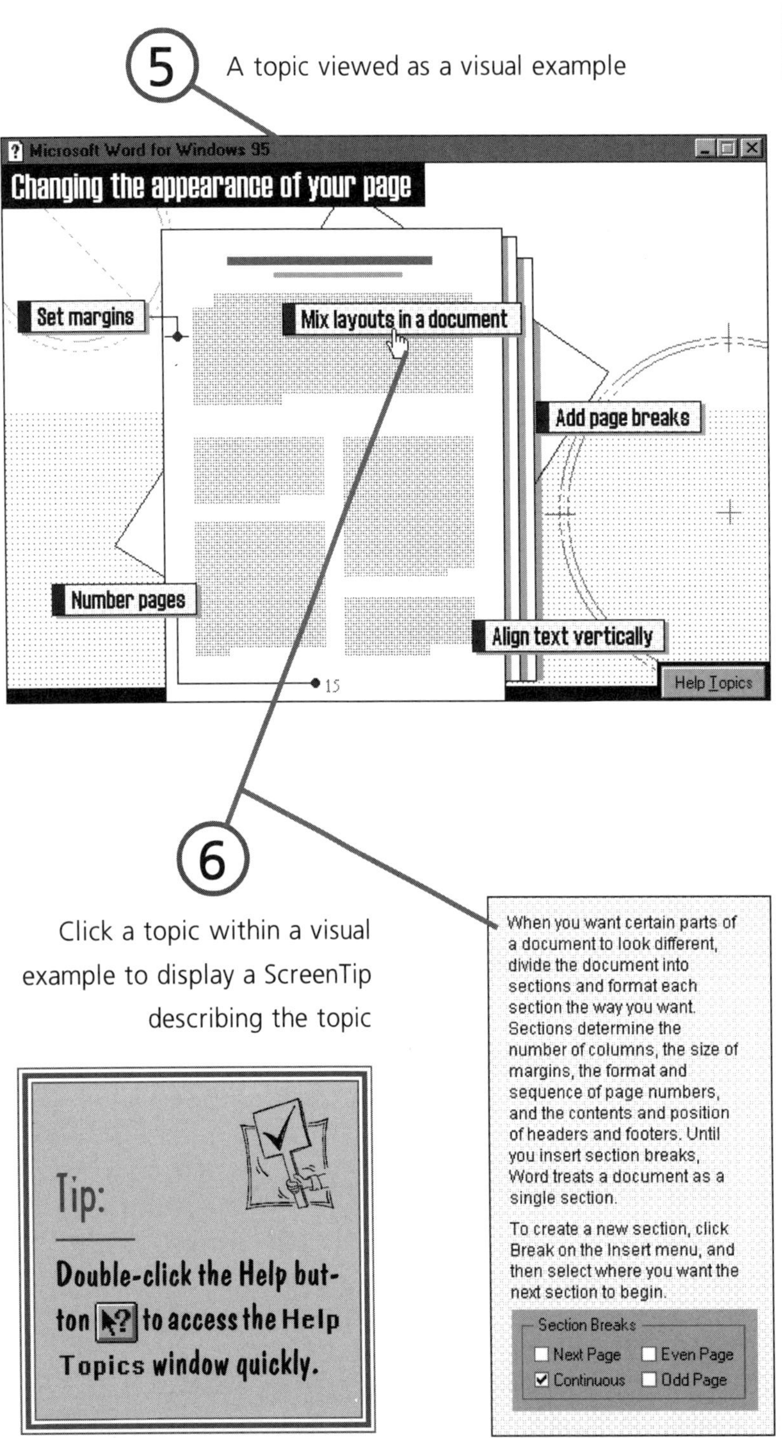

5
A topic viewed as a visual example
Microsoft Word for Windows 95
Changing the appearance of your page
Set margins
Mix layouts in a document
Add page breaks
Number pages
Align text vertically
15
Help Topics
6
When you want certain parts of a document to look different, divide the document into sections and format each section the way you want. Sections determine the number of columns, the size of margins, the format and sequence of page numbers, and the contents and position of headers and footers. Until you insert section breaks, Word treats a document as a single section.
To create a new section, click Break on the Insert menu, and then select where you want the next section to begin.
Section Breaks
Next Page
Even Page
Continuous
Odd Page

Click a topic within a visual example to display a ScreenTip describing the topic

Tip:

Double-click the Help button to access the Help Topics window quickly.

Basic steps (contd):

5 When you reach the topic you want to view, it is displayed as a visual example (as left), a step-by-step procedure, or another form of help.

6 In a visual example, click the topic you want more help about, to call up a ScreenTip.

HELP BY INDEX

1 Choose **Help→Microsoft Word Help Topics** to call up the **Help Topics** window.

2 Click the **Index** tab.

3 Type in a few letters of the topic you want help with — as you do, the list of entries jumps to the respective entry.

4 Click **Display** (or double-click the entry) to display the topic.

1 Call up the **Help Topics** window

2 Click the **Index** tab

3 Type in the first letters of the subject you want

4 Click to access the topic

Basic steps (contd):

HELP BY FIND

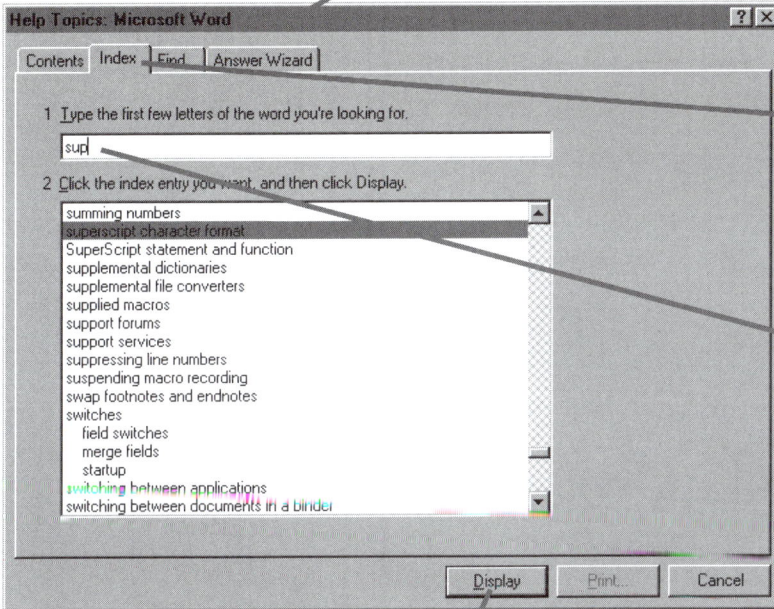

1. Choose **Help→Microsoft Word Help Topics** to call up the **Help Topics** window.
2. Click the **Find** tab.
3. Click **Next** and step through the following sequence of dialog boxes to set up the Find Wizard.

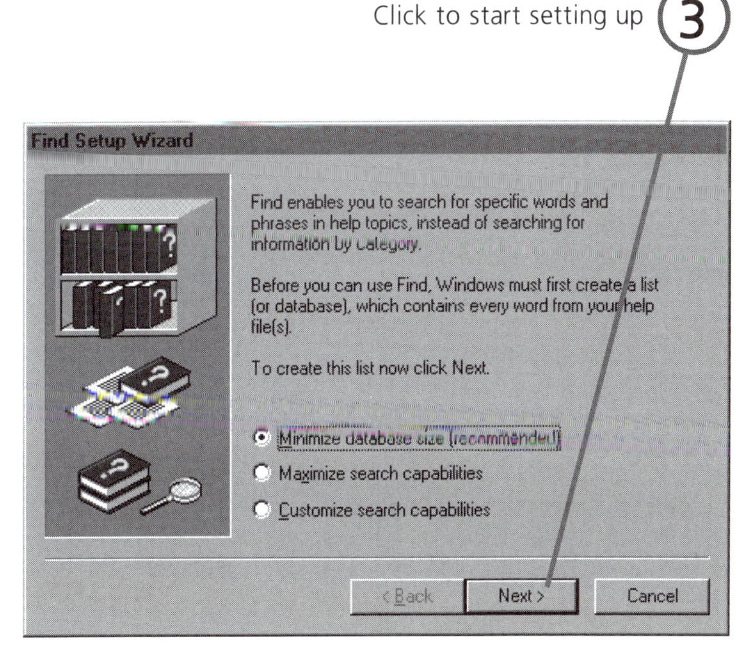
Click to start setting up
3
Find Setup Wizard
Find enables you to search for specific words and phrases in help topics, instead of searching for information by category.
Before you can use Find, Windows must first create a list (or database), which contains every word from your help file(s).
To create this list now click Next.
Minimize database size (recommended)
Maximize search capabilities
Customize search capabilities
< Back
Next >
Cancel

...still drowning (contd)!

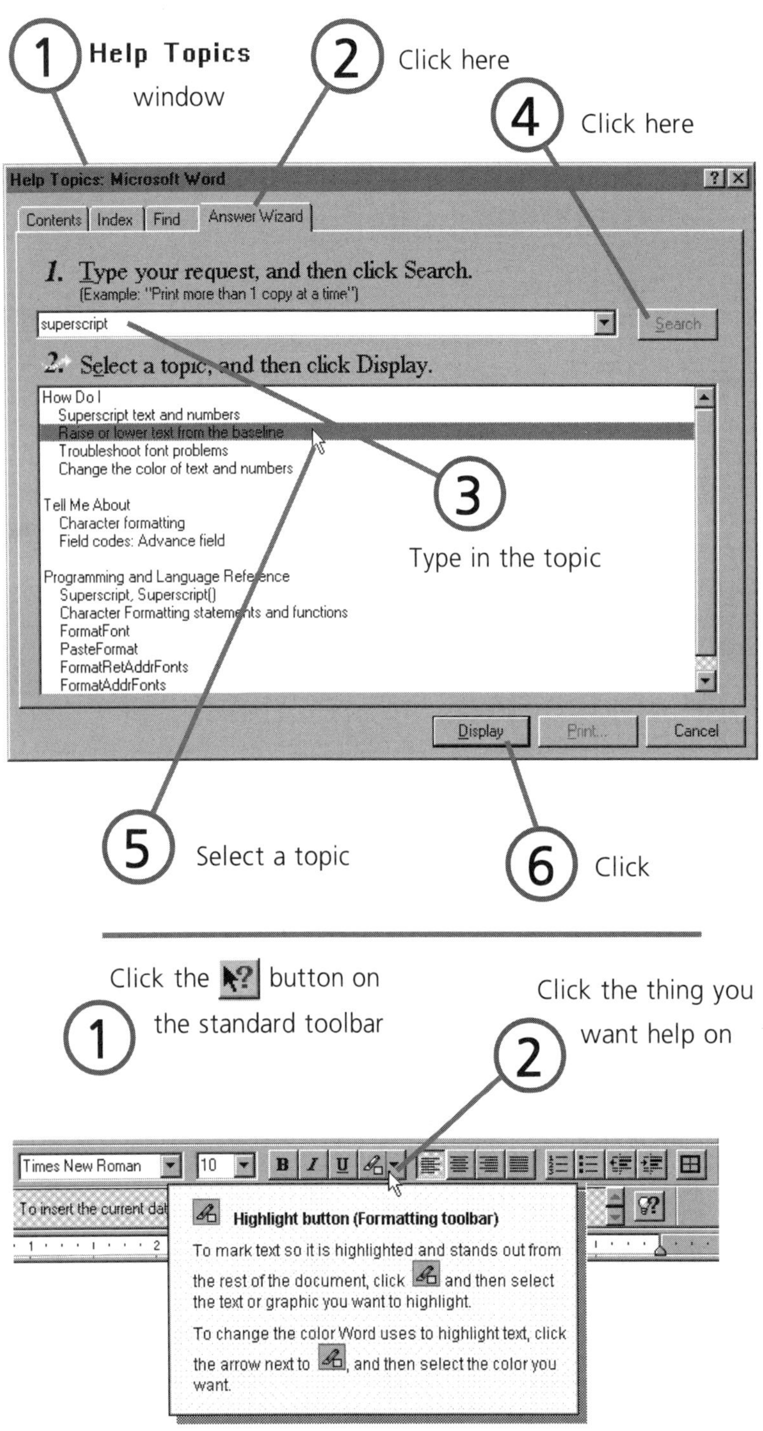

1 Help Topics window
2 Click here
4 Click here
Help Topics: Microsoft Word
Contents
Index
Find
Answer Wizard
1. Type your request, and then click Search.
(Example: "Print more than 1 copy at a time")
superscript
Search
2. Select a topic, and then click Display.
How Do I
Superscript text and numbers
Raise or lower text from the baseline
Troubleshoot font problems
Change the color of text and numbers
Tell Me About
Character formatting
Field codes: Advance field
Programming and Language Reference
Superscript, Superscript()
Character Formatting statements and functions
FormatFont
PasteFormat
FormatRetAddrFonts
FormatAddrFonts
Display
Print...
Cancel
3 Type in the topic
5 Select a topic
6 Click
1 Click the button on the standard toolbar
2 Click the thing you want help on
Times New Roman
10
To insert the current dat
Highlight button (Formatting toolbar)
To mark text so it is highlighted and stands out from the rest of the document, click and then select the text or graphic you want to highlight.
To change the color Word uses to highlight text, click the arrow next to , and then select the color you want.

Basic steps (contd):

HELP BY ANSWER WIZARD

1 Choose **Help→Microsoft Word Help Topics** to call up the **Help Topics** window.

2 Click the **Answer Wizard** tab.

3 Type in the topic you want help with.

4 Click **Search**.

5 Select a topic in the topic list.

6 Click **Display** to prompt the **Answer Wizard** to show you the procedure.

SCREENTIPS HELP

1 Click the help button. The pointer changes to the help pointer.

2 Click the button, object, or even menu command you want help with, and the Help system goes straight to the information you need, displaying it as a ScreenTip.

Help – I'm not so Perfect!

If you've previously used WordPerfect as your word processor, then some of Word's features will probably be confusing to you.

Not to worry, though: help is at hand in the form of a system which correlates specific WordPerfect commands to those in Word.

Basic steps:

1 Type Alt+H, then W, or choose **Help→WordPerfect Help** — or more quickly — double-click the WordPerfect help button WPH on the status bar. This calls up the **Help for WordPerfect Users** dialog box.

2 Select the WordPerfect command name in the command keys box.

3 Read the information about the command.

4 For a demonstration of the command, click **Demo**.

The **Help for WordPerfect Users** dialog box

Select the WordPerfect command you are familiar with here

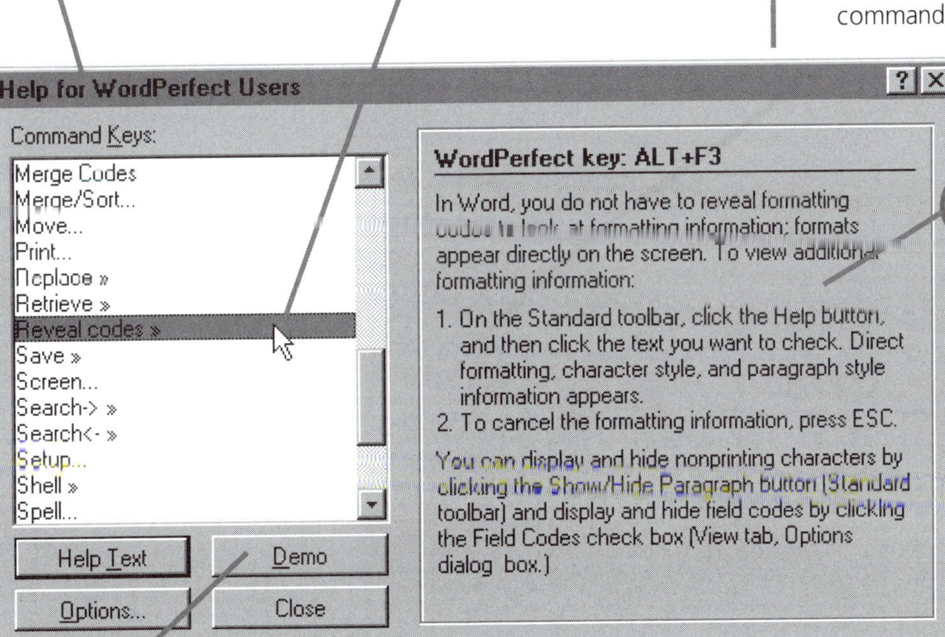
1
2
Help for WordPerfect Users
Command Keys:
Merge Codes
Merge/Sort...
Move...
Print...
Replace »
Retrieve »
Reveal codes »
Save »
Screen...
Search-> »
Search<- »
Setup...
Shell »
Spell...
Help Text
Demo
Options...
Close
WordPerfect key: ALT+F3
In Word, you do not have to reveal formatting codes to look at formatting information; formats appear directly on the screen. To view additional formatting information:
1. On the Standard toolbar, click the Help button, and then click the text you want to check. Direct formatting, character style, and paragraph style information appears.
2. To cancel the formatting information, press ESC.
You can display and hide nonprinting characters by clicking the Show/Hide Paragraph button (Standard toolbar) and display and hide field codes by clicking the Field Codes check box (View tab, Options dialog box.)
4

3 Read information about your selected command

Click for a demonstration

Toolbars

Basic steps:

Apart from choosing commands in menus, Word is controlled by on-screen buttons, found in toolbars. The two most obvious toolbars are at the top of a Word document but, as we'll see, there are others, too — and further — Word lets you customize them to your heart's content — see page 146 for more details.

1 To display any particular toolbar, choose **View↳Toolbar**.

2 In the **Toolbars** dialog box, choose which toolbars you want displayed by checking them.

3 Click **OK**.

The standard toolbar — buttons used for common everyday tasks

The formatting toolbar — containing buttons you use to stylize text within documents

Create your own toolbars with this button

Click to display toolbars in list

Reset a selected toolbar to its original state

Change buttons and positions in existing or new toolbars with this button

Turn off those irritating ToolTips

2 Check more boxes to display more toolboxes

Turn off/on color buttons with this check box

Get larger buttons with this check box

Display shortcut keys with ToolTips

Toolbars

Toolbars:

Standard
Formatting
Borders
Database
Drawing
Forms
Microsoft
Word for Windows 2.0
Tip Wizard

OK
Cancel
New...
Reset...
Customize...

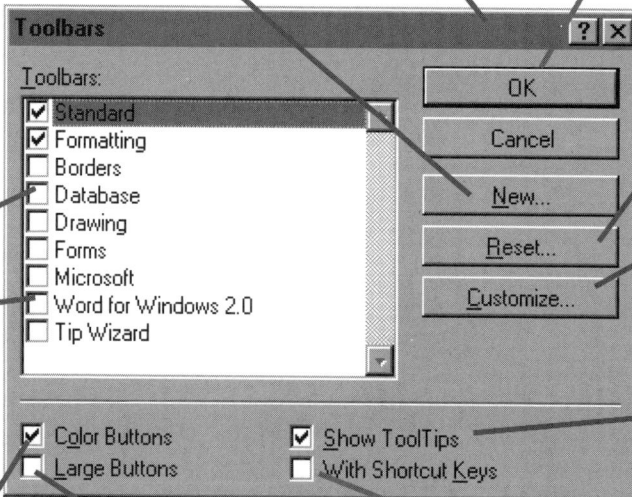

Color Buttons
Large Buttons
Show ToolTips
With Shortcut Keys

Toolbars (contd)

You can turn off any existing toolbar, or turn on any of the other toolbars (see previous page) on-the-fly in Word by clicking on any toolbar with the right mouse button. This calls up a drop-down menu from which you can choose the toolbar you want displayed.

Basic steps (contd):

4 Alternatively, use the mouse shortcut — click any toolbar with the right mouse button.

5 Click the toolbar you want turned on or off.

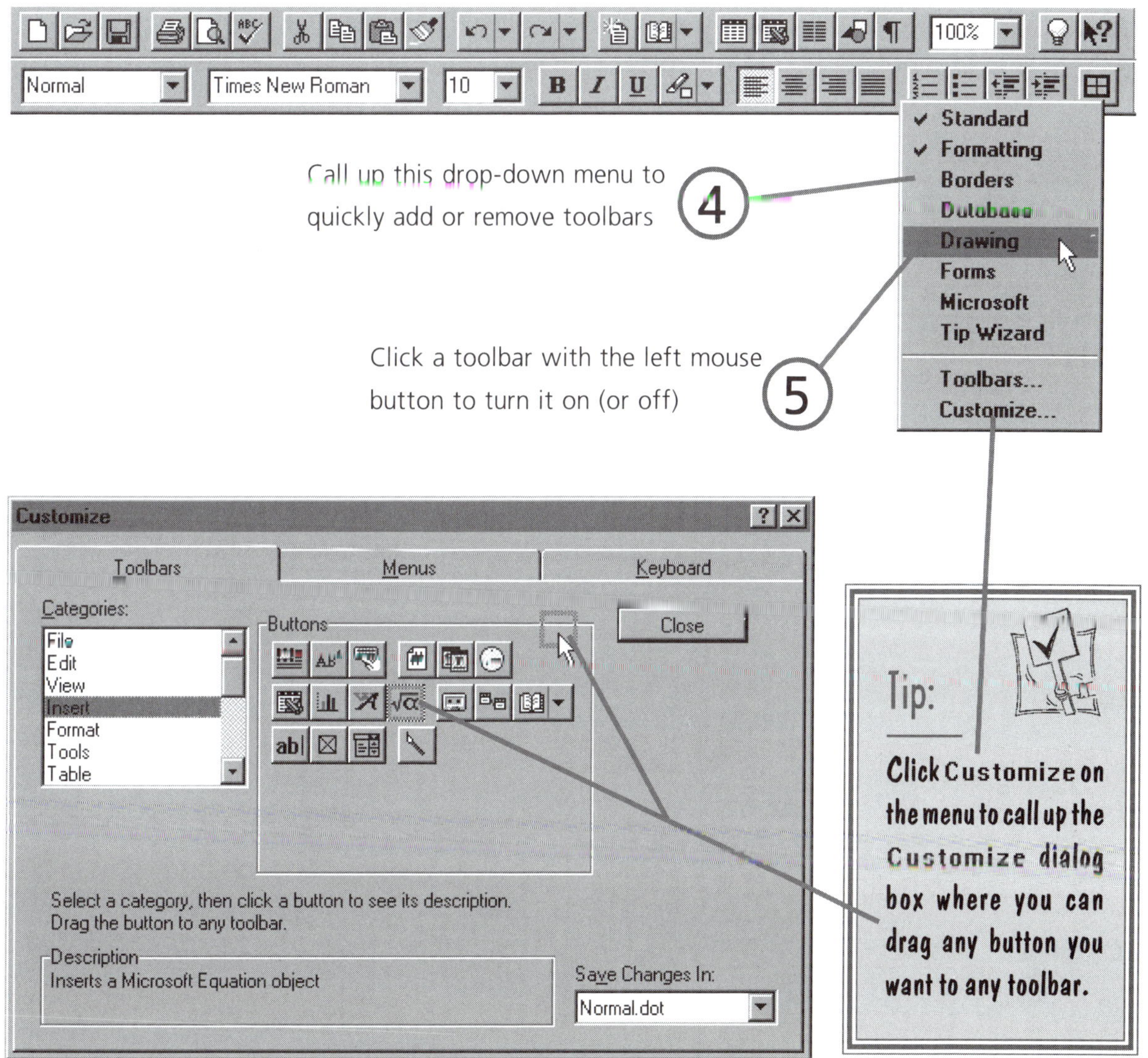

Normal
Times New Roman
10
100%
Standard
Formatting
Borders
Database
Drawing
Forms
Microsoft
Tip Wizard
Toolbars...
Customize...
Call up this drop-down menu to quickly add or remove toolbars
4
Click a toolbar with the left mouse button to turn it on (or off)
5
Customize
Toolbars
Menus
Keyboard
Categories:
File
Edit
View
Insert
Format
Tools
Table
Buttons
Close
Select a category, then click a button to see its description.
Drag the button to any toolbar.
Description
Inserts a Microsoft Equation object
Save Changes In:
Normal.dot

Tip:

Click Customize on the menu to call up the Customize dialog box where you can drag any button you want to any toolbar.

Other toolbars

All default toolbars in Word are displayed below. While most are fixed in position in the document window, two — the Microsoft and the Forms toolbars — are floating — that is, you can move them by dragging their title bars as you do any window in Windows. Any new toolbars you create for yourself (page 147) float, too.

Finally, remember that you can customize default toolbars, as well as any of your own creations, by moving, removing, adding, or creating buttons.

> **Tip:**
>
> **If you've used Word 2, and the interface for Word for Windows 95 seems alien to you, turn off the Standard toolbar and use the Word 2 toolbar instead. That way you'll feel right at home.**

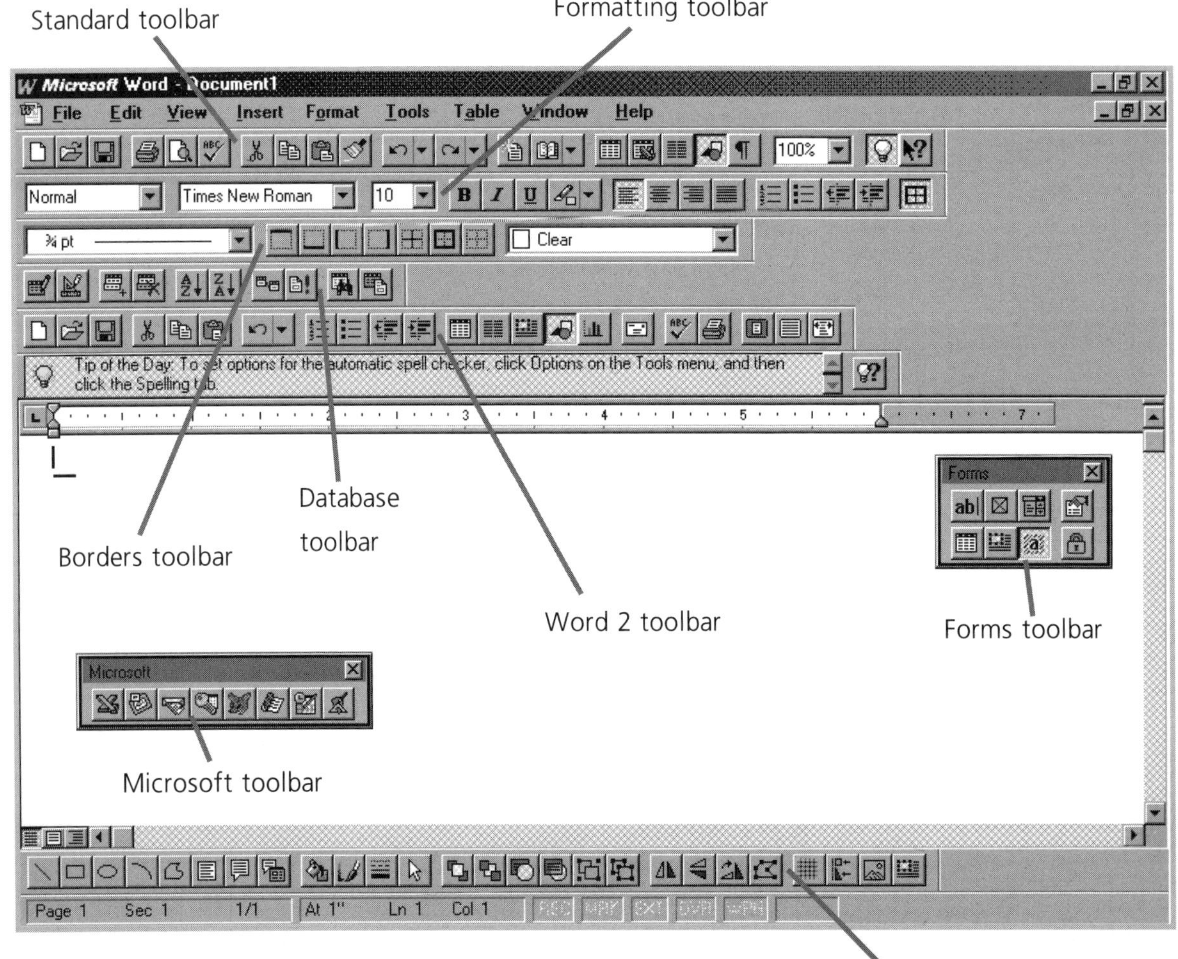
Standard toolbar
Formatting toolbar
Microsoft Word - Document1
File Edit View Insert Format Tools Table Window Help
Borders toolbar
Database toolbar
Word 2 toolbar
Forms toolbar
Microsoft toolbar
Drawing toolbar

Buttons

Buttons on toolbars are graphically representative of their function. As a result, it's easy to see what most of them do. However, some buttons are a little more obscure. Here the standard and formatting toolbar buttons are listed as a reference, together with brief explanations.

> **Take note:**
>
> **There are many, many more buttons hidden within Word's interface, either pre-formatted onto other toolbars, or unused in a default installation. There's nothing to stop you using other toolbars, customizing existing toolbars, or even creating your own buttons from scratch.**

— new document
— open document
— save document
— print document
— print preview
— spelling check
— cut
— copy
— paste
— format painter
— undo
— redo
— autoformat

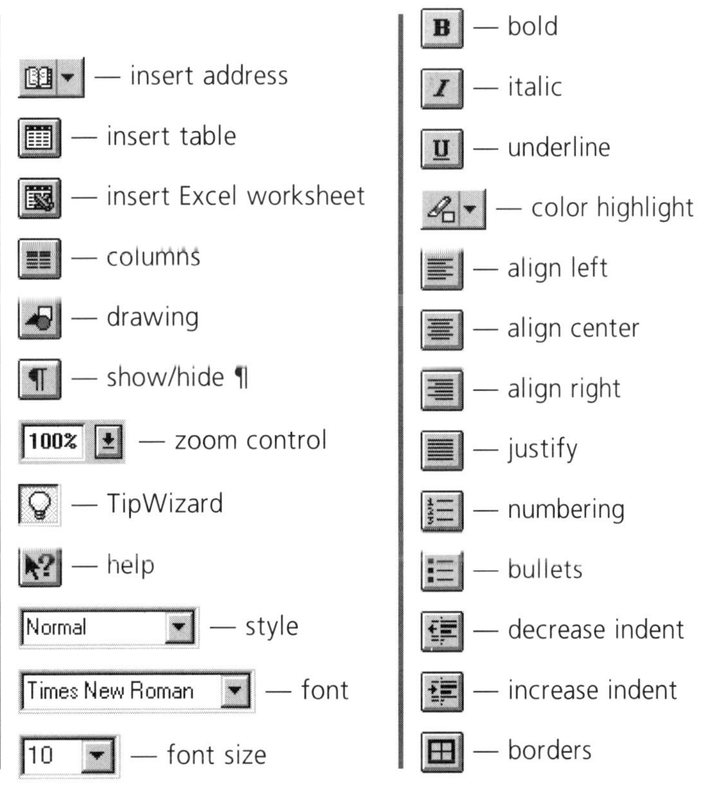
— insert address
— insert table
— insert Excel worksheet
— columns
— drawing
— show/hide ¶
100%
— zoom control
— TipWizard
— help
Normal
— style
Times New Roman
— font
10
— font size
B
— bold
I
— italic
U
— underline
— color highlight
— align left
— align center
— align right
— justify
— numbering
— bullets
— decrease indent
— increase indent
— borders

Normal view

Basic steps:

Word allows a number of views of your document — normal view is simply the one new documents usually default to. It's important to remember, though, that each view of a document makes no difference to what's actually in the document — it's just one way of looking at it.

1 Your document is probably already in normal view (see below). If not, choose **View→Normal**, or type [Alt]+[N], or (best) click the Normal view button at the bottom left of your document window.

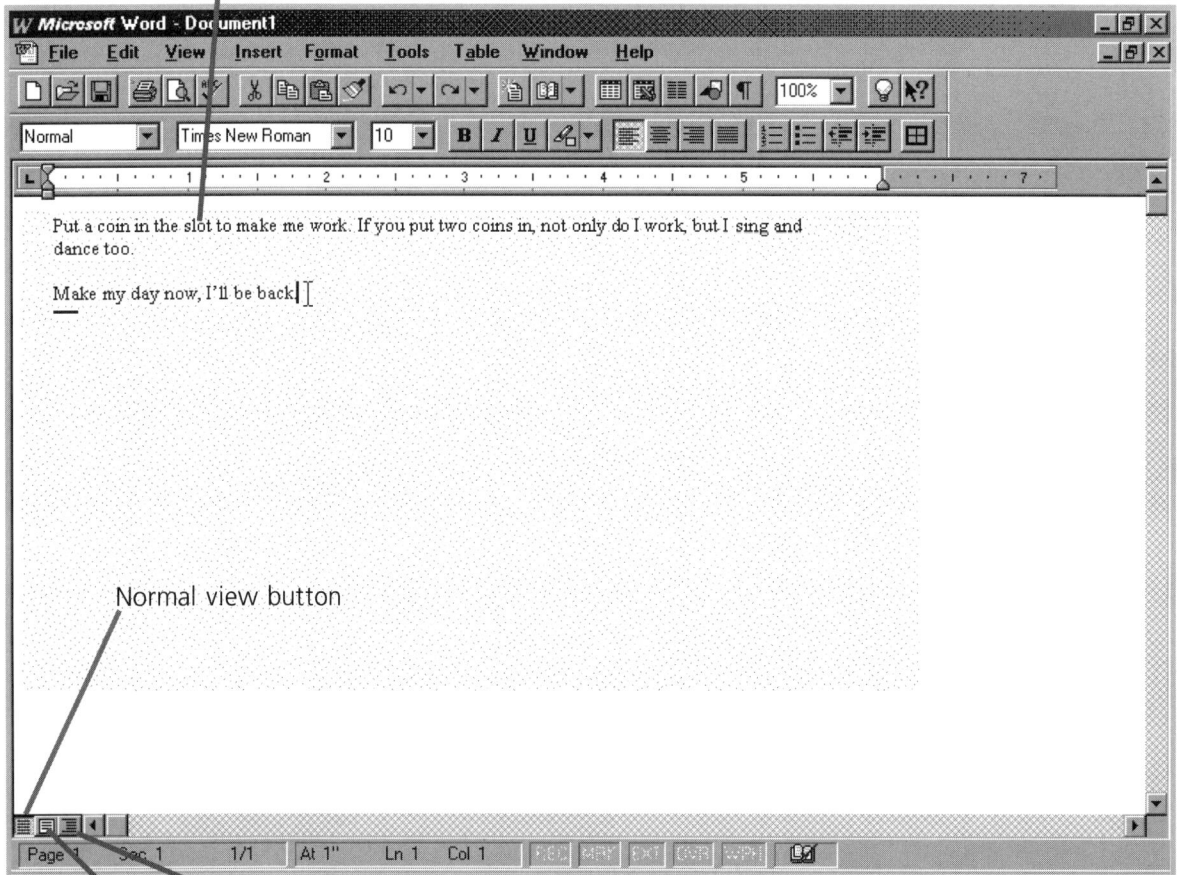

1 Normal view

Put a coin in the slot to make me work. If you put two coins in, not only do I work, but I sing and dance too.

Make my day now, I'll be back.

Normal view button

Page layout and outline view buttons

Page layout view

This view lets you see how the printed page will appear — *what you see is what you get* (WYSIWYG). Margins and borders around text are shown, as well as positions of graphics. This is a useful view to check the final appearance of your document before printing. However, general operation becomes a little slower.

Basic steps:

1 Choose **View→Page Layout**, or type [Alt]+[V] then [P], or (best) click the Page Layout button at the bottom left of your document window.

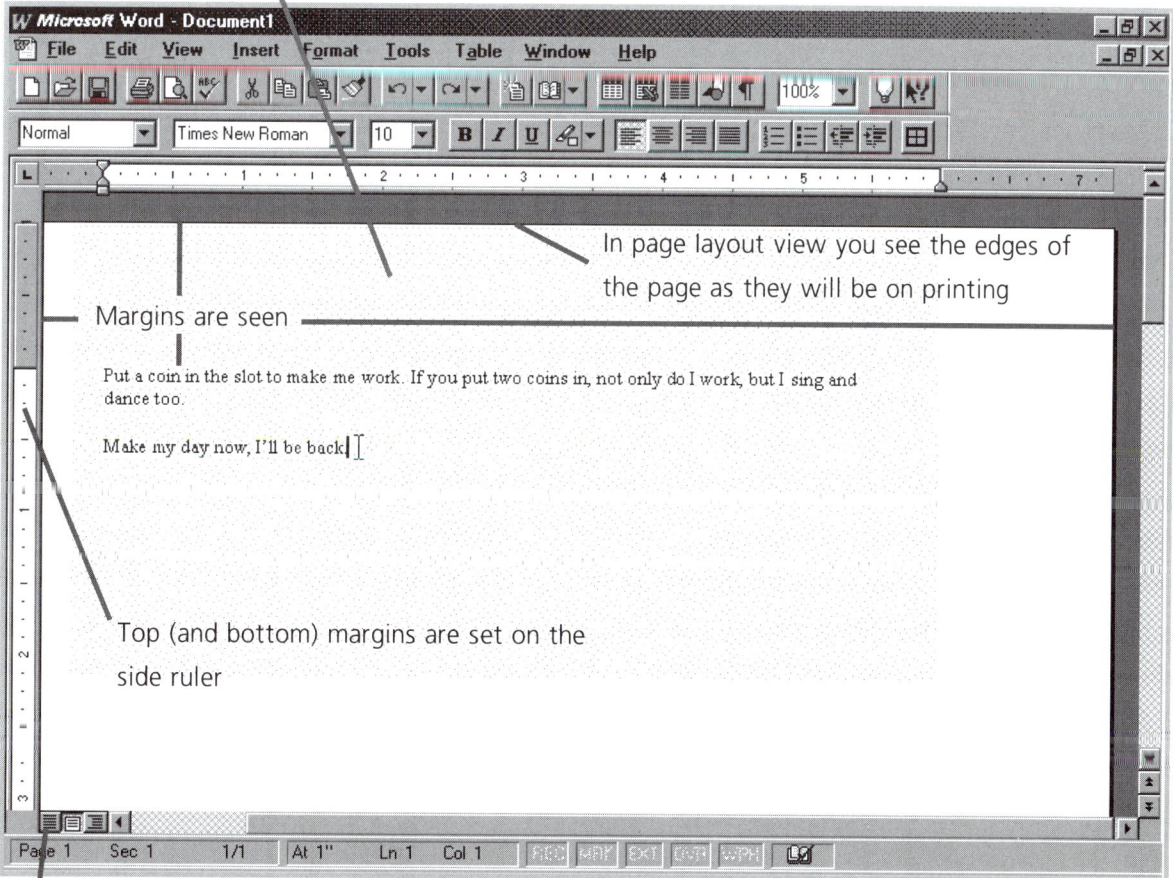

1 Page layout view
Microsoft Word - Document1
File Edit View Insert Format Tools Table Window Help
Normal
Times New Roman
10
100%
In page layout view you see the edges of the page as they will be on printing
Margins are seen
Put a coin in the slot to make me work. If you put two coins in, not only do I work, but I sing and dance too.
Make my day now, I'll be back.
Top (and bottom) margins are set on the side ruler
Page 1 Sec 1 1/1 At 1" Ln 1 Col 1
Get back to normal view with this button

Outline view

Basic steps:

Outline view allows you to control how the various levels of headings and subheadings in your document are displayed (or not displayed) and organized. It is the ideal method for rearranging documents by moving parts of text long distances within the document, or changing the hierarchy of headings. See page 104 for fuller details of outlining.

1 Choose **View→Outline**, or type Alt+V then O, or (best) click the Outline button at the bottom left of your document window.

(1) Outline view

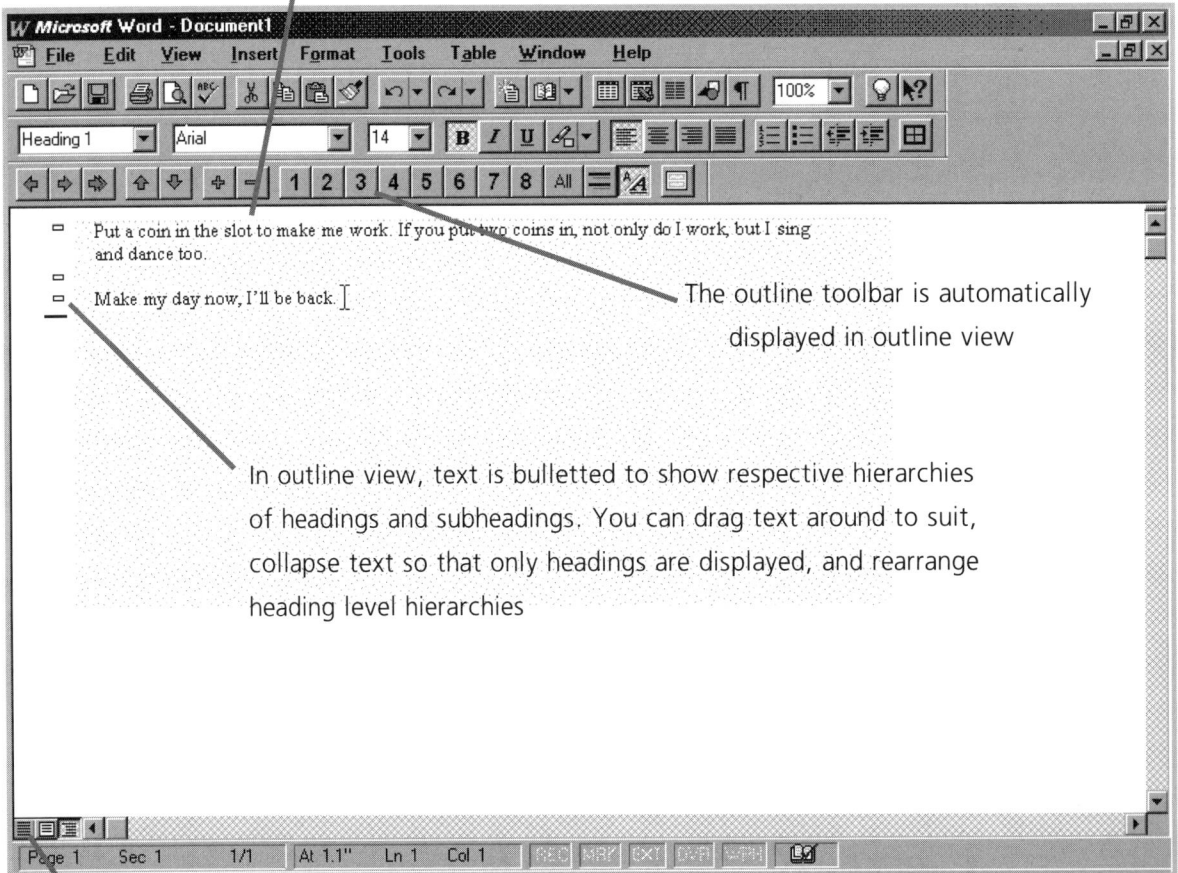

Microsoft Word - Document1

File Edit View Insert Format Tools Table Window Help

Heading 1 | Arial | 14

Put a coin in the slot to make me work. If you put two coins in, not only do I work, but I sing and dance too.

Make my day now, I'll be back.

Page 1 Sec 1 1/1 At 1.1" Ln 1 Col 1

The outline toolbar is automatically displayed in outline view

In outline view, text is bulletted to show respective hierarchies of headings and subheadings. You can drag text around to suit, collapse text so that only headings are displayed, and rearrange heading level hierarchies

Get back to normal view with this button

Full screen view

Word has a neat facility to get rid of all the on-screen clutter such as toolbars, menu line, scroll boxes, and so on. Full screen view can improve your outlook on, say, a small monitor screen, yet you can still get back to normal view with just a click of the mouse.

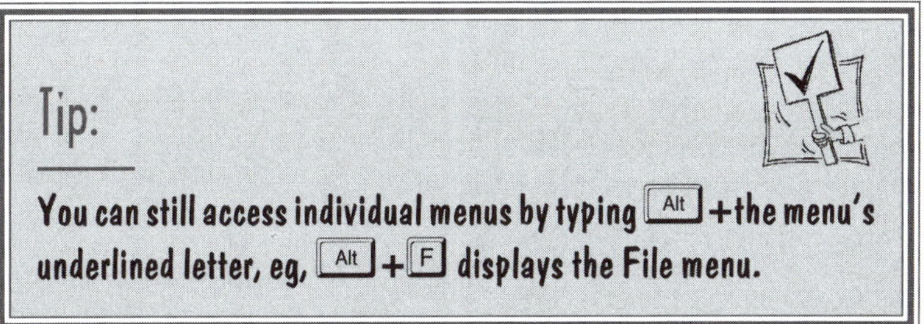

Tip:

You can still access individual menus by typing [Alt]+the menu's underlined letter, eg, [Alt]+[F] displays the File menu.

Basic steps:

1 Choose **View→Full Screen**, or type [Alt]+[V] then [U]. The screen display changes to full screen view — showing nothing except text or graphic elements you have entered, and the Full Screen toolbar at the bottom right.

Put a coin in the slot to make me work. If you put two coins in, not only do I work, but I sing and dance too.

Make my day now, I'll be back

1 Full screen view

To get back to normal view, click the full screen button on the full screen toolbar

Full

Zooming

Basic steps:

You can magnify or reduce part of a document page in Word, to get a close up or overall view of the page. This is known as zooming.

1 Click on the down arrow of the zoom control button of the standard toolbar.

2 From the resultant drop-down menu, choose your desired zoom percentage.

3 As an alternative, you can choose **View→Zoom** to call up the **Zoom** dialog box, and select a zoom value there.

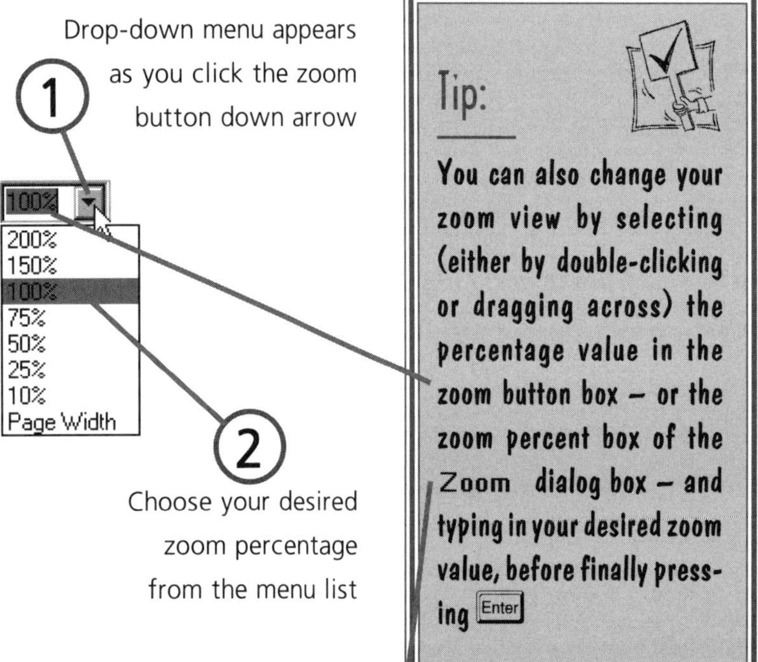
Drop-down menu appears as you click the zoom button down arrow
1
100%
200%
150%
100%
75%
50%
25%
10%
Page Width
2
Choose your desired zoom percentage from the menu list

Tip:

You can also change your zoom view by selecting (either by double-clicking or dragging across) the percentage value in the zoom button box – or the zoom percent box of the Zoom dialog box – and typing in your desired zoom value, before finally pressing Enter

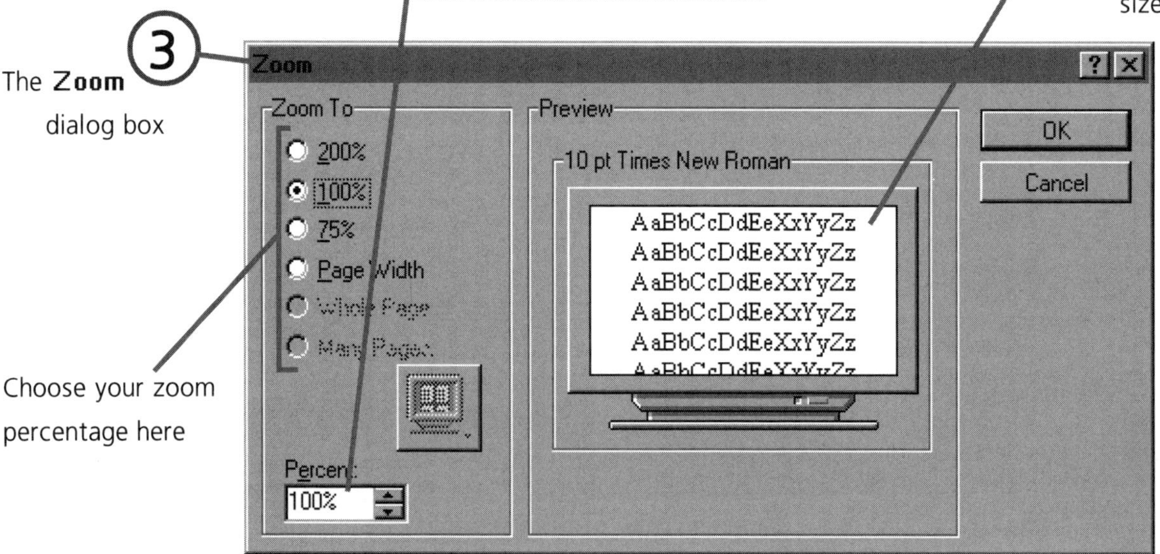
A preview gives you some idea of text size
3
The **Zoom** dialog box
Zoom
Zoom To
200%
100%
75%
Page Width
Whole Page
Many Pages:
Percent:
100%
Preview
10 pt Times New Roman
AaBbCcDdEeXxYyZz
AaBbCcDdEeXxYyZz
AaBbCcDdEeXxYyZz
AaBbCcDdEeXxYyZz
AaBbCcDdEeXxYyZz
OK
Cancel
Choose your zoom percentage here

Saving a document

Basic steps:

Once you've worked on a document you need to save it onto disk:

- the document remains in computer memory only as long as Word is running
- if you quit Word, or turn off your machine without saving the document to disk it is lost forever — **RIP**

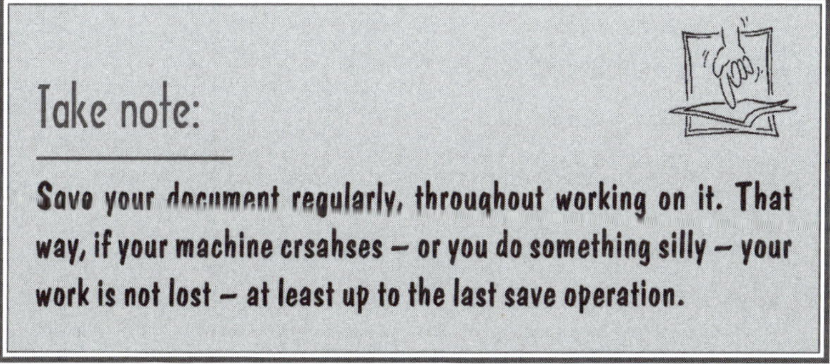

Take note:

Save your document regularly, throughout working on it. That way, if your machine crsahses – or you do something silly – your work is not lost – at least up to the last save operation.

1 Choose **File→Save**, or type [Alt]+[F] then [S], or type [Ctrl]+[S], or click the Save button, to call the **Save As** dialog box if this is the first time you have saved the document. If you have already saved the document the **Save As** dialog box isn't even called up — the document is simply saved over itself with the same file name.

2 Enter a name in the **File Name** box.

3 Locate the directory you want, then click **Save** to save the document.

1 The **Save As** dialog box

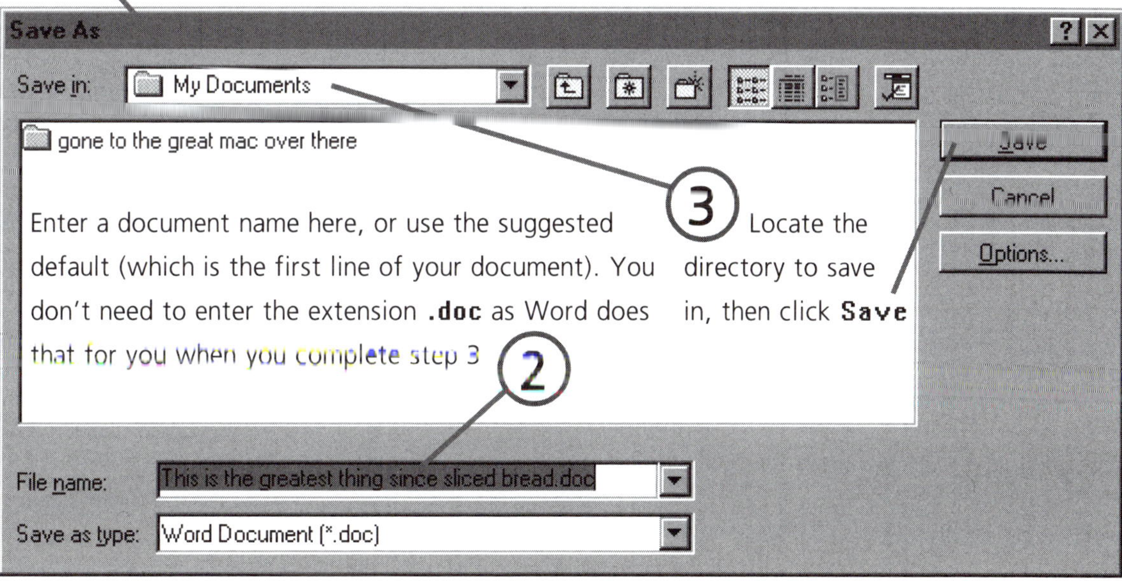
Save As
Save in: My Documents
gone to the great mac over there
Save
Cancel
Options...
File name: This is the greatest thing since sliced bread.doc
Save as type: Word Document (*.doc)
Enter a document name here, or use the suggested default (which is the first line of your document). You don't need to enter the extension .doc as Word does that for you when you complete step 3
2
3 Locate the directory to save in, then click Save

Opening documents

Basic steps:

When you first start up Word a new document is created automatically for you, ready for you to enter text. There are other times, however, when you need to create another new document, or open existing documents you have previously saved.

1 Choose **File→Open**, or type [Alt]+[F] then [O], or type [Ctrl]+[O], or click the Open button. The **Open** dialog box is shown.

2 Locate the document you wish to open in its drive and directory.

3 Click the Preview button to see a preview of any selected document.

4 Click **Open**.

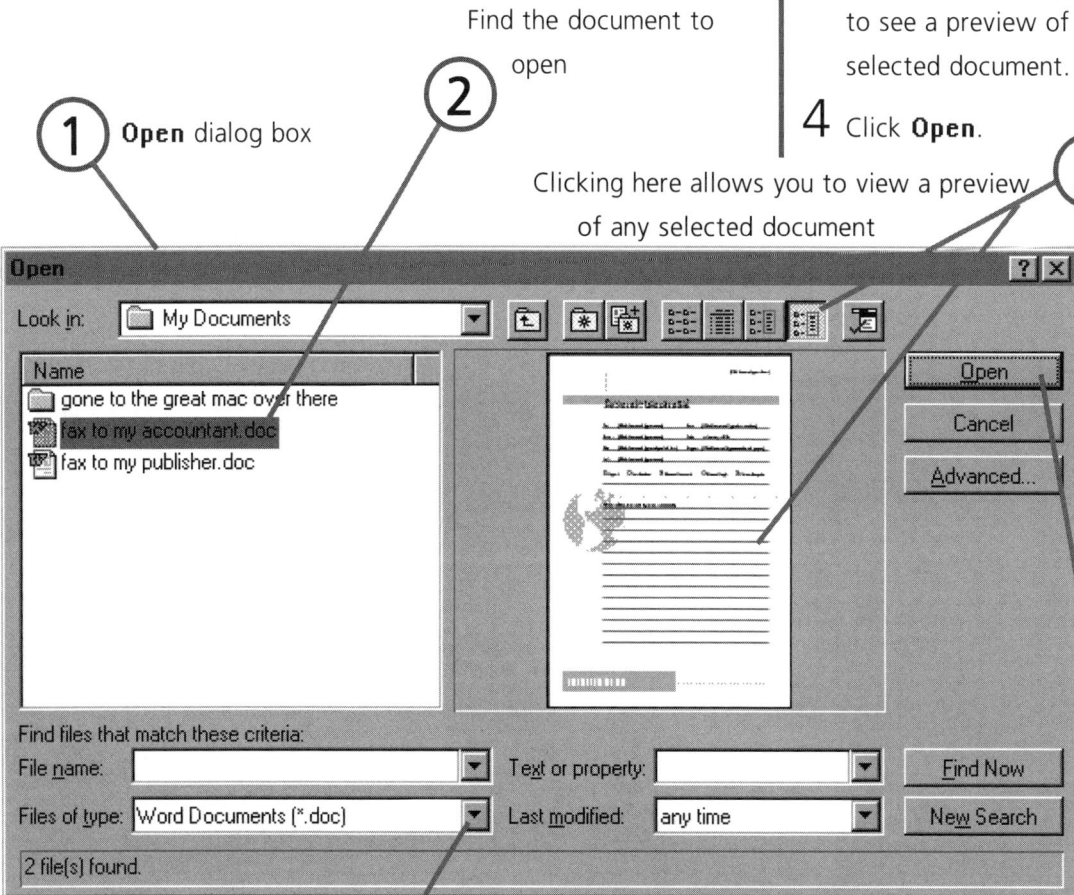

(1) **Open** dialog box

(2) Find the document to open

(3) Clicking here allows you to view a preview of any selected document

If the document isn't a Word document (with the **.doc** extension), this drop-down box lets you see other openable document types

Click (4)

Creating new documents

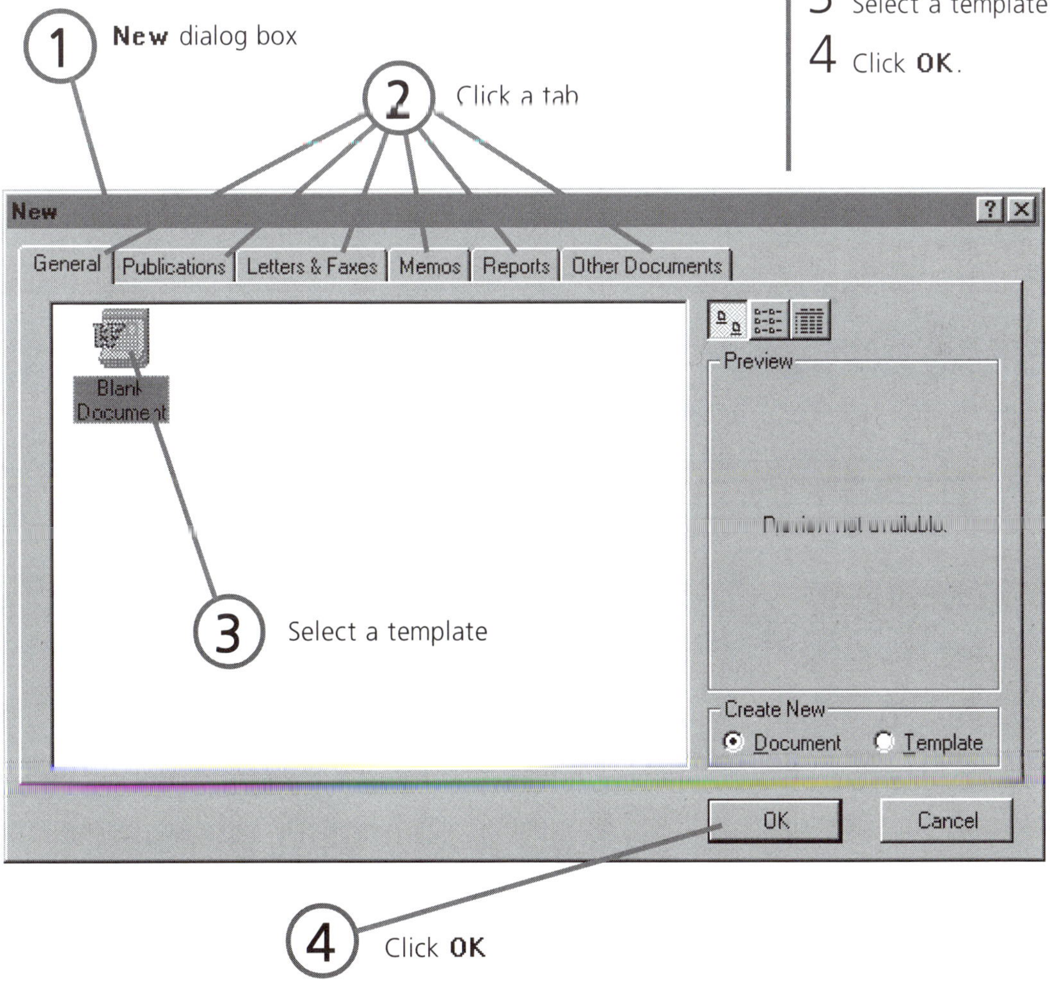

Basic steps:

Creating a new document is just as easy as opening an existing document. Word creates a new document as the image of a template. Templates are ready-built and installed document *plans*, complete with styles and formats you might want to use for any particular type of document (see page 132 for further details of templates).

Templates are arranged in sections, accessed in the New dialog box with tabs.

1 **New** dialog box
2 Click a tab
New
General
Publications
Letters & Faxes
Memos
Reports
Other Documents
Blank Document
Preview
Create New
Document
Template
OK
Cancel
3 Select a template
4 Click **OK**

CREATING A NEW DOCUMENT

1. Choose **File→New**, or type Alt+F then N, or type Ctrl+N. The **New** dialog box is called up.
2. Click a tab with the generic heading of the document type you want to create.
3. Select a template.
4. Click **OK**.

Creating... (contd)

Basic steps:

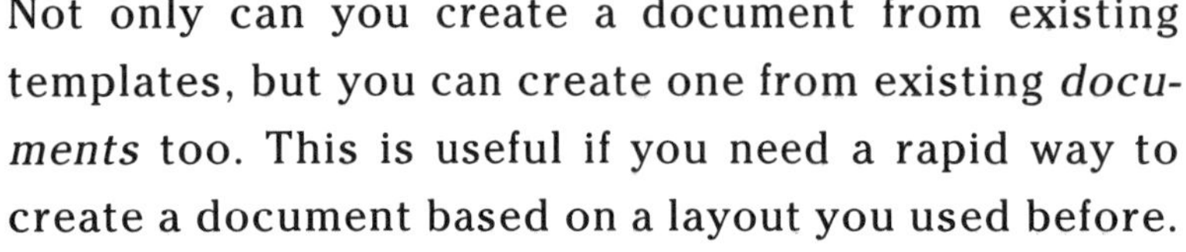

Not only can you create a document from existing templates, but you can create one from existing *documents* too. This is useful if you need a rapid way to create a document based on a layout you used before.

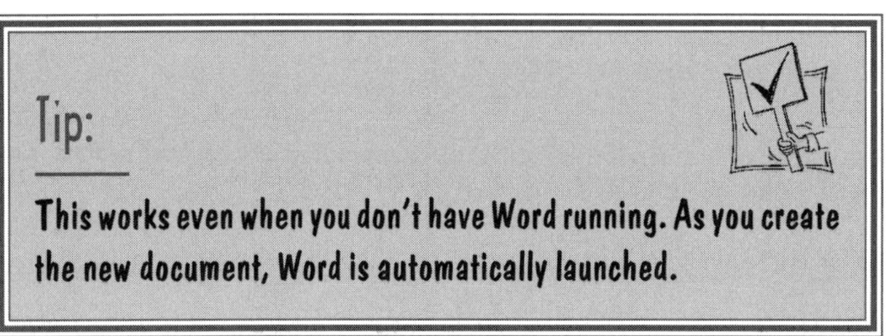

Tip:

This works even when you don't have Word running. As you create the new document, Word is automatically launched.

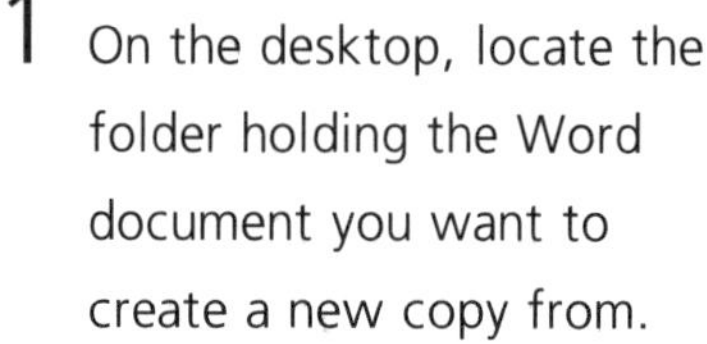

1. On the desktop, locate the folder holding the Word document you want to create a new copy from.
2. Click the document with the right mouse button.
3. In the shortcut menu, click **New** with your left mouse button — a copy of the document is opened.

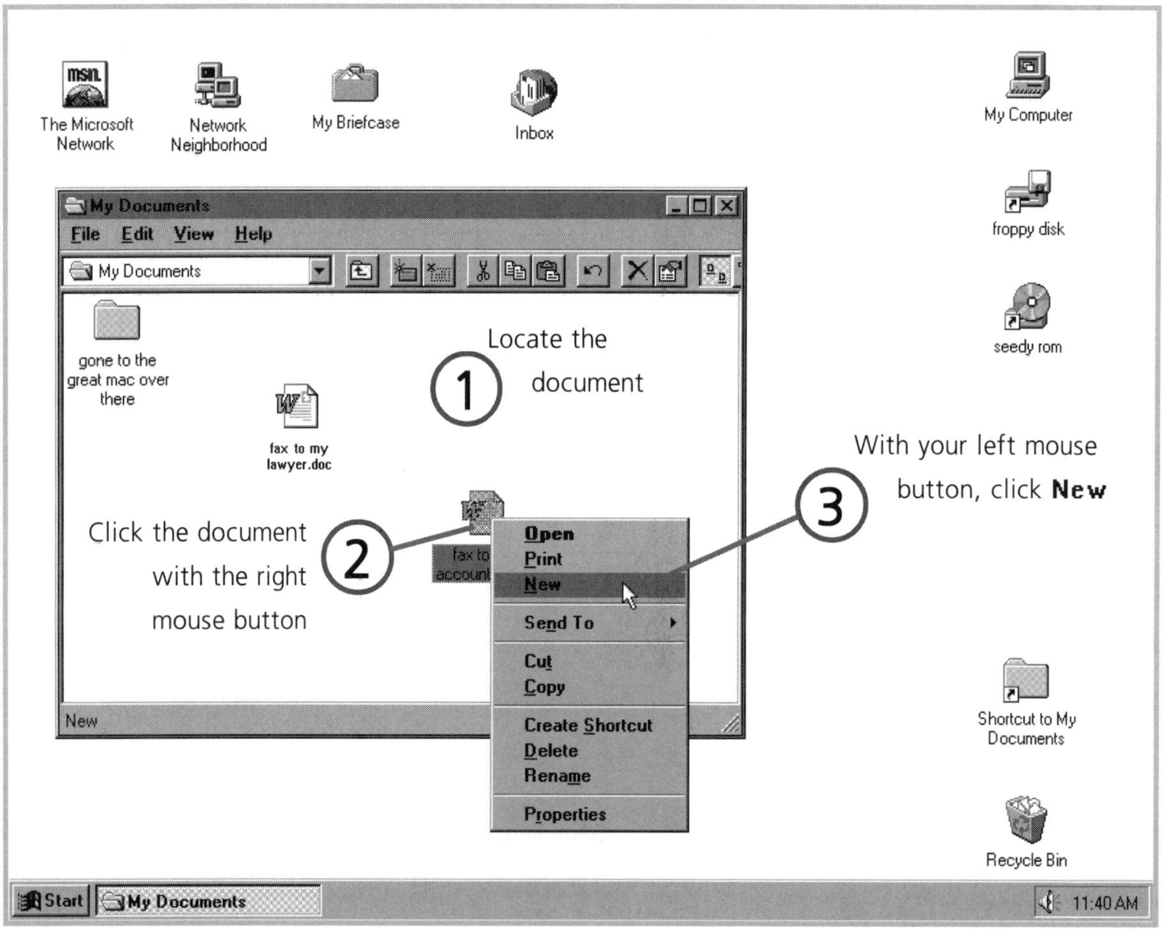

1 Locate the document

2 Click the document with the right mouse button

3 With your left mouse button, click **New**

Good-bye – or just au revoir?

After you've finished using a computer program it's usual to exit or quit it. If you're only trying to clear the screen for a short while, on the other hand, there are alternatives.

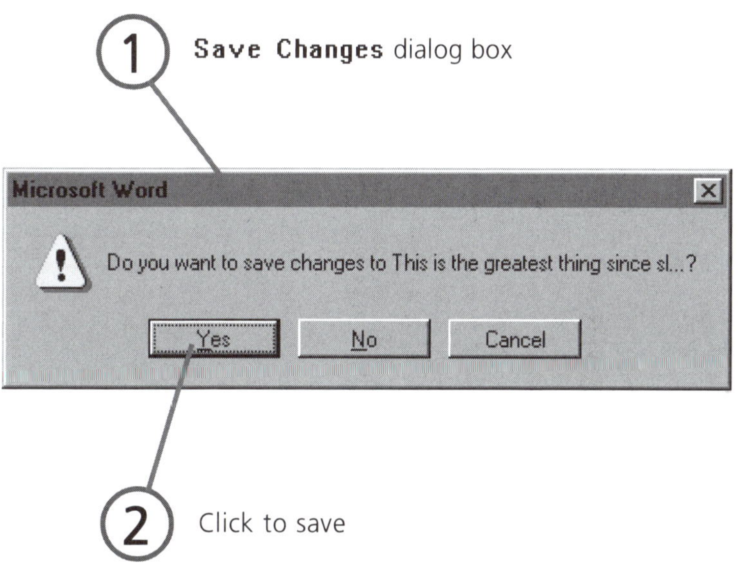

1 **Save Changes** dialog box
Microsoft Word
Do you want to save changes to This is the greatest thing since sl...?
Yes
No
Cancel
2 Click to save

Basic steps:

1. Choose **File→Exit**, or type Alt+F then X. If you have recently saved the document or documents you are working on and have not worked on them since, Word quits right away. If you have worked on a document since last saving it (or have not saved it at all) the **Save Changes?** dialog box is displayed
2. If you click **Yes**, Word calls up the **Save As** dialog box, as on page 21.

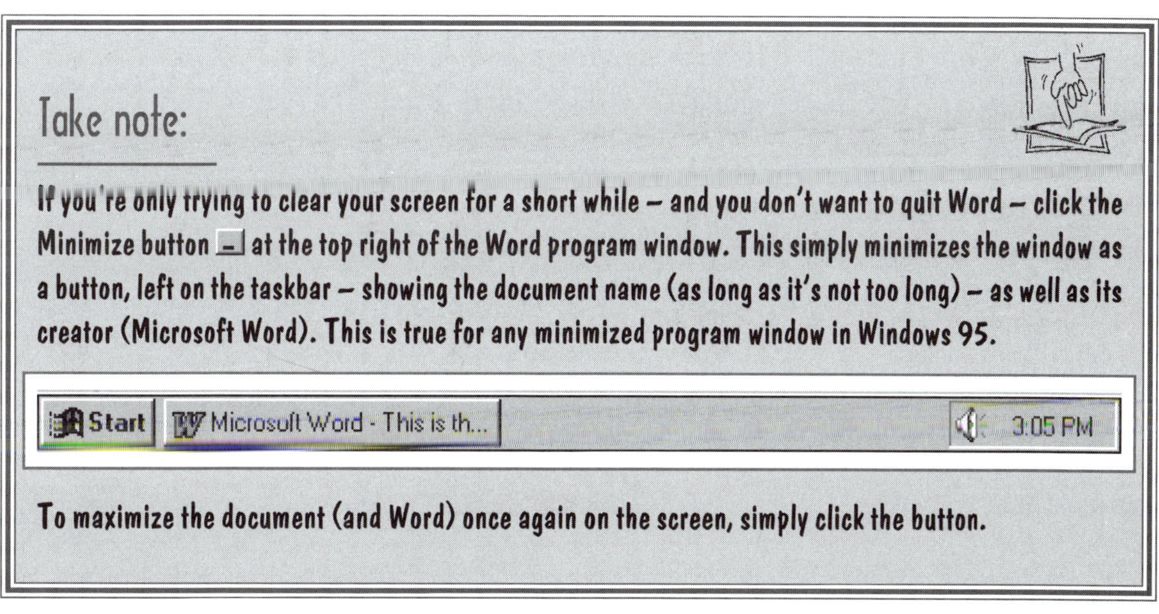

Take note:

If you're only trying to clear your screen for a short while – and you don't want to quit Word – click the Minimize button at the top right of the Word program window. This simply minimizes the window as a button, left on the taskbar – showing the document name (as long as it's not too long) – as well as its creator (Microsoft Word). This is true for any minimized program window in Windows 95.

Start
Microsoft Word - This is th...
3:05 PM

To maximize the document (and Word) once again on the screen, simply click the button.

Summary for Section 1

- Start up Word by choosing Start↳**Programs**↳**Microsoft Word**, or Start↳**Programs**↳**Microsoft Office**↳**Microsoft Word** from the taskbar.
- Get on-line help by double-clicking the Help button in the standard toolbar. Then select the topic you want help on.
- Get faster on-line help by single-clicking the Help button, then click the button, object, or even menu command you need help with.
- Access toolbars by either clicking on any toolbar with the right mouse button then selecting the one you want, or choose **View**↳**Toolbars** to call up the **Toolbars** dialog box.
- Change document view between normal, page layout, and outline to suit the way you work.
- Page layout view lets you see the page as it will be printed.
- Outline view lets you rearrange headings and their hierarchies, as well as dragging text large distances easily in the document.
- Remove all on-screen clutter with full screen view by choosing **View**↳**Full Screen**.
- Open existing Word documents — or other applications' documents — from the **Open** dialog box.
- Create a new document — in the form of a selected template — in the **New** dialog box.

2 Text essentials

Entering text 28
Editing text 30
Selecting text 32
Ooops – a mistake! 36
Cut, copy, and paste 38
Drag-and-drop editing 40
Entering symbols 42
Summary for Section 2 44

Entering text

As a word processor, of course, Word's main function is to store straightforward text. As you start up Word, or create a new document, you can begin to enter text immediately.

Basic steps:

1 Simply type something. It doesn't matter what — a few lines of rubbish will do nicely.

2 If the document is important, remember to save it.

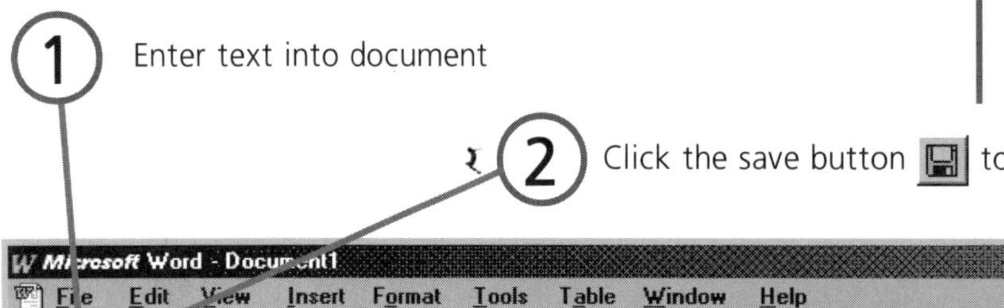

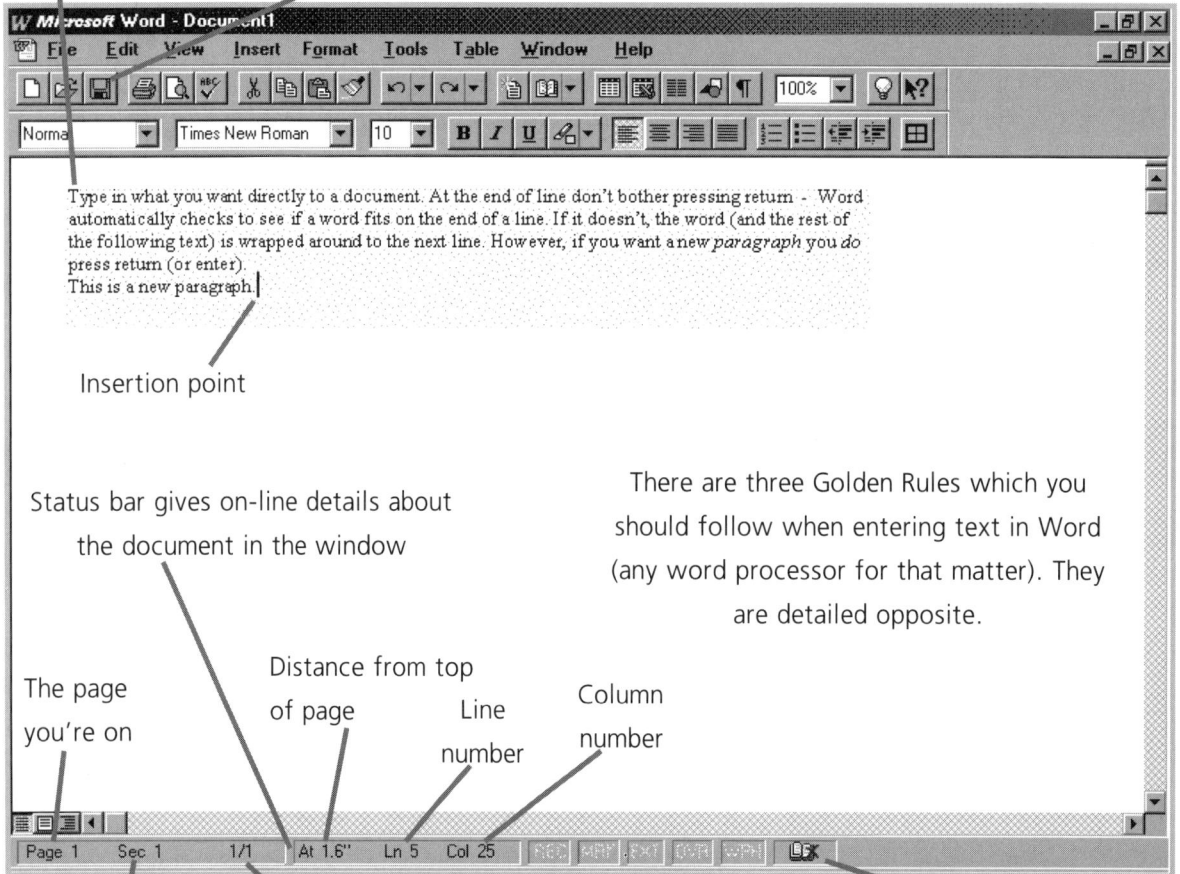

1 Enter text into document
2 Click the save button to save your document
Microsoft Word - Document1
File Edit View Insert Format Tools Table Window Help
Normal
Times New Roman
10
100%
Type in what you want directly to a document. At the end of line don't bother pressing return - Word automatically checks to see if a word fits on the end of a line. If it doesn't, the word (and the rest of the following text) is wrapped around to the next line. However, if you want a new *paragraph* you *do* press return (or enter).
This is a new paragraph.
Insertion point
Status bar gives on-line details about the document in the window
There are three Golden Rules which you should follow when entering text in Word (any word processor for that matter). They are detailed opposite.
The page you're on
Distance from top of page
Line number
Column number
Page 1 Sec 1 1/1 At 1.6" Ln 5 Col 25
Which section of the document you're in
Page number of total
Insertion point location on page
Modes
Spelling button

The status bar

Get into the habit of looking at the status bar. It gives some explicit information about what's happening within your Word document, such as:

- page number, section (you can break your document up into smaller sections, to make it more manageable — see page 74) number, and total number of pages
- location of the insertion point (that is, the point within the text where your keyboard entries appear on screen)
- mode buttons — accessed by double-clicking — of these only two are of importance here, and are:
- WPH — on-line help for ex-WordPerfect users. See page 11 for details
- OVR — active when blacked (that is, not grayed). See next page for details
- spelling button — if the button displays an ✘ mark, Word has found an error

Take note:

The Golden Rules of Word

1 Never, never, never, never, never, never, never, never, never, never (get the message?) put two spaces together. The old typists' routine of putting two spaces at the end of a sentence should not be done in a word processor because spaces aren't generally of a fixed width. A program like Word adjusts spaces to ensure the text fits its given column width and looks good. Two or more spaces together may be adjusted in width to give ridiculously wide spaces between words. For the same reason, text which is formed into tabular columns mustn't be created by inserting spaces to line columns up – it might look aligned on screen, but when it prints you can't guarantee it – use tabs instead (see page 60).

2 Never, never, never, never (oh, here we go again) put two carriage returns together. Actually, this isn't quite so critical as Golden Rule number 1, but important nevertheless. Spaces between paragraphs are best controlled by creating styles for each paragraph type (see section 6) which incorporate spaces before and after them.

3 Never (once is enough this time, I'm sure) press ↵ or Enter at the end of a line of text – unless the end of the line is also the end of a paragraph. There is simply no need – and carriage returns fix the text to those line lengths. Use Word's word-wrapping facility to do it automatically – then any textual style changes will automatically create consequent new word-wraps, too.

Editing text

Basic steps:

Inevitably you will make mistakes in your work. This is where a word processor like Word shows its strength. On a typewriter, mistakes have to be erased and re-typed, usually resulting in a shoddy document. In a word processor, on the other hand, mistakes are simply edited on-screen before printing. Even if a mistake slips by you, and you only see it after printing, you can correct it and reprint the document.

Even if your required corrections aren't due to mistakes, but are straightforward editorial changes, Word has some unbeaten facilities for making any kind of textual change necessary in a document.

There are several ways you can edit text. The simplest — covered here — is overtyping.

All editing procedures, on the other hand, rely on the principle of placing the insertion point at the point which requires editing! If you learn nothing else from this page, learn this fact.

OVERTYPE EDITING

1 If you spot a mistake which requires you to retype part or all of a word or sentence, position the insertion point at the beginning of the mistake.

2 Look at the OVR button on the status bar. If it is grayed, you are in insert edit mode; if it is black you are in overtype edit mode. Double-click it to toggle between the two modes. Make sure you are in overtype edit mode (the button should be in blackface (ie OVR).

As you move the mouse pointer over text it changes to the I-beam pointer I. When you position the pointer over the point to edit, then click, the insertion point of Word becomes active at that point. This whole process of pointing and clicking with the I-beam pointer I is known as *positioning the insertion point.*

Remember it — because all editing relies on it!

1

There was a cow stupefied on a hill. If it hasn't gonn it will be their still.
Now is the time for all good men to come to the aid of the party

3 Retype the section of text — this overtypes text already there.

4 Move to any other areas you need to overtype as in Step 1.

5 When you have finished overtyping, double-click the overtype button OVR again to return to insertion mode

Take note:

Editing in any word processor worth its salt is most often a combination of techniques – not just one. In other words – find out about all techniques to take full advantage of Word.

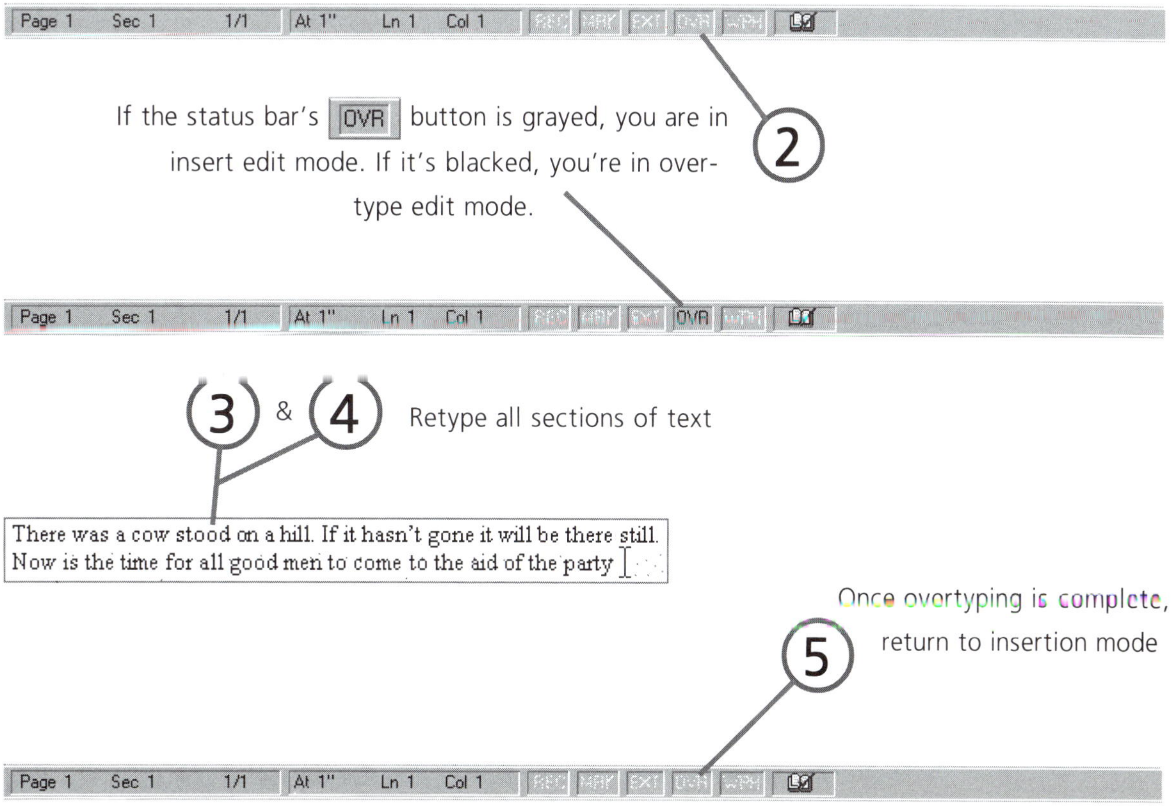

Page 1 Sec 1 1/1 At 1" Ln 1 Col 1 REC MRK EXT OVR WPH

2

If the status bar's OVR button is grayed, you are in insert edit mode. If it's blacked, you're in overtype edit mode.

Page 1 Sec 1 1/1 At 1" Ln 1 Col 1 REC MRK EXT OVR WPH

3 & 4 Retype all sections of text

There was a cow stood on a hill. If it hasn't gone it will be there still.
Now is the time for all good men to come to the aid of the party

5 Once overtyping is complete, return to insertion mode

Page 1 Sec 1 1/1 At 1" Ln 1 Col 1 REC MRK EXT OVR WPH

Selecting text

Whenever you want to edit text (that is, apart from when you overtype — see previous page) you need to select the particular text you want to change:

- Word allows you to do this in various ways
- no single way is best
- instead, a combination of selecting techniques — depending on what is to be selected — should be used
- selection of text is sometimes known by different names such as blocking or highlighting. These names are often merely descriptive of the selection process — text which is selected becomes highlighted or blocked and that's how you know the text happens to be selected!

Basic steps:

1. You can select any letter, word, sentence, paragraph, or any part of these by dragging over the required text.
2. To select a single word, double-click the word.
3. To select more than one word, drag from one word across to the next, or further if you want more words to be selected.
4. To select a whole line of text, click in the selection bar to the left of the line.

(1) Drag the I-beam pointer over the letters, or words, or sentences, or paragraphs you want to be selected

No, no, no, said the Giant. There can be no suggestion of a compromise. I am going to eat you all up, because that's the sort of thing giants are known to do.

As you drag over your selected text and release the mouse button, the selected text becomes highlighted.

(2) You can select a single word most quickly by double-clicking the word

Highlighted text is simply the visible sign that the text is selected

No, no, no, said the Giant. There can be no suggestion of a compromise. I am going to eat you all up, because that's the sort of thing giants are known to do.

3

Drag over words to select them. As you drag over each new part of a word the whole word becomes selected automatically

No, no, no, said the Giant. There can be no suggsetion of a compromise. I am going to eat you all up, because that's the sort of thing giants are known to do.

Tip:

When you begin selecting in the middle of a word, then drag to include part of another word, Word automatically selects both words (and any subsequent ones too), as well as any space after the words.

4

Select whole lines of text by clicking in the selection bar

The selection bar is to the left of the text on any Word document page

No, no, no, said the Giant. There can be no suggsetion of a compromise. I am going to eat you all up, because that's the sort of thing giants are known to do.

Take note:

All of these selection techniques can be used to select graphic items, such as pictures, as well as text.

Selecting text (contd)

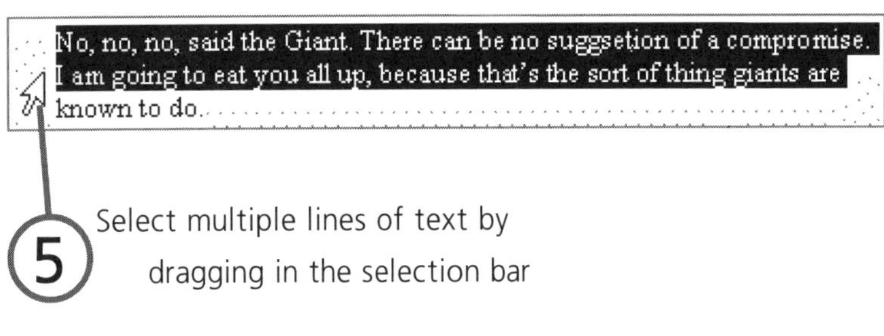

No, no, no, said the Giant. There can be no suggsetion of a compromise.
I am going to eat you all up, because that's the sort of thing giants are
known to do.

5 Select multiple lines of text by dragging in the selection bar

6 Select a single sentence by holding down Ctrl and clicking in the sentence

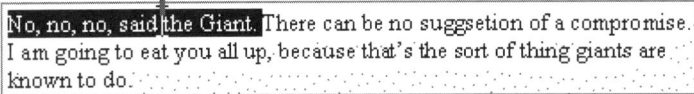

No, no, no, said the Giant. There can be no suggsetion of a compromise.
I am going to eat you all up, because that's the sort of thing giants are
known to do.

7 Double-click in the selection bar (or triple-click in the text) to select a paragraph

No, no, no, said the Giant. There can be no suggsetion of a compromise.
I am going to eat you all up, because that's the sort of thing giants are
known to do.

8 Drag across paragraphs in the selection bar to select multiple paragraphs

No, no, no, said the Giant. There can be no suggsetion of a compromise.
I am going to eat you all up, because that's the sort of thing giants are
known to do.

With that he picked up Jack and lifted him towards his mouth. Once
inside the Giant's mouth Jack realised his time was nigh unless he did
some quick thinking. He decided to go for broke and tickled the Giant's
tonsils.

Basic steps:

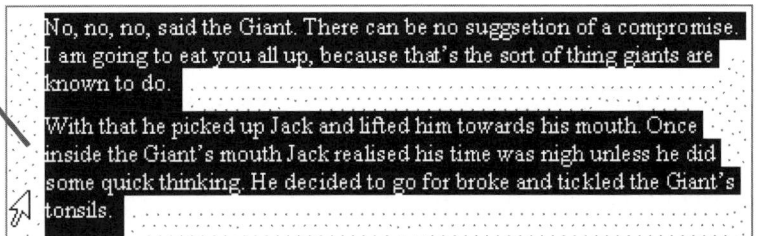

5 To select multiple lines of text, drag in the selection bar to the left of the lines.

6 To select a sentence, hold down Ctrl and click anywhere in the sentence.

7 To select a paragraph, either double-click in the selection bar to the left of the paragraph, or triple-click anywhere in the text.

8 To select multiple paragraphs, drag in the selection bar to the left of the paragraphs.

9 To select an entire document, triple-click in the selection bar.

10 Select text which isn't a word, sentence, or paragraph by positioning the insertion point at the beginning of the text, then holding down Shift while you click at the end.

Select an entire document's text by triple-clicking in the selection bar

9

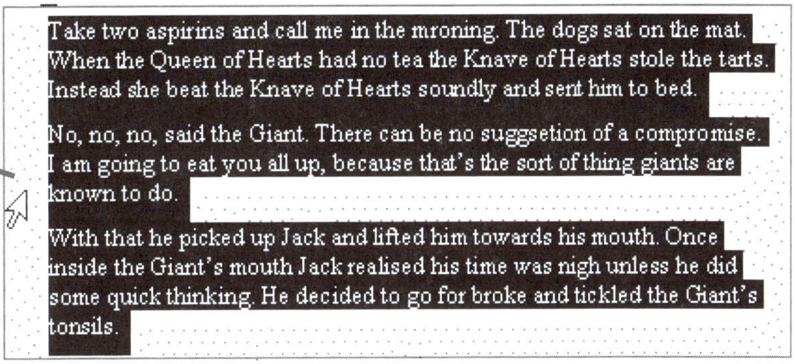

Take two aspirins and call me in the mroning. The dogs sat on the mat. When the Queen of Hearts had no tea the Knave of Hearts stole the tarts. Instead she beat the Knave of Hearts soundly and sent him to bed.

No, no, no, said the Giant. There can be no suggsetion of a compromise. I am going to eat you all up, because that's the sort of thing giants are known to do.

With that he picked up Jack and lifted him towards his mouth. Once inside the Giant's mouth Jack realised his time was nigh unless he did some quick thinking. He decided to go for broke and tickled the Giant's tonsils.

> **Tip:**
>
> **Cancel a selection by clicking outside of it, or pressing any arrow key.**

By clicking at the starting point, then holding down Shift and clicking at the finishing point, a complete block of text can be selected

10

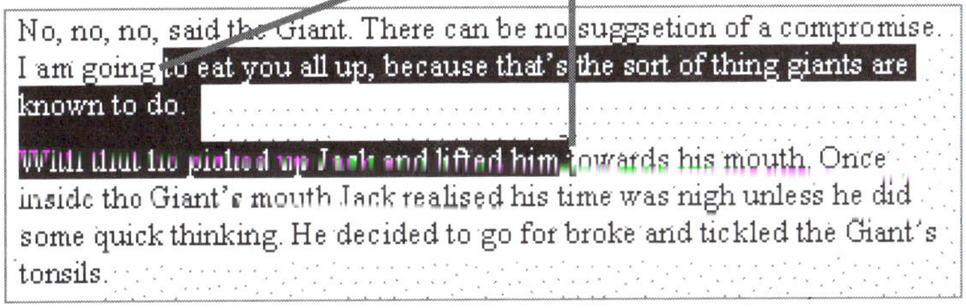

No, no, no, said the Giant. There can be no suggsetion of a compromise. I am going to eat you all up, because that's the sort of thing giants are known to do.

With that he picked up Jack and lifted him towards his mouth. Once inside the Giant's mouth Jack realised his time was nigh unless he did some quick thinking. He decided to go for broke and tickled the Giant's tonsils.

> **Tip:**
>
> **Whatever you do in Word – writing, editing, stylizing, formatting and so on – relies on being able to select text.**
>
> **No single selection method is best for all purposes. Depending on what you want to select, you should choose the preferred method. Sometimes you should use the mouse, sometimes you should use the keyboard.**
>
> **The only way you can make sure you use the preferred method for any particular purpose is to learn how to use all methods.**

Keyboard shortcuts

You can select text with the keyboard, too:

One character right	Shift + →
One character left	Shift + ←
To the end of a word	Ctrl + Shift + →
To the beginning of a word	Ctrl + Shift + ←
To the end of a line	Shift + End
To the beginning of a line	Shift + Home
One line down	Shift + ↓
One line up	Shift + ↑
To the end of a paragraph	Ctrl + Shift + ↓
To the beginning of a paragraph	Ctrl + Shift + ↑
One screen down	Shift + Page Down
One screen up	Shift + Page Up
To end of document	Ctrl + Shift + End
To beginning of document	Ctrl + Shift + Home
Entire document	Ctrl + A
To a specific location	F8 +arrow keys

Ooops – a mistake!

Word processors are meant to make the correction of mistakes as simple as possible. Apart from the editing facilities of Word we've already seen, however, are extra goodies which make the correction of simple typing errors almost as easy as making the mistakes in the first place — but not qwite, if you see what I mean!

It's best to know all these goodies to get the best out of Word. The mistakes we're concerned with here are those which you notice almost as you make them:

- obvious spelling errors
- mis-hit keys
- style changes which shouldn't have been made

and so on.

Basic steps:

1 If you have just a few letters you want to delete, a quick solution can be to press [Back space], or [Delete]:

- [Back space] deletes the character before the insertion point
- [Delete] deletes the character after the insertion point
- [Ctrl]+[Back space] deletes the word before the insertion point
- [Ctrl]+[Delete] deletes the word after the insertion point

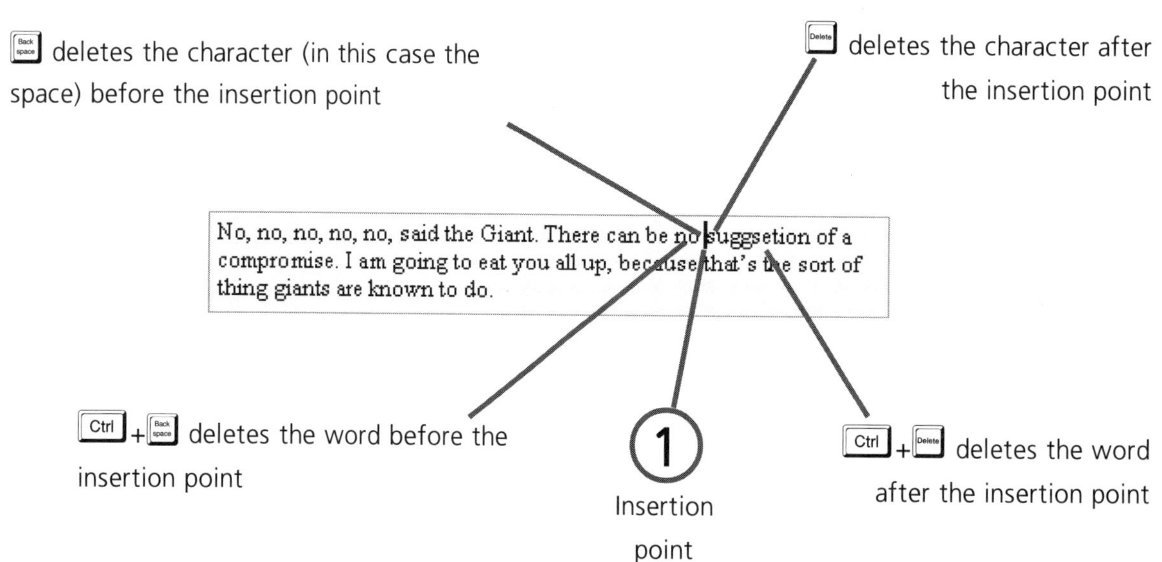
[Back space] deletes the character (in this case the space) before the insertion point
[Delete] deletes the character after the insertion point
No, no, no, no, no, said the Giant. There can be no suggsetion of a compromise. I am going to eat you all up, because that's the sort of thing giants are known to do.
[Ctrl]+[Back space] deletes the word before the insertion point
1
Insertion point
[Ctrl]+[Delete] deletes the word after the insertion point

2 You can very often *undo* a mistake or change you make in a Word document, because Word features a multiple undo facility. Just click the Undo button [Undo button] after you have made a mistake or change you want to undo and a drop-down box lists all your recent actions in reverse order — your most recent action at the top of the list.

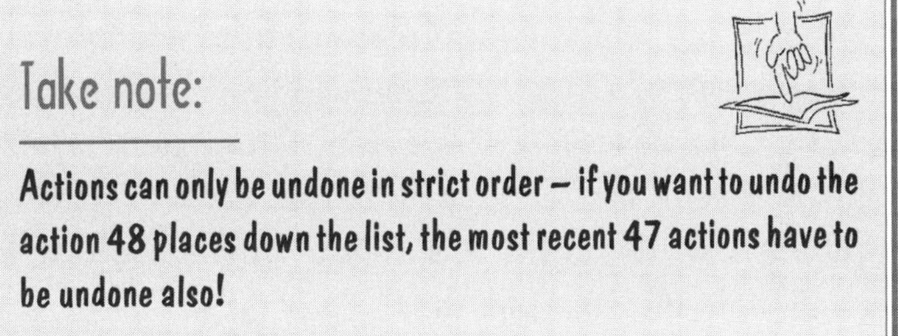

Take note:

Actions can only be undone in strict order – if you want to undo the action 48 places down the list, the most recent 47 actions have to be undone also!

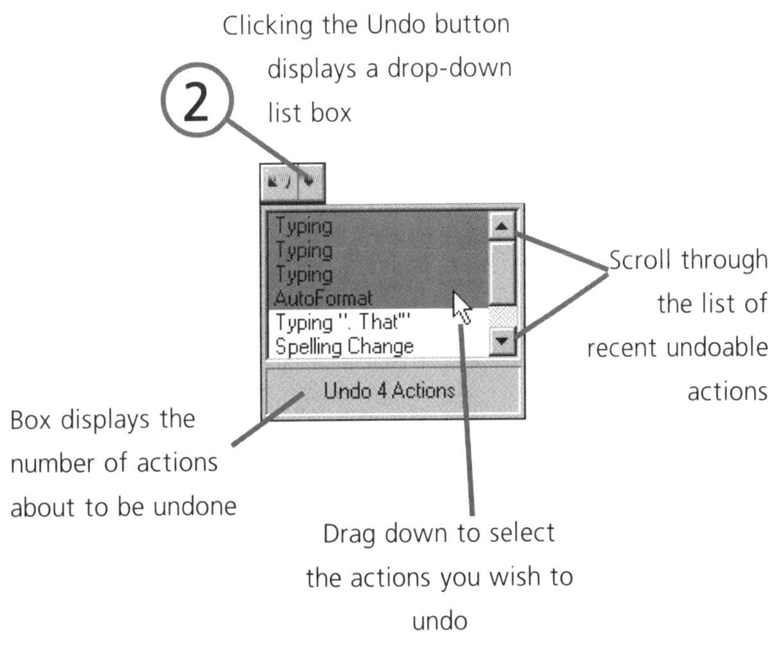
Clicking the Undo button displays a drop-down list box
2
Typing
Typing
Typing
AutoFormat
Typing ". That"
Spelling Change
Undo 4 Actions
Scroll through the list of recent undoable actions
Box displays the number of actions about to be undone
Drag down to select the actions you wish to undo

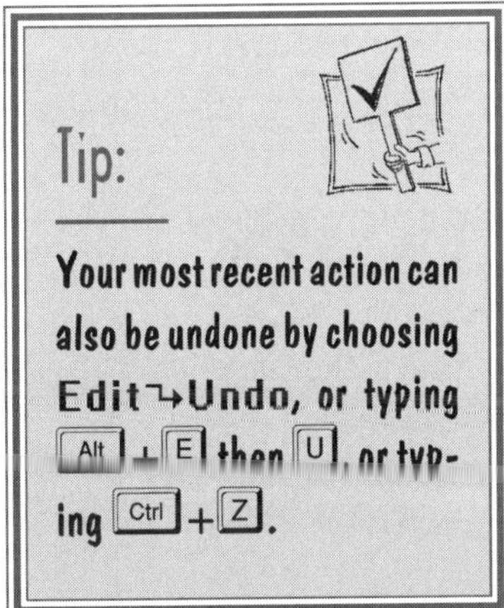

Tip:

Your most recent action can also be undone by choosing Edit→Undo, or typing Alt + E then U, or typing Ctrl + Z.

Tip:

If you undo an action by mistake, click the Redo button [Redo button] to undo the undo!

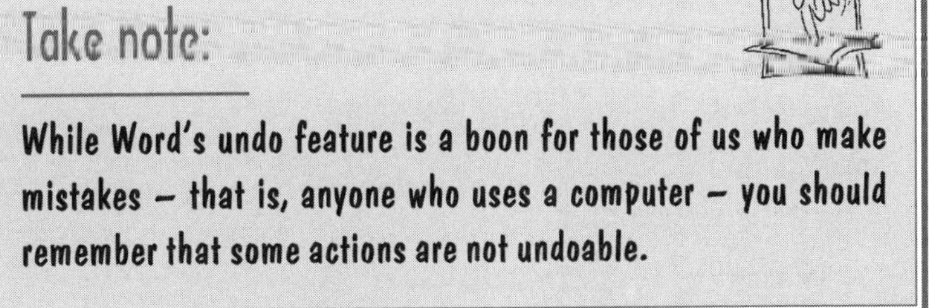

Take note:

While Word's undo feature is a boon for those of us who make mistakes – that is, anyone who uses a computer – you should remember that some actions are not undoable.

Cut, copy, and paste

Basic steps :

Word (like any Windows application) uses a temporary storage area known as the Clipboard to keep items you want to move or copy within a Word document. These items can be of text or graphic forms (or a mixture of both). Using the Clipboard to do this is known as cutting, copying, and pasting:

- you *cut* an item onto the Clipboard when you want to remove it from one place in a document and move it to another place
- you *copy* an item onto the Clipboard when you want it to occur at more than one place in your document
- taking an item from the Clipboard and putting it in your document is known as *pasting*.

CUTTING

1 Select the item or items you want to cut onto the Clipboard. This can be a selection of text, a graphical item, or a combination of the two.

2 Choose **Edit→Cut**, or type Alt+E then T, or type Ctrl+X, or simply click the Cut button to cut the selected item — it disappears from your Word document and is moved onto the Clipboard.

Come and see the show

On the other hand, this is a boring part of this document. Let's liven it up by moving the graphic down here!

1 & 3 Select the item or items to be cut or copied

Use whichever selection method is appropriate for the text (or graphic in this case) to be copied or cut. To select this graphic, clicking in the selection bar is fastest.

2 Cut the item or items (now you see it — now you don't!)

Come and see the show

On the other hand, this is a boring part of this document. Let's liven it up by moving the graphic down here!

Position the insertion point before pasting 5

COPYING

3 Select the item or items you want to copy.

4 Choose **Edit➜Copy**, or type Alt+E then C, or type Ctrl+C, or click the Copy button — the selection stays in your document but is copied onto the Clipboard, too.

PASTING

5 Position the insertion point where you want the item or items stored on the Clipboard to be pasted.

6 Choose **Edit➜Paste**, or type Alt+E then P, or type Ctrl+V, or click the Paste button to paste the item or items into your document.

Tip:

Items on the Clipboard remain there until you cut or copy another item onto the Clipboard (or until you exit Word). In other words, you can paste an item into your document over and over again if you want.

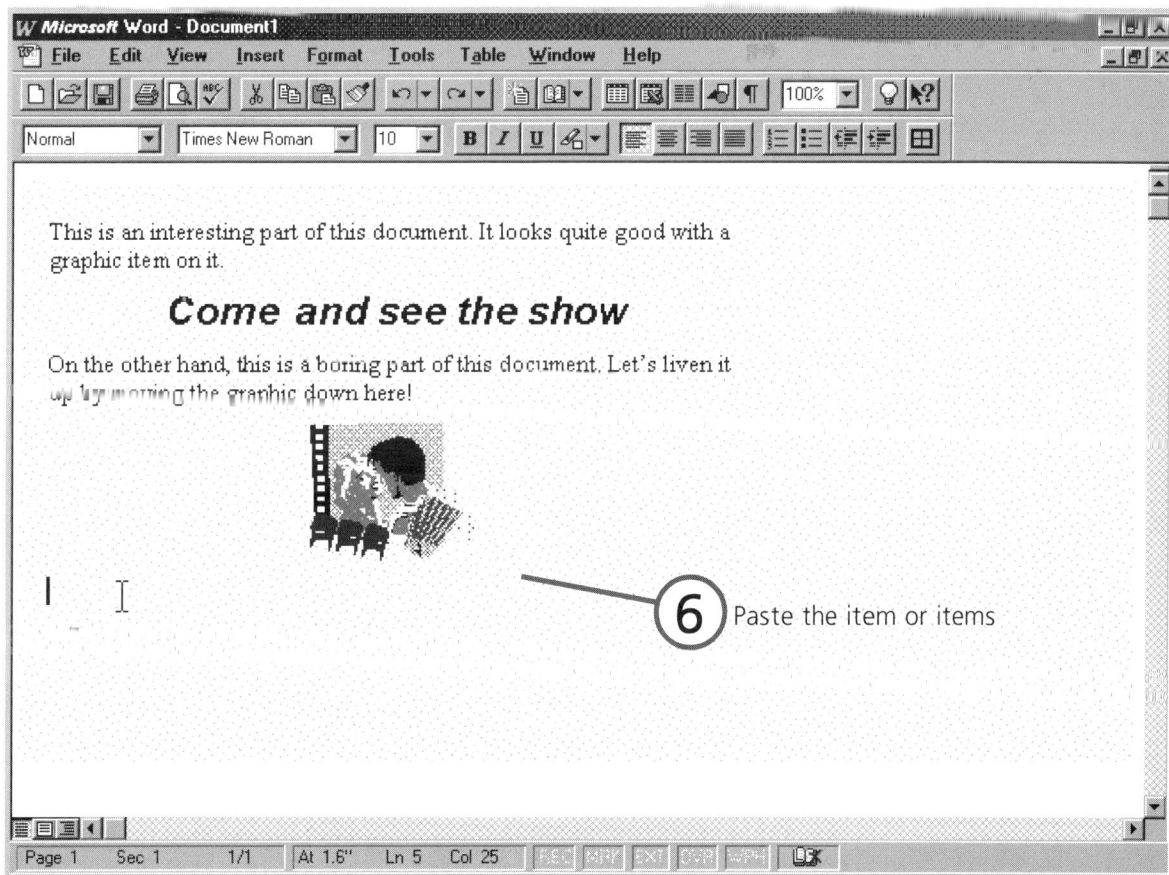

W Microsoft Word - Document1

File Edit View Insert Format Tools Table Window Help

This is an interesting part of this document. It looks quite good with a graphic item on it.

Come and see the show

On the other hand, this is a boring part of this document. Let's liven it up by moving the graphic down here!

6 Paste the item or items

Page 1 Sec 1 1/1 At 1.6" Ln 5 Col 25

Drag-and-drop editing

Word has an extremely useful feature in its ability to allow selected text to be moved or copied by dragging. Proper use of this drag-and-drop editing can speed up incorporation of revisions in a document.

1 Select the text

Take two aspirins and call me in the mroning. The dogs sat on the mat.
When the Queen of Hearts had no tea the Knave of Hearts stole the tarts.
Instead she beat the Knave of Hearts soundly and sent him to bed.

2 The arrow pointer replaces the I-beam pointer over selected text

Take two aspirins and call me in the mroning. The dogs sat on the mat.
When the Queen of Hearts had no tea the Knave of Hearts stole the tarts.
Instead she beat the Knave of Hearts soundly and sent him to bed.

3 As you drag the selected text, the drag-and-drop pointer is displayed

Take two aspirins and call me in the mroning. The dogs sat on the mat.
When the Queen of Hearts had no tea the Knave of Hearts stole the tarts.
Instead she beat the Knave of Hearts soundly and sent him to bed.

4 The dotted insertion point tells you where the text will be moved to

5 The text moves as you let go of the mouse button

Take two aspirins and call me in the mroning. The dogs sat on the mat.
When the Knave of Hearts stole the tarts the Queen of Hearts had no tea.
Instead she beat the Knave of Hearts soundly and sent him to bed.

Basic steps:

MOVING SELECTED TEXT

1 Select the text to be moved .

2 Position the pointer over the selected text (the I-beam pointer changes to the arrow pointer).

3 Click on the selected text and drag the pointer — it changes to the drag-and-drop pointer .

4 As you drag the drag-and-drop pointer to a new position, the dotted insertion point follows, indicating where the selected text will be dragged to.

5 When you have located the dotted insertion point where you want, release the mouse button. The selected text moves to the new location.

Copying selected text

6 Select text as before.

7 Drag the selected text as before.

8 Locate the position you wish to copy text to as before (with the dotted insertion point).

9 Before you let go of the mouse button, press and hold down Ctrl (the drag-and-drop pointer changes to show a plus symbol indicating Word is ready to copy — not just move — text).

10 Let go of the mouse button. The selected text is copied to the new location.

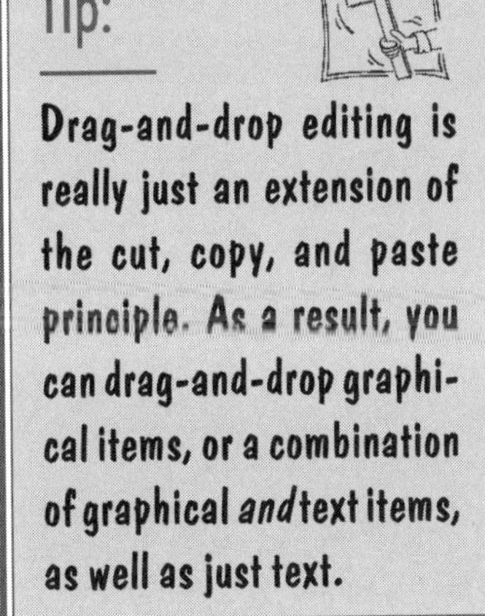
Tip:
Drag-and-drop editing is really just an extension of the cut, copy, and paste principle. As a result, you can drag-and-drop graphical items, or a combination of graphical *and* text items, as well as just text.

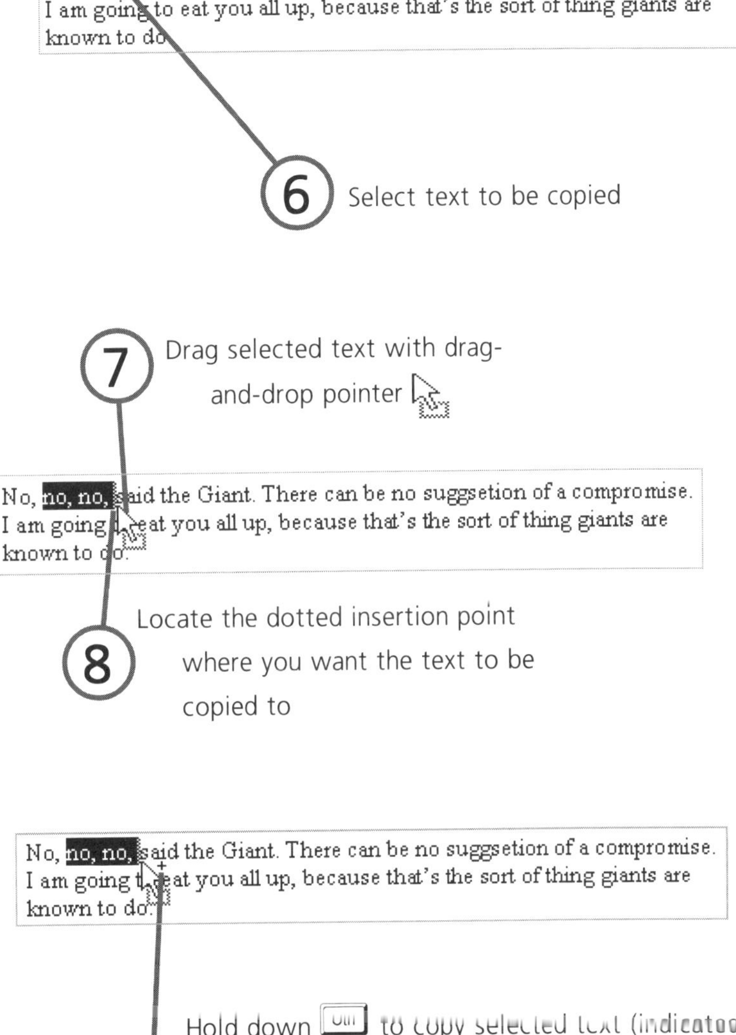
No, no, no, said the Giant. There can be no suggsetion of a compromise. I am going to eat you all up, because that's the sort of thing giants are known to do.
6 Select text to be copied
7 Drag selected text with drag-and-drop pointer
No, no, no, said the Giant. There can be no suggsetion of a compromise. I am going to eat you all up, because that's the sort of thing giants are known to do.
8 Locate the dotted insertion point where you want the text to be copied to
No, no, no, said the Giant. There can be no suggsetion of a compromise. I am going to eat you all up, because that's the sort of thing giants are known to do.

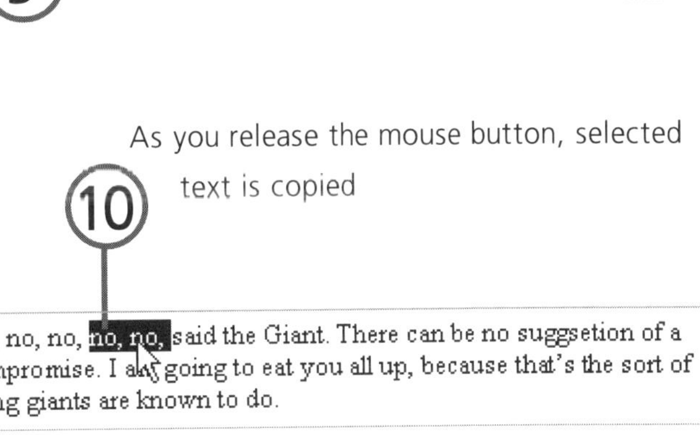
9 Hold down Ctrl to copy selected text (indicated by + symbol on drag-and-drop pointer)
10 As you release the mouse button, selected text is copied
No, no, no, no, no, said the Giant. There can be no suggsetion of a compromise. I am going to eat you all up, because that's the sort of thing giants are known to do.

Entering symbols

Although Word is a *word* processor, very often it's necessary to include symbols within text. Examples of such symbols are:

- mathematical or scientific symbols — Ω µ ß ∝, for example (however, if you want to include complete mathematical formulae or expressions into your work it is best to use Word's integral equation editor, which is beyond the scope of this book)
- dingbats — the blob or bullet (●) at the left of this list is an example of a dingbat. Others are ✄ ☞ ✣ ❐ ♠, which can be used to embellish text
- typographical symbols and marks — the most obvious examples of typographical marks are curly quotes (' and ") which differentiate properly typeset text from typewritten text (with straight quotes — ' and ") as well as en dashes (–) and em dashes (—)
- foreign letters with accents — é ü å õ ç

and so on. The ability to enter such symbols rapidly greatly enhances a word processor. Word has a special Symbol command which simplifies the task.

Tip:

Use typographer's symbols and marks to give your work that professional edge. Automatically include curly quotes using Word's AutoCorrect feature (page 100). Use an en dash to combine number ranges (eg, pages 44–56) and use an em dash to separate emphasizing text – just like that!

Basic steps:

1 Position the insertion point where you want the symbol to be (if you are typing in text and want to enter the symbol as you go, the insertion point is already positioned correctly). Now choose **Insert→Symbol**, or type [Alt]+[I] then [S]. This calls up the **Symbol** dialog box which automatically displays symbols available in fonts.

2 Click a symbol and it is displayed enlarged. Click Insert if you want the symbol in your text. Alternatively, double-click the symbol you want. It is placed in the text at the position of the insertion point.

3 Display and choose a different font, if you want, with the **Font** drop-down list box.

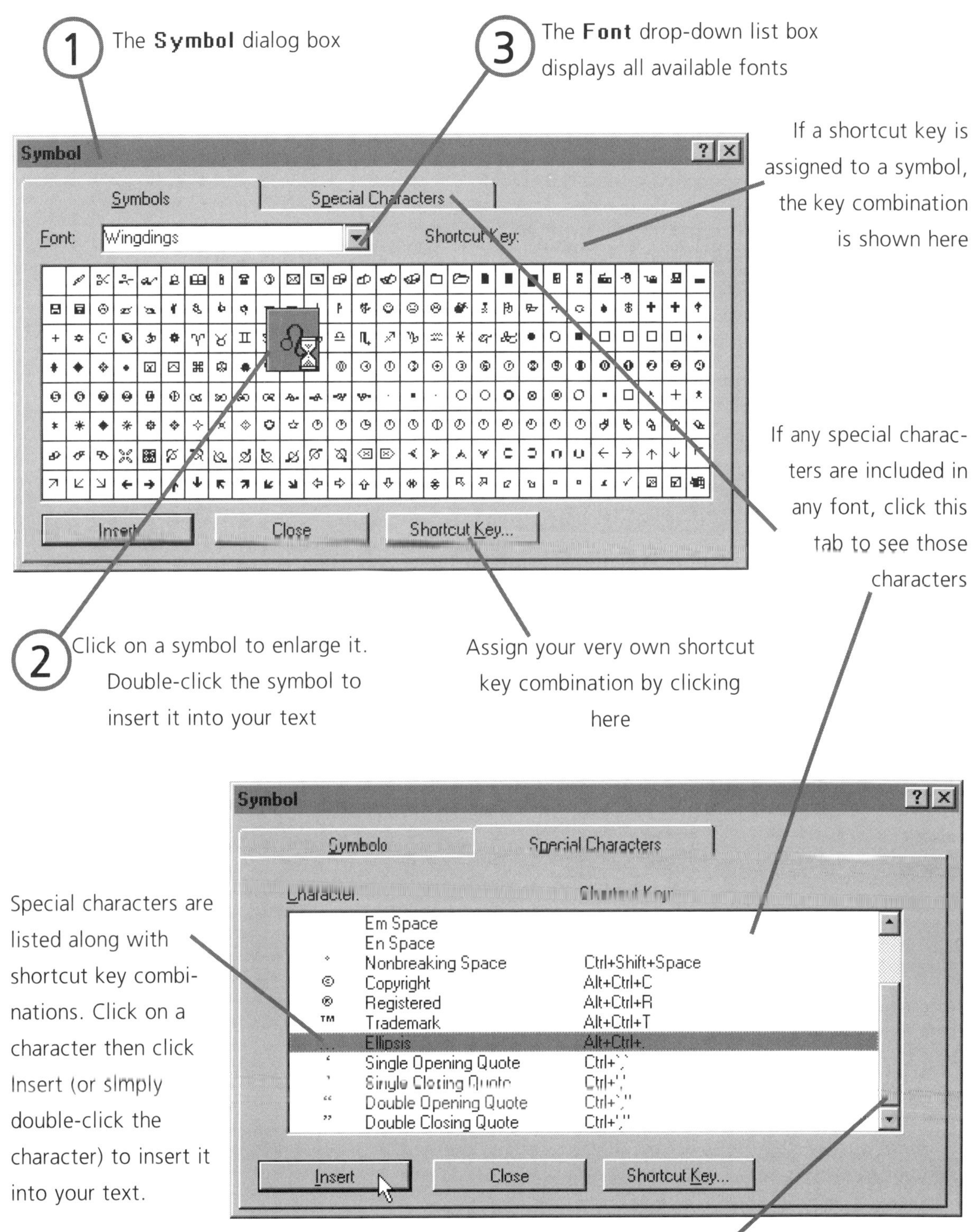

1
The Symbol dialog box
3
The Font drop-down list box displays all available fonts
If a shortcut key is assigned to a symbol, the key combination is shown here
Symbol
Symbols
Special Characters
Font:
Wingdings
Shortcut Key:
Insert
Close
Shortcut Key...
If any special characters are included in any font, click this tab to see those characters
2
Click on a symbol to enlarge it. Double-click the symbol to insert it into your text
Assign your very own shortcut key combination by clicking here
Special characters are listed along with shortcut key combinations. Click on a character then click Insert (or simply double-click the character) to insert it into your text.
Character:
Shortcut Key:
Em Space
En Space
Nonbreaking Space Ctrl+Shift+Space
© Copyright Alt+Ctrl+C
® Registered Alt+Ctrl+R
™ Trademark Alt+Ctrl+T
… Ellipsis Alt+Ctrl+.
‘ Single Opening Quote Ctrl+`,`
’ Single Closing Quote Ctrl+','
“ Double Opening Quote Ctrl+`,"
” Double Closing Quote Ctrl+',"
Scroll through the list to see more characters

Summary for Section 2

- Follow the three Golden Rules:
  1. never put two spaces together
  2. never put two carriage returns together
  3. never press ↵ or Enter at the end of a line of text — unless it is also the end of a paragraph.

- Get into the habit of checking the status bar regularly.

- If you're an ex-WordPerfect user (and who wouldn't be now that Word 7 for Windows 95 is here), remember to access Word's on-line help system for WordPerfect users.

- Learn how to select text using *all* of the available methods — no one method is best for all cases, and you really need to know them all.

- Use the cut, copy, and paste facility to speed up your work. Learn the keyboard shortcuts (Ctrl+X to cut, Ctrl+C to copy, Ctrl+V to paste), or use the buttons (, , and).

- Use drag-and-drop editing — although a little tricky to get the hang of, it's an extremely good editing aid.

- Word's multiple undo feature can save you hours of work if you make a mistake.

- Access symbols and special characters with the **Symbol** dialog box.

- Use typographer's special marks and symbols to give your work a truly professional look.

3 Formatting text

About formatting 46
Character formats 48
Painting a format 53
Paragraph formats 54
Tabs 60
Simple tables 62
More about tabs 64
Borders and shading 66
Summary for Section 3 72

About formatting

When you first enter text at the keyboard in Word it is generally unformatted. That is, it is plain, unembellished, with no changes applied to alter its appearance. Generally, it will be in the default font (say, Times New Roman) and a default size (say, 10 point).

Making alterations to text's appearance is known as formatting the text. There are several ways this can be done:

- formatting can be applied by the user to individual or grouped characters — this is known as *character formatting*
- formatting can be applied by the user to whole paragraphs — called (fancy that) *paragraph formatting*
- formatting can be applied automatically by Word — either as you enter text or afterwards, and either across a whole document (using Word's *AutoFormat* feature), or to paragraphs (using *paragraph styles*).

While character and paragraph formatting are both very powerful tools and can give you the visual effects you might require in a document, the *real* power of a word processor like Word lies in its ability to apply automatic formatting.

Take note:

Use character and paragraph formatting by all means – and they're going to be described over the next few pages so you can get to grips with them – but bear in mind that only when you use them to build *automatic* formatting features do they *really* become useful.

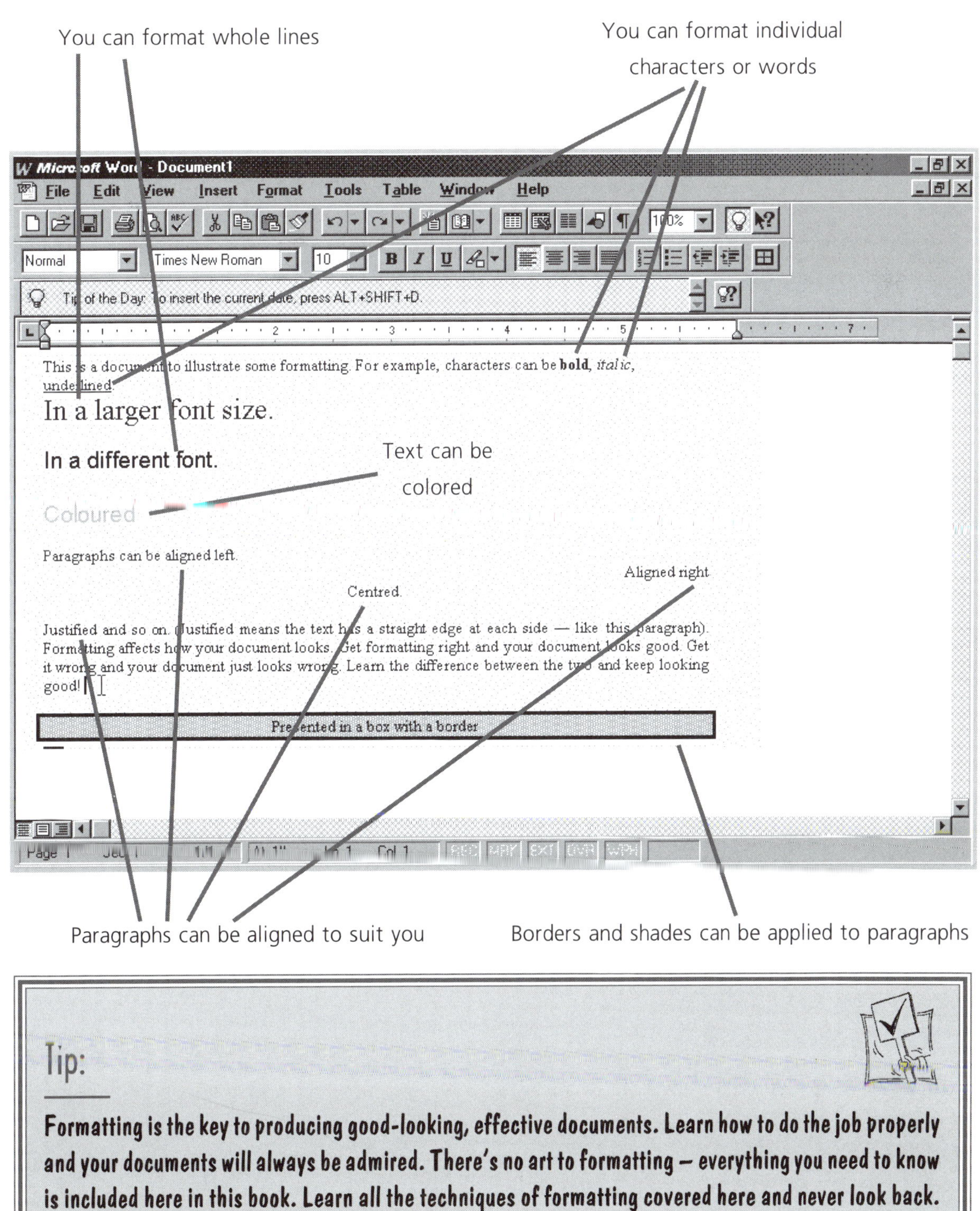

You can format whole lines
You can format individual characters or words
Microsoft Word - Document1
File Edit View Insert Format Tools Table Window Help
Normal
Times New Roman
10
Tip of the Day: To insert the current date, press ALT+SHIFT+D.
This is a document to illustrate some formatting. For example, characters can be bold, italic, underlined.
In a larger font size.
In a different font.
Text can be colored
Coloured
Paragraphs can be aligned left.
Aligned right
Centred.
Justified and so on. (Justified means the text has a straight edge at each side — like this paragraph). Formatting affects how your document looks. Get formatting right and your document looks good. Get it wrong and your document just looks wrong. Learn the difference between the two and keep looking good!
Presented in a box with a border
Paragraphs can be aligned to suit you
Borders and shades can be applied to paragraphs

Tip:

Formatting is the key to producing good-looking, effective documents. Learn how to do the job properly and your documents will always be admired. There's no art to formatting – everything you need to know is included here in this book. Learn all the techniques of formatting covered here and never look back.

Character formats

Basic steps:

Character formatting is a matter of selecting the text you wish to format, then applying the format change you want.

Many of the most common formats are available as buttons or options on the formatting toolbar. Some, however, are accessed by menus.

1 Select the text to be formatted.

2 Apply the new format or formats.

Select the text to be formatted — this can be an individual letter, a word, group of words, sentence, paragraph, or even the whole document

This is a sample of text in Times New Roman font at 10 point. It will be used to illustrate character formatting.

Format the selected text as you wish — this example shows the selected text bolded

This is a sample of text in Times New Roman font at 10 point. It will be used to **illustrate character formatting**

Text you format is displayed formatted on screen. There are no formatting codes (as in some — let's say — lesser-capable word processors). What you see on-screen is more or less what you get in the printout.

Tip:

To format a single word you don't need to select the word in the usual manner – all you have to do is click anywhere in the word, then apply the format changes you want.

Basic steps:

There are three main ways you can apply formatting to text:

1 From the formatting toolbar — buttons or options.

The formatting toolbar gives the easiest options to change common formats

Click buttons to apply (or remove) bold, italic, underline, and highlight

Change font with this drop-down list box

Change font size with this drop-down list box

If you have many fonts in your system you can jump in the list by entering the font's initial letter in the font name box — the list jumps directly to fonts with that initial letter for you to select

If the font size you want isn't listed, just enter your desired size at the keyboard — if you are using a TrueType or PostScript font it will display and print correctly for just about any size you want

The fonts you've used most recently are listed in the top of the list, above this line

A TrueType font

A font available on the printer currently selected

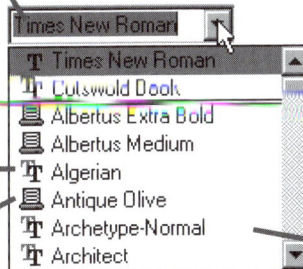

All fonts are listed alphabetically below the line

Character formats (contd)

Basic steps:

2 From the **Font** dialog box (choose **Format↳Font**, or type Alt+O then F to display it).

The **Font** dialog box gives some more formatting options

Click this tab to see more options regarding letter spacing and vertical positioning

List box for font size

List box for available fonts

Drop-down list box for special underlining effects

Check box options for various formats

List box of bold and italic format options

Drop-down list box holding available colors to format text with

Preview box, to see the effects of formats you have selected

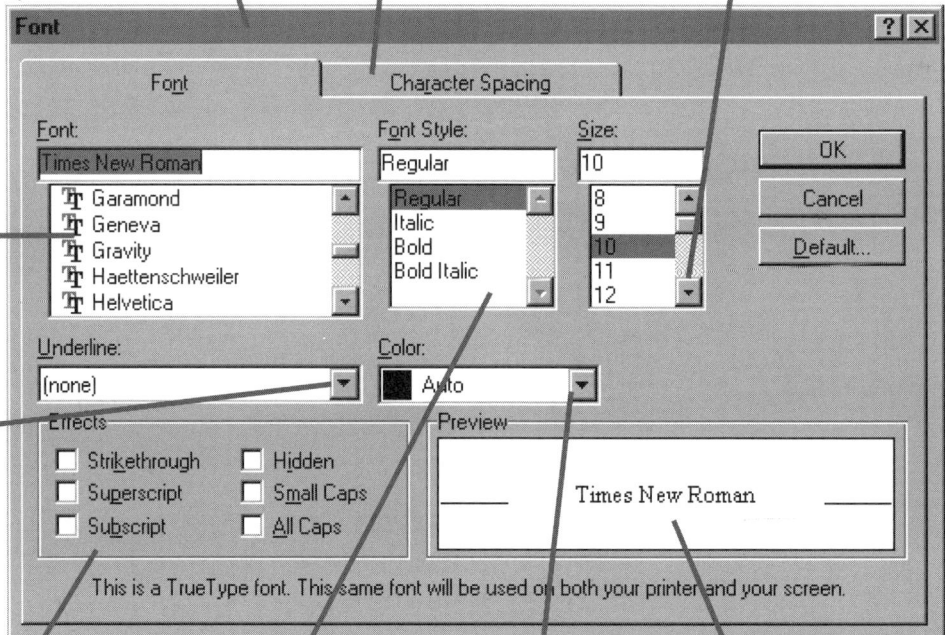

3 With keyboard combinations. These can very often provide the quickest methods of applying formats.

KEYBOARD SHORTCUT COMBINATIONS

Many formatting options can best be applied with a keyboard shortcut:

Format	Shortcut
Bold	Ctrl + B
Italic	Ctrl + I
Underline	Ctrl + U
Word underline	Ctrl + Shift + W
Double underline	Ctrl + Shift + D
Subscript	Ctrl + =
Superscript	Ctrl + Shift + =
Small caps	Ctrl + Shift + K
All caps	Ctrl + Shift + A
Change case	Shift + F3
Hidden text	Ctrl + Shift + H
Copy formats	Ctrl + Shift + C
Paste formats	Ctrl + Shift + V
Remove formats	Ctrl + SPACEBAR
Font	Ctrl + Shift + F
Symbol font	Ctrl + Shift + Q
Point size	Ctrl + Shift + P
next up	Ctrl + >
next down	Ctrl + <
up one point	Ctrl +]
down one point	Ctrl + [

Tip:

You can apply a format to the insertion point, too. This way, anything you type after the format is applied has that format, until you change it again. This is useful for, say, italicizing a single word for emphasis as you type it – just apply the italic format before you type the word, then remove the italic format (hence returning to regular text) after the word is finished.

Character formats (contd)

There are some points worth remembering about character formatting in Word. These are shown here as tips for you to use as reference.

Tip:

Your last formatting action can be repeated by choosing Edit↳Repeat Formatting, or typing Alt+E then R, or typing Ctrl+Y.

Note that all formats applied via the Font dialog box will be reapplied as one, whereas only the last individual formatting action applied with, say, buttons on the Formatting toolbar is reapplied.

Tip:

Removing a character format follows the same procedure as applying it in the first place. You first select the character, characters, word, words, sentence, paragraph, and so on, then you go through the same steps you took to originally apply it. If a word is bold, for example, you simply select it then click the Bold button **B** on the formatting toolbar to remove the format.

Tip:

You can remove *all* formatting applied by the methods shown over these last few pages, by first selecting the text then typing

Ctrl+SPACEBAR.

Note, though, that this does not remove formatting applied as part of styles (see page 118).

Painting a format

If you see text which is formatted the way you want another selection of text to be formatted, you can copy the formatting onto further text with the Format Painter button on the Standard toolbar.

1 Select the text with the format you want to copy (in this case an italicized word)

Take it from me. There's no *point* in trying to pass your driving test. Within ten years at most — more likely five — there'll be so many cars on the road that no-one will be able to drive more than 35 miles per hour anyway. And where's the fun in that?

3 Select the text to be formatted

Take it from me. There's no *point* in trying to pass your driving test. Within ten years at most — more likely five — there'll be so many cars on the road that no-one will be able to drive more than 35 miles per hour anyway. And where's the fun in that?

Once selected, the text is automatically formatted

Take it from me. There's no *point* in trying to pass your driving test. Within ten years at most — more likely five — there'll be so many cars on the road that no-one will be able to *drive more than 35 miles per* hour anyway. And where's the fun in that?

Tip:

You don't even need to select a single word if you want to paint another word's format onto it with the format painter pointer. Just click anywhere inside the word and the format is painted over the whole word.

Basic steps:

1. Select the text, part of text, or simply position the insertion point anywhere inside the text you wish to copy the formatting from.
2. Click the Format Painter button on the Standard toolbar. The pointer changes to the format painter pointer.
3. Select the text you want to be formatted.

Tip:

If you double-click the Format Painter button after selecting text with the format you want to copy, the format painter pointer remains active after you have painted the format to further text. You can continue to paint the format for as long as you want onto more selections of text. Click the Format Painter button again to deactivate the format painter pointer.

Paragraph formats

Whereas character formats affect just the *characters* you select, paragraph formats control the — you've got it — *paragraphs*. In other words, complete blocks of text and their line spacings, indents, or alignments, are affected by paragraph formats. Paragraph formats *do not just affect* single characters, words, or sentences.

Paragraph marks (¶) indicate where a paragraph ends

This·is·a·left-aligned·paragraph.¶

This·is·a·right-aligned·paragraph.¶

This·is·a·centred·paragraph.¶

This·paragraph·has·single·line-spacing·and·is·indented·by·a·small·amount·on·its·first·line.·Lines·are·close·together,·set·by·Word·itself.·This·is·a·standard·setting·unless·you·change·the·default·style·(covered·later·in·the·book).¶

This·paragraph·has·double·line-spacing·and·is·indented·on·its·first·line·by·a·slightly·larger·amount.·Lines·are·obviously·wider·apart·than·the·previous·paragraph.·It's·possible·to·do·this·all·in·Word·quite·simply·when·you·know·what·you're·doing.¶

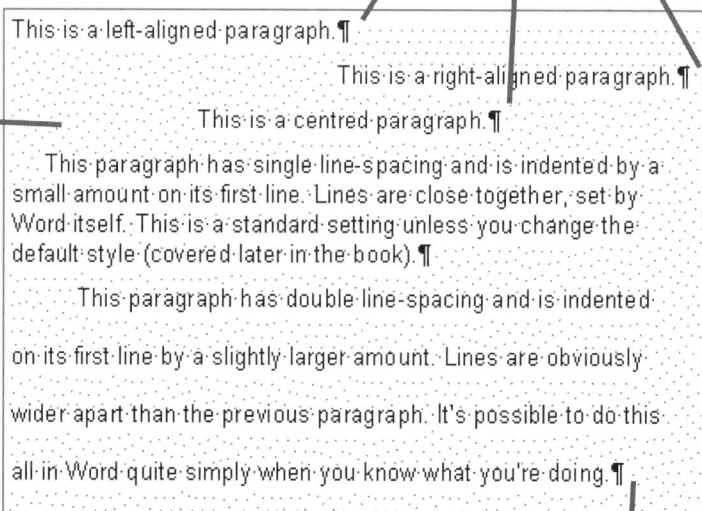

Note that while all these paragraphs in this screenshot of a Word document have the same character formats (they are all in the same font, size, and so on) they still *appear* different, because their paragraph formats are different

Paragraph marks (¶) are used by Word to store a paragraph's formatting

Take note:

A paragraph is defined as any block of text – no matter how short, or how long – ending with a paragraph mark ¶. A paragraph mark is added to your text each time you press Enter or ↵.

Paragraph marks *may* be hidden – to display them (or hide them if they are currently displayed) click the Show/Hide ¶ button ¶ on the Standard toolbar.

Basic steps:

1 First select the paragraph or paragraphs you intend to format.

2 Apply the new paragraph format or formats.

To apply a paragraph format to a paragraph, you use the same techniques you use to apply a character format to a character.

(1) Select the paragraph or paragraphs (in this example there are two paragraphs) you want to format

Here we go, here we go, here we go. It's another fine, fine day down at the ranch. The brunch is cooking and the horses are lively. After we've eaten we'll get going and round-up the cattle. Never in the field of human conflict has so much been eaten by so few.¶

Inevitably, there will be a cut in resources. There's now so little money to go round that it's just a question of jobs or the tools to do those jobs. If we want to maintain current levels of employment, we'll all just have to do with less to spend.¶

Take note:

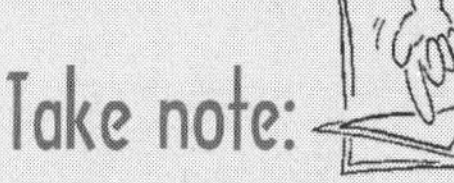

You don't have to select a whole paragraph before you apply paragraph formatting to it. If you position the insertion point *anywhere* within the paragraph, then apply paragraph formatting, the *entire* paragraph is formatted.

Tip:

If you are currently typing text into a formatted paragraph, then press [Enter] or [↵], the new paragraph so created continues with the format of the preceding paragraph. In other words, if you have formatted a paragraph to the paragraph style you want, each subsequent paragraph has the same format.

(2) Apply the paragraph formats — here the paragraphs have been indented on their first lines and justified

Here we go, here we go, here we go. It's another fine, fine day down at the ranch. The brunch is cooking and the horses are lively. After we've eaten we'll get going and round-up the cattle. Never in the field of human conflict has so much been eaten by so few.¶

Inevitably, there will be a cut in resources. There's now so little money to go round that it's just a question of jobs or the tools to do those jobs. If we want to maintain current levels of employment, we'll all just have to do with less to spend.¶

Paragraph formats (contd)

Like character formats, paragraph formats can be applied to text in three main ways.

Basic steps:

1 Paragraph formats can be applied from the Formatting toolbar (some are applied from the ruler, too).

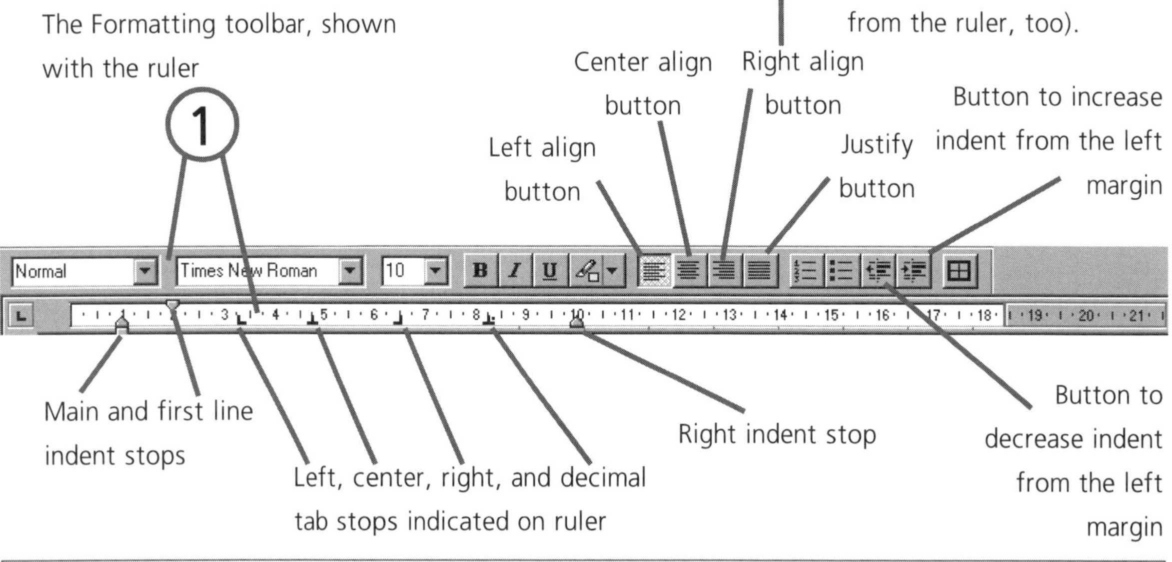
The Formatting toolbar, shown with the ruler
1
Center align button
Right align button
Button to increase indent from the left margin
Left align button
Justify button
Normal
Times New Roman
10
Main and first line indent stops
Left, center, right, and decimal tab stops indicated on ruler
Right indent stop
Button to decrease indent from the left margin

Tip:

Unlike some word processors, Word does not use formatting codes. The formats you apply are visible directly on-screen, so you can see how they will print. If, however, you want to see the particular paragraph (or character) formats applied, click the Help button on the Standard toolbar, then click in the paragraph.

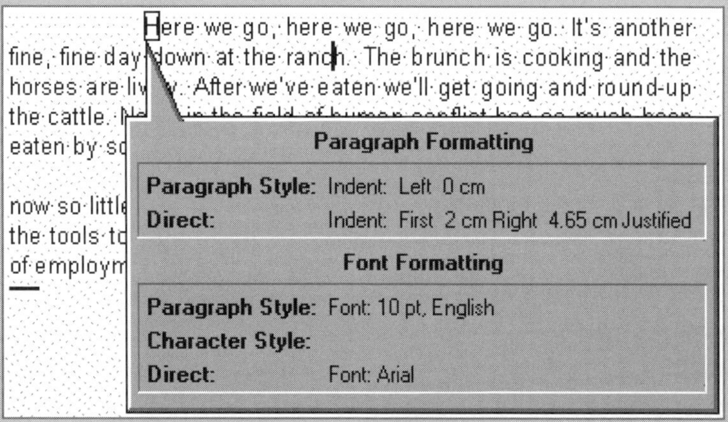

A Paragraph Formatting dialog box is displayed which shows the formatting applied. Click again, or press Esc to get rid of it.

Here we go, here we go, here we go. It's another fine, fine day down at the ranch. The brunch is cooking and the horses are liv... After we've eaten we'll get going and round-up the cattle. ... eaten by so... now so littl... the tools to... of employm...

Paragraph Formatting

Paragraph Style: Indent: Left 0 cm
Direct: Indent: First 2 cm Right 4.65 cm Justified

Font Formatting

Paragraph Style: Font: 10 pt, English
Character Style:
Direct: Font: Arial

2 Formats can be applied from the **Paragraph** dialog box (to display it choose **Format**↳ **Paragraph**, or type Alt+O then P).

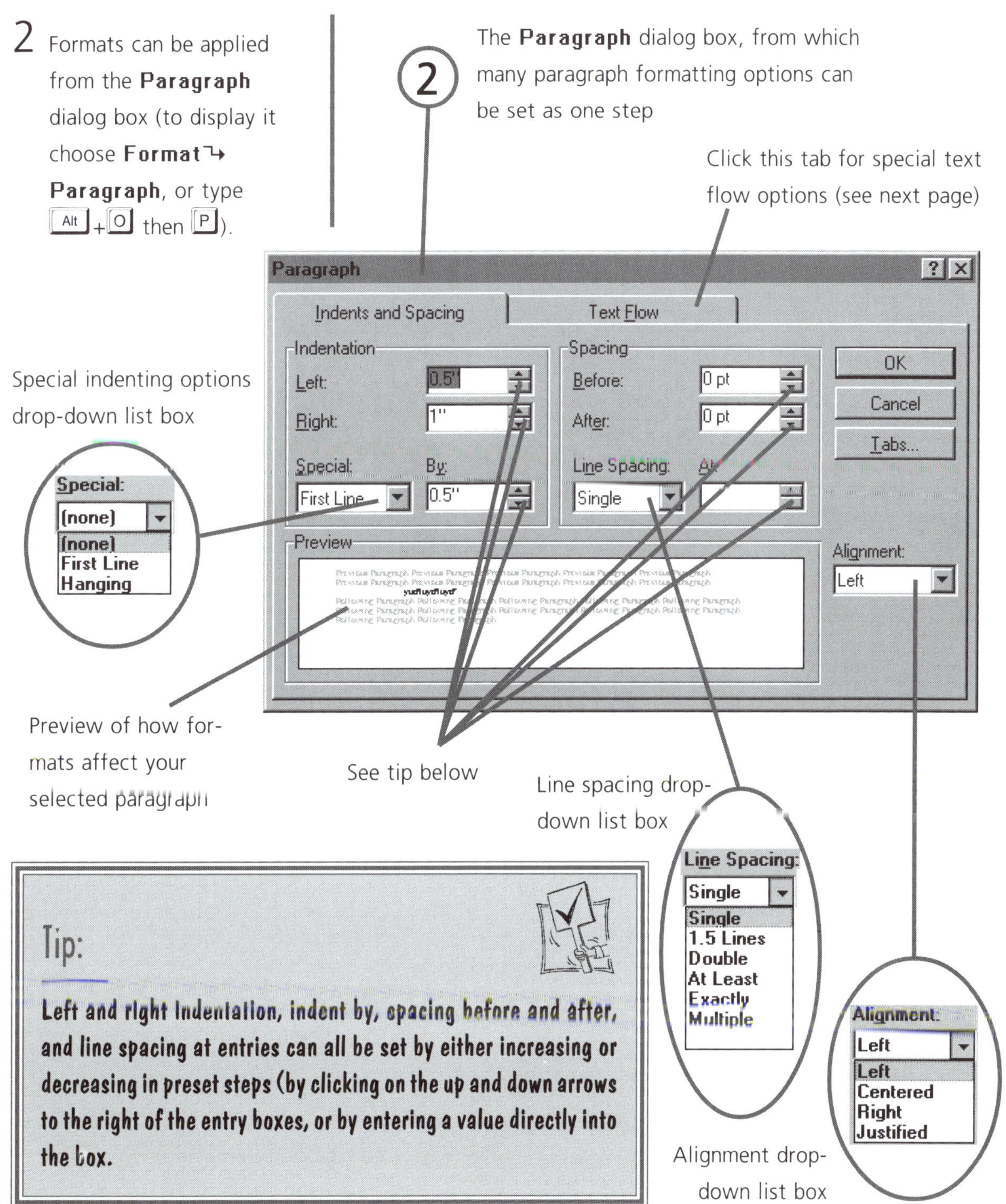

2
The **Paragraph** dialog box, from which many paragraph formatting options can be set as one step
Click this tab for special text flow options (see next page)
Paragraph
Indents and Spacing
Text Flow
Indentation
Left:
0.5"
Right:
1"
Special:
By:
First Line
0.5"
Spacing
Before:
0 pt
After:
0 pt
Line Spacing:
At:
Single
OK
Cancel
Tabs...
Preview
Alignment:
Left
Special indenting options drop-down list box
Special:
(none)
(none)
First Line
Hanging
Preview of how formats affect your selected paragraph
See tip below
Line spacing drop-down list box
Line Spacing:
Single
Single
1.5 Lines
Double
At Least
Exactly
Multiple
Alignment:
Left
Left
Centered
Right
Justified
Alignment drop-down list box

Tip:

Left and right indentation, indent by, spacing before and after, and line spacing at entries can all be set by either increasing or decreasing in preset steps (by clicking on the up and down arrows to the right of the entry boxes, or by entering a value directly into the box.

Paragraph formats (contd)

Special paragraph formatting attributes are available from the **Text Flow** tab option of the **Paragraph** dialog box. These attributes affect the way text flows between pages of a document. Main ones are labelled and described.

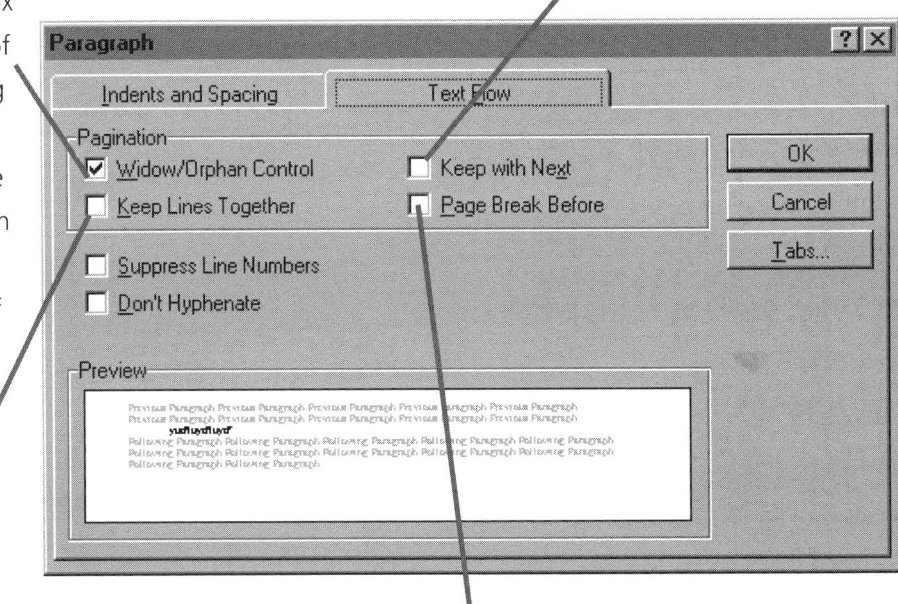

Paragraph
Indents and Spacing
Text Flow
Pagination
Widow/Orphan Control
Keep Lines Together
Keep with Next
Page Break Before
Suppress Line Numbers
Don't Hyphenate
Preview
OK
Cancel
Tabs...

Checking this prevents a paragraph from being split from the following paragraph

Checking this check box prevents the last line of a paragraph from being printed at the top of a page (a widow), or the first line of a paragraph from being printed alone at the bottom of a page (an orphan)

Checking this prevents a paragraph from being split across pages

Checking this inserts a page break before a paragraph (in other words, the paragraph will be at the top of a new page)

Tip:

These attributes can make a document look much better and prevent anomalies. If the Keep with Next option is checked for a paragraph formatted as a heading which by chance falls at the bottom of a page, for example, it will be forced onto the next page along with its accompanying text.

Basic steps:

3 Paragraph formats can be applied directly with keyboard shortcut combinations. Like character formatting keyboard combinations, these are very often the quickest ways of applying certain formats.

Tip:

You can most quickly indent selected paragraphs using either the keyboard shortcut combinations above right, or (even better) using the Decrease Indent or Increase Indent buttons on the Formatting toolbar.

While changes due to either of these methods are in fixed increments, you can always later change them by dragging indent markers on the ruler.

KEYBOARD SHORTCUT COMBINATIONS

Left-align text	Ctrl + B
Center align text	Ctrl + E
Right-align text	Ctrl + R
Justify text	Ctrl + J
Indent from left margin	Ctrl + M
Decrease indent	Ctrl + Shift + M
Create a hanging indent	Ctrl + T
Decrease a hanging indent	Ctrl + Shift + T
1 line space	Ctrl + 1
1.5 line space	Ctrl + 5
2 line space	Ctrl + 2
Add or remove 12 points of space before a paragraph	Ctrl + 0
Remove paragraph formats not applied by a style	Ctrl + Q
Restore Normal style	Ctrl + Shift + N
Display or hide nonprinting characters (¶ and so on)	Ctrl + *

Take note:

While character and paragraph formats are all very nice, and very good, and used properly can greatly improve the look of a document, bear in mind you have to apply every one of them individually.

On the other hand, you can apply formats automatically by using styles (page 118). Automatic formatting is much quicker and, because you can use both methods across documents, ensures that documents you create can have a unified style, or set of styles, giving a much more professional appearance to your work.

Tabs

Like a typewriter, any word processor has the ability to define tab stops. These are used to help align text, so that tables or columns of figures can be neatened up and aligned underneath each other.

Better than a typewriter, on the other hand, word processors usually have more than one type of tab stop. Where typewriters only align text so that text is left-aligned after the tab stop, Word allows text to be:

- left-aligned — as on a typewriter, with text aligned after the tab stop
- center-aligned — with text centered around the tab stop
- right-aligned — where text is aligned to the right of the tab stop
- decimal-aligned — with monetary figures, say, aligned so their decimal points are aligned directly on the tab stop
- bar-aligned — Word creates a vertical line in your document, the height of the text line, at the tab stop.

Tip

You move to a tab stop when you're typing simply by pressing Tab. This action moves the insertion point to the next tab stop, after which you can carry on typing. Note (see illustration below) that a character → indicates a tab entry in text. These are special characters which are not printed (like paragraph marks ¶) and can be hidden or displayed (just like paragraph marks) by clicking the Show/Hide ¶ button ¶ on the Standard toolbar.

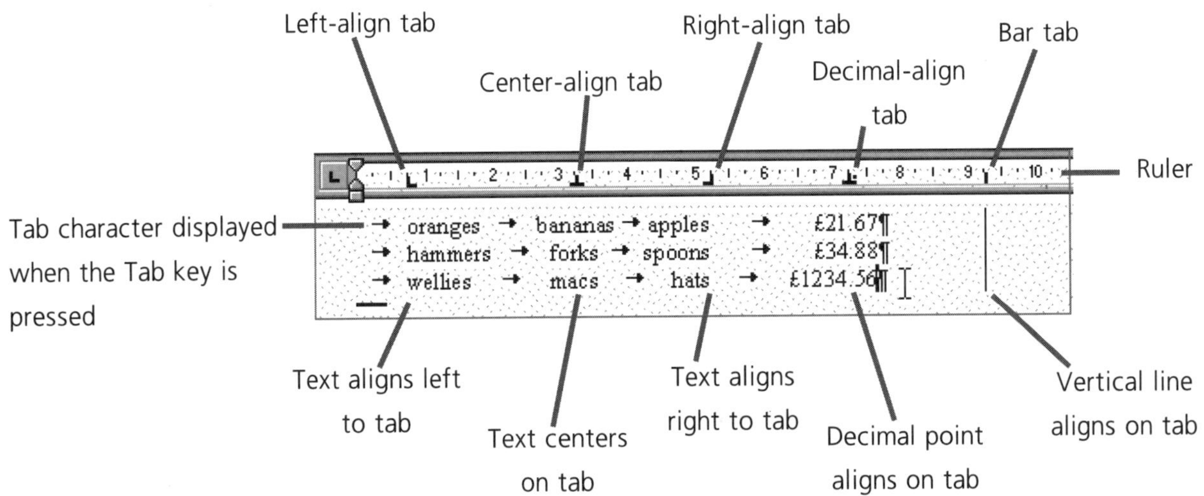

Left-align tab
Right-align tab
Bar tab
Center-align tab
Decimal-align tab
Ruler
Tab character displayed when the Tab key is pressed
→ oranges → bananas → apples → £21.67¶
→ hammers → forks → spoons → £34.88¶
→ wellies → macs → hats → £1234.56¶
Text aligns left to tab
Text centers on tab
Text aligns right to tab
Decimal point aligns on tab
Vertical line aligns on tab

Basic steps:

The most straightforward way of setting tabs is with the ruler:

1 Repeatedly click the Tab Alignment button (preset as [L]) until the type of tab you require is displayed

- [L] — align left
- [⊥] — align center
- [┘] — align right
- [⊥.] — align to decimal point.

2 Click in the ruler at the position you want the tab stop. It is displayed in the ruler as a symbol (according to which tab stop type you selected).

3 Adjust the tab stop if you need to, by dragging it along the ruler to its new position.

Take note:

Tabs are a paragraph format. In other words, they are set for and remain in force for a paragraph – no matter how many lines the paragraph contains.

Take note:

As you insert a new tab stop, any default tab stops to its left – literally – disappear.

1 The Tab Alignment button — keep clicking it until the tab type you want is selected (align left is default)

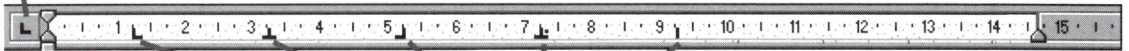

2 After selecting a tab stop type, click in the ruler to position your tab stop. The tab stop is displayed by one of four symbols (plus the bar tab symbol)

Old tab position

New tab position

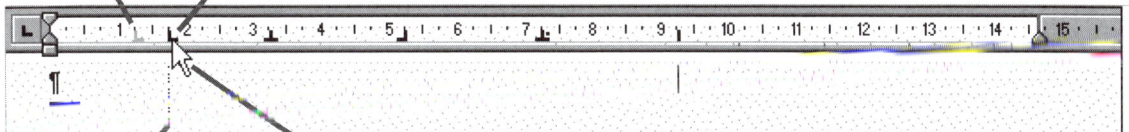

As you drag, a line shows you the new tab position in the document

3 You can adjust a tab stop's position by dragging it along the ruler to where you want it

Simple tables

To create a simple table you can use tabs. Because tabs are a paragraph format, you need to select the paragraphs which form the table before setting the tabs — in exactly the same ways described when we selected text previously. Once the paragraphs forming the table are selected, the tab changes you make affect all those paragraphs.

Take note:

Never, never, never, never, never (enough to make you see the importance?) press [Tab] more than once to align text. It doesn't matter if text doesn't align as you want while you're entering it (see Tip below) – it's still better to change the tabs later to suit your layout requirements. That way you can see the effects of changes you make to the text directly. If you set the tab stops *before* you enter the text, you're just guessing where they need to be, and you'll almost certainly have to change them anyway!

Basic steps:

1 After you've typed in the paragraphs you want to become a table, select them.

2 Set your tabs (don't worry if they're not exact — just set them approximately).

3 Adjust the tabs (by dragging them along the ruler) until the text tabulates as you want — by typing text in first using the default tab stops, followed by setting your own tabs, then adjusting them, you can see the effects of adjustment on-screen.

4 Make any changes to character or other paragraph formats you want.

Tip:

While tab stops have to be set prior to text entry on a typewriter, this is not the case with Word. In fact, it is better simply to enter the text which is to be tabulated before setting tabs at all. The default tabs in a Word document (set at every half inch – or 1.27 centimeter) will let you tabulate the text initially (it probably won't align at all as you type it in – but don't worry). Once the text is completely entered you can select it, then put the tab stops where you want. Even once you've set the tab stops you can change them, until you get the text looking as you want it.

1 Select the paragraphs you want — note the heading of the table isn't selected here

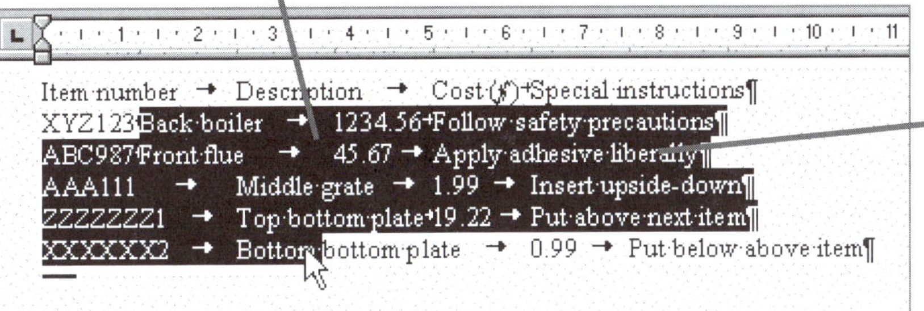

Item·number → Description → Cost·(£)→Special·instructions¶
XYZ123→Back·boiler → 1234.56→Follow·safety·precautions¶
ABC987→Front·flue → 45.67 → Apply·adhesive·liberally¶
AAA111 → Middle·grate → 1.99 → Insert·upside-down¶
ZZZZZZZ1 → Top·bottom·plate→19.22 → Put·above·next·item¶
XXXXXX2 → Bottom·bottom·plate → 0.99 → Put·below·above·item¶

Note how the default tab stops render the table somewhat unattractive — it doesn't matter at this stage because step 3 tidies it up.

2 Set the tabs you want for each column of the table (see pages 60–61)

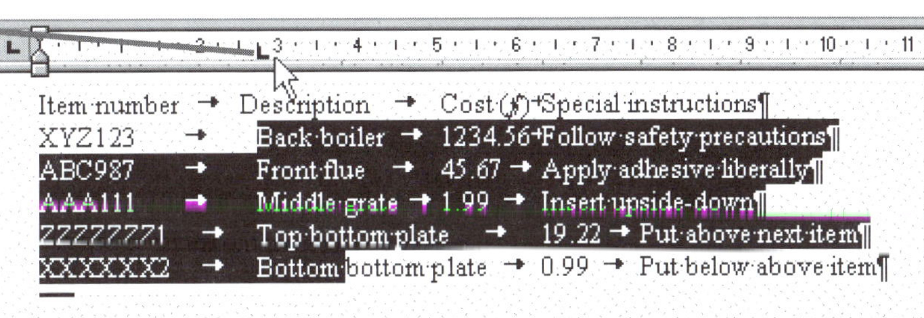

Item·number → Description → Cost·(£)→Special·instructions¶
XYZ123 → Back·boiler → 1234.56→Follow·safety·precautions¶
ABC987 → Front·flue → 45.67 → Apply·adhesive·liberally¶
AAA111 → Middle·grate → 1.99 → Insert·upside-down¶
ZZZZZZZ1 → Top·bottom·plate → 19.22 → Put·above·next·item¶
XXXXXX2 → Bottom·bottom·plate → 0.99 → Put·below·above·item¶

3 Adjust the tabs to suit the table and the appearance you want

Item·number → Description → Cost·(£)→Special·instructions¶
XYZ123 → Back·boiler → 1234.56 → Follow·safety·precautions¶
ABC987 → Front·flue → 45.67 → Apply·adhesive·liberally¶
AAA111 → Middle·grate → 1.99 → Insert·upside-down¶
ZZZZZZZ1 → Top·bottom·plate → 19.22 → Put·above·next·item¶
XXXXXX2 → Bottom·bottom·plate →0.99 → Put·below·above·item¶

Now the heading can be tabulated to fit

4 Make character and other paragraph formatting changes you want

Item·number → ***Description*** → ***Cost·(£)*** → ***Special·instructions***¶
XYZ123 → Back·boiler → 1234.56 → Follow·safety·precautions¶
ABC987 → Front·flue → 45.67 → Apply·adhesive·liberally¶
AAA111 → Middle·grate → 1.99 → Insert·upside-down¶
ZZZZZZZ1 → Top·bottom·plate → 19.22 → Put·above·next·item¶
XXXXXX2 → Bottom·bottom·plate →0.99 → Put·below·above·item¶

More about tabs

Basic steps:

While the ruler affords by far the easiest method of setting and adjusting tabs, it is actually quite inexact and some tab options aren't available from it. Total control over tabs (both setting and adjusting) is available from the **Tabs** dialog box.

1 Display the **Tabs** dialog box by choosing **Format↳Tabs** or by typing [Alt]+[O] then [T] (or by clicking on the **Tabs** buttons in the **Paragraph** dialog box — see page 57).

2 Set tab stop positions, alignment types, and leaders (if required).

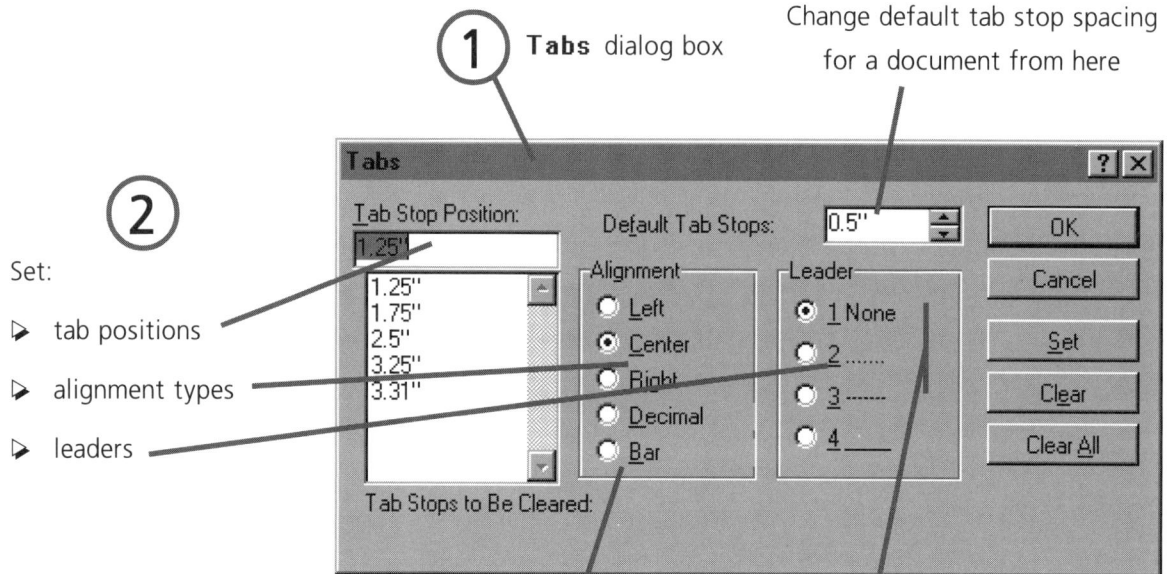

1 **Tabs** dialog box

Change default tab stop spacing for a document from here

2

Set:

- tab positions
- alignment types
- leaders

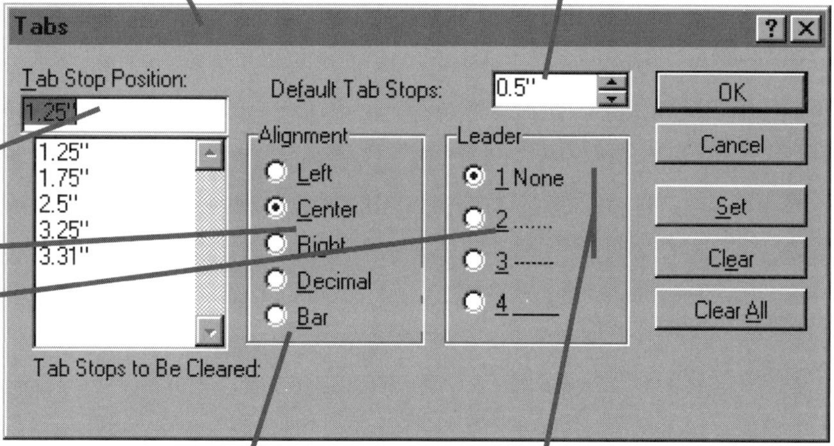

Note that a bar tab can only be set from the **Tabs** dialog box — not from the ruler (although you can adjust it — once set — from the ruler)

You can clear tabs with these buttons, or set those you enter

There are two options to clear tabs:

1 You can use the clear buttons in the **Tabs** dialog box (see below left).

2 You can literally drag the tabs off the ruler so they disappear. This is by far the faster method where only a few tabs are to be cleared.

Tip:

Tabs – as we've already seen – are paragraph formats. Like all the other paragraph formats, they remain in operation after each paragraph, until you change them.

If you want tab settings to remain in operation for a few paragraphs, you can set them before you start, then type away. As you press Enter or ↵ to begin a new paragraph, the formats (including tab settings) are carried over.

Tip:

You can fill the empty space before a tab stop with dotted, dashed, or solid lines called leaders. They can give a professional finish to contents pages, where a contents list is separated from its page number list by some considerable space.

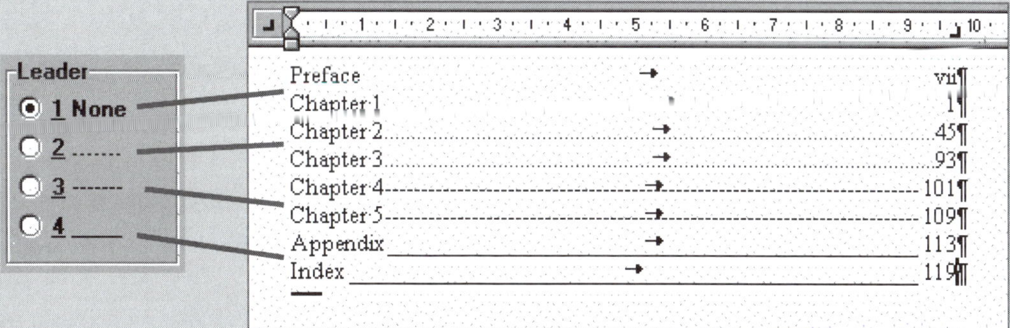
Leader
1 None
2 ....
3 -------
4 ____
Preface vii¶
Chapter 1 1¶
Chapter 2 45¶
Chapter 3 93¶
Chapter 4 101¶
Chapter 5 109¶
Appendix 113¶
Index 119¶

Take note:

You can only set or clear leaders from the Tabs dialog box.

Borders and shading

Basic steps:

Two other paragraph formats which can be used to create a professional appearance in Word documents are paragraph borders and shading.

Borders are rules around a paragraph (which may, or may not, be thick enough to see — a border of zero thickness is still there, albeit not visible). Shadings are the background shades of colors or grays which go inside borders.

Borders and shadings are set up and adjusted in one of two ways:

- through the Borders toolbar
- with the **Paragraph Borders and Shading** dialog box.

The easiest way to apply borders and shading is with the Borders toolbar.

1 If it's not already displayed, call up the Borders toolbar by clicking the Borders button on the Formatting toolbar.

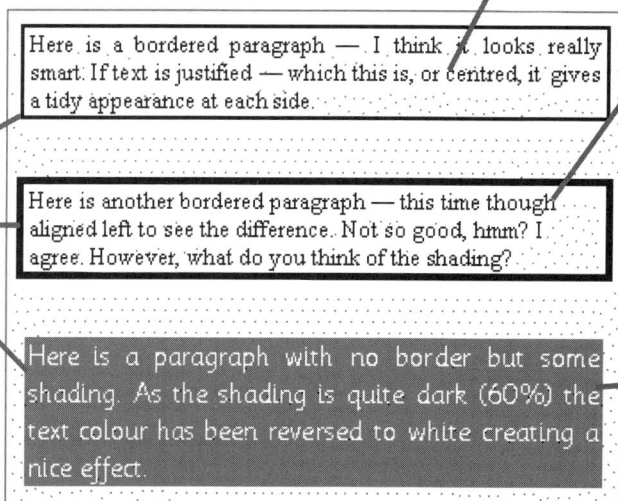

How the paragraph is formatted is very important to how the bordered and shaded paragraph will look. Justified or centered text always looks better than left- or right-aligned text, simply because the borders (and resultant shading) are evenly placed around the text.

Borders can be:

- thinner
- thicker
- nonexistent

Here is a bordered paragraph — I think it looks really smart. If text is justified — which this is, or centred, it gives a tidy appearance at each side.

Here is another bordered paragraph — this time though aligned left to see the difference. Not so good, hmm? I agree. However, what do you think of the shading?

Here is a paragraph with no border but some shading. As the shading is quite dark (60%) the text colour has been reversed to white creating a nice effect.

For a paragraph you intend to shade darkly, consider reversing text to create a pleasant effect.

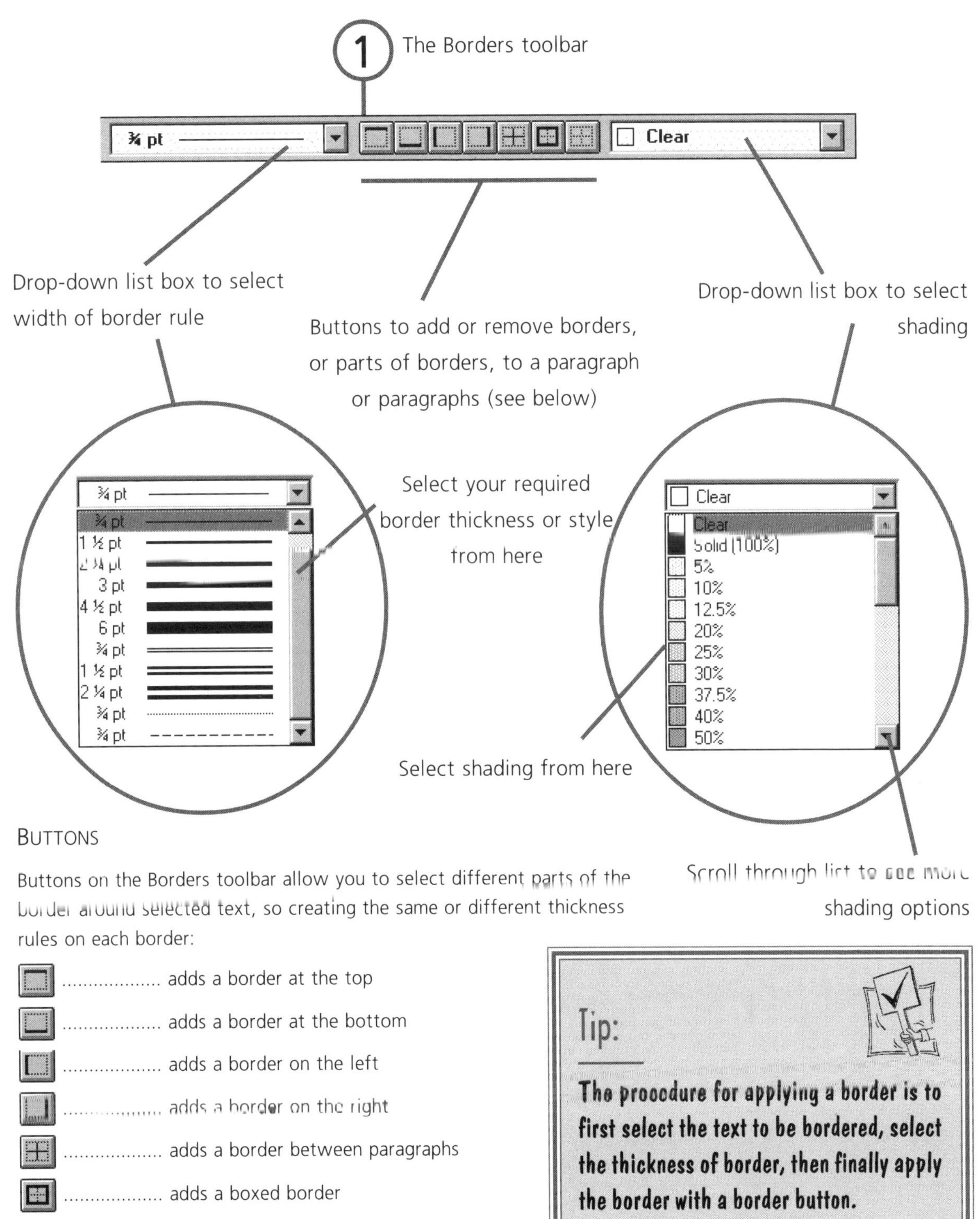

1
The Borders toolbar
¾ pt
Clear
Drop-down list box to select width of border rule
Buttons to add or remove borders, or parts of borders, to a paragraph or paragraphs (see below)
Drop-down list box to select shading
Select your required border thickness or style from here
Select shading from here
Scroll through list to see more shading options

BUTTONS

Buttons on the Borders toolbar allow you to select different parts of the border around selected text, so creating the same or different thickness rules on each border:

- .... adds a border at the top
- .... adds a border at the bottom
- .... adds a border on the left
- .... adds a border on the right
- .... adds a border between paragraphs
- .... adds a boxed border
- .... removes all borders

Tip:

The procedure for applying a border is to first select the text to be bordered, select the thickness of border, then finally apply the border with a border button.

Borders & shading (contd)

Basic steps:

When you add a border to text it extends around the full size of the paragraph the text is formatted to. In other words, the width and height of the paragraph will be the width and height of the border — regardless of whether the text itself totally fills the border. This can result in unusual (and unattractive) borders.

1. Select the text to be bordered.
2. Select the thickness or style of border and shading required.
3. Apply the border.
4. Adjust the right indent of the paragraph to be the same width as the text itself.

(1) Select the text to have a border — remember (as borders and shades are paragraph formats) you only need to click in the paragraph to select the whole paragraph

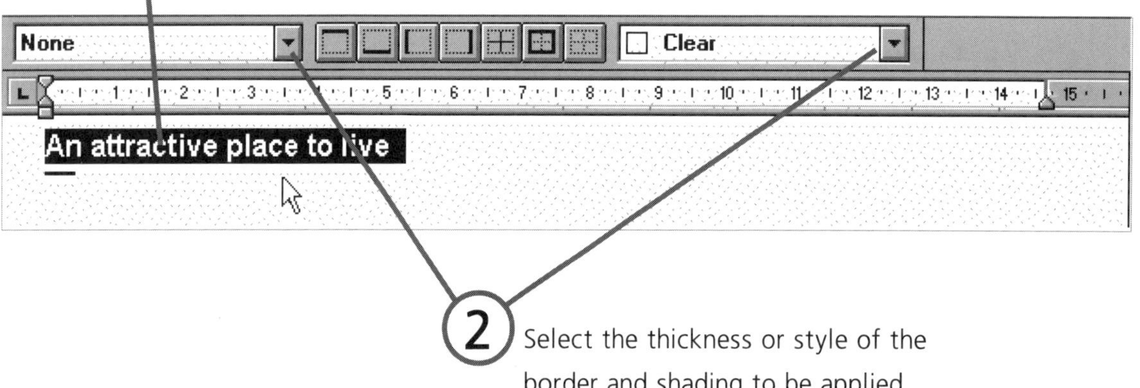

None
Clear
An attractive place to live

(2) Select the thickness or style of the border and shading to be applied

(3) Apply the border — this one is a boxed border, applied with the boxed border button

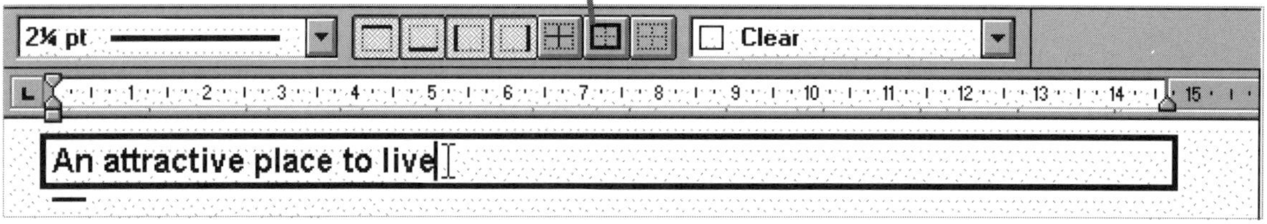

4 Drag the right indent marker of the ruler until the indent is just to the right of the text in the paragraph

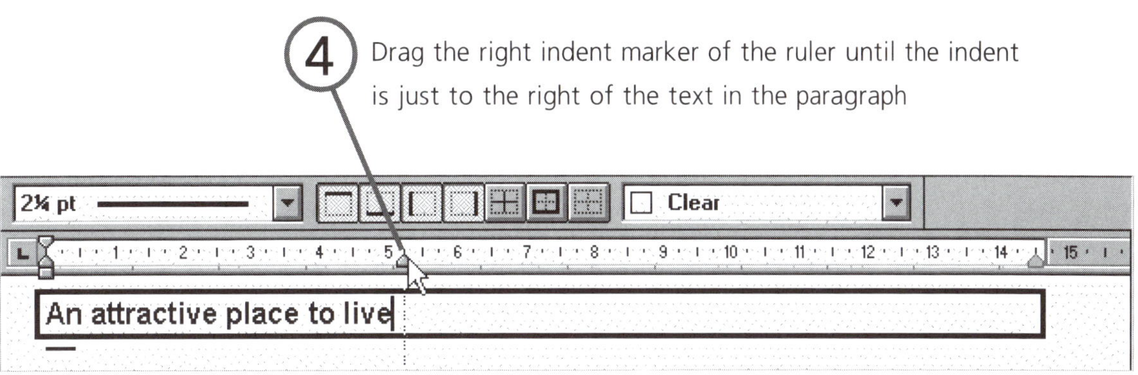
2¼ pt
Clear
An attractive place to live

The paragraph is now boxed properly and attractively — note that if you now add to the text in the bordered paragraph the border will still be the correct width as the text simply overflows onto the next line which is of the same width. The border's bottom rule remains below the bottom line of the paragraph however many lines it has.

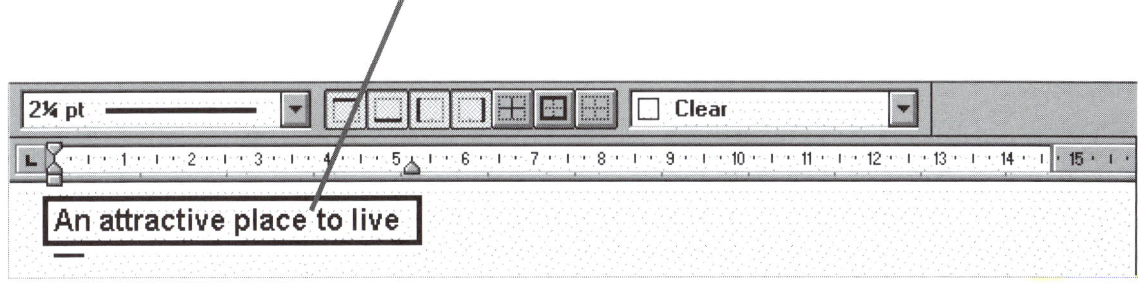
2¼ pt
Clear
An attractive place to live

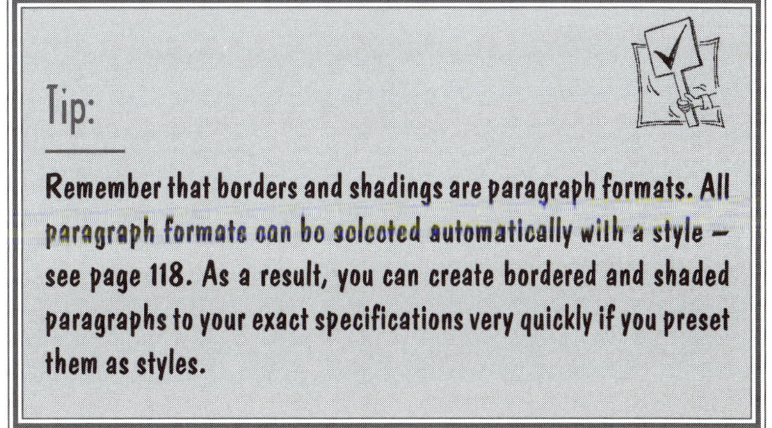

Tip:

Remember that borders and shadings are paragraph formats. All paragraph formats can be selected automatically with a style – see page 118. As a result, you can create bordered and shaded paragraphs to your exact specifications very quickly if you preset them as styles.

Borders & shading (contd)

Basic steps:

You can create and adjust borders and shadings through the **Paragraph Borders and Shading** dialog box, too. While this isn't as quick as using the Borders toolbar, it does provide some options not otherwise available.

1 To call up the **Paragraph Borders and Shading** dialog box choose **Format→Borders and Shading**, or type [Alt]+[O] then [B].

The **Paragraph Borders and Shading** dialog box

1

Click this tab to see the shading options (see opposite)

Some borders are preset — just click the one you want

Preview shows effects and allows you to select the border (or borders) you want to create — just click on the border you want at the edge of the text in the preview

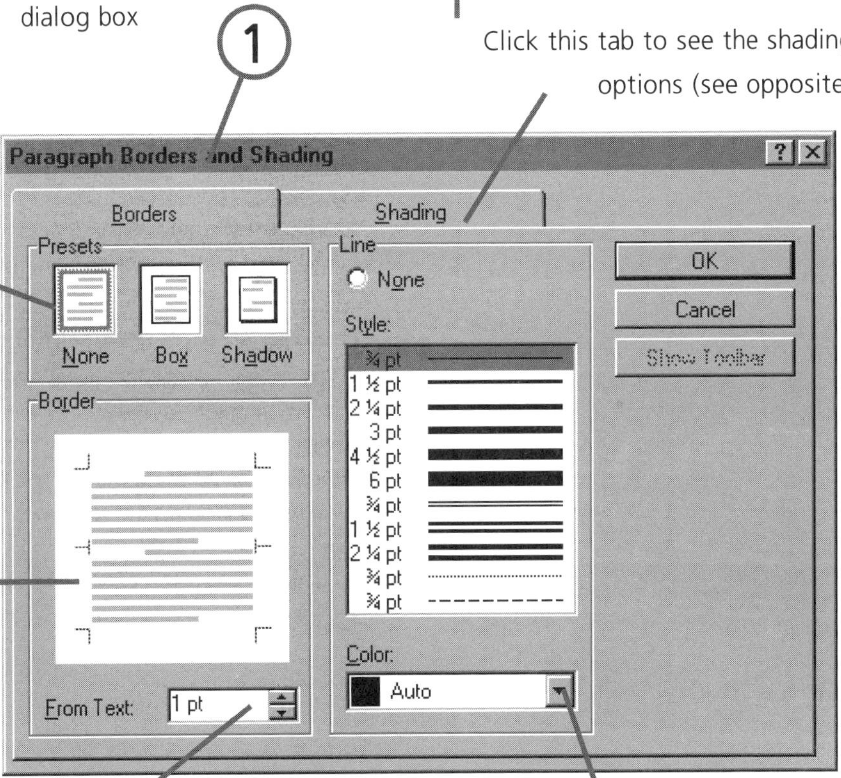

You can specify that a border is spaced a greater distance from the edge of text (default is 1 point) by increasing the measurement in this entry box

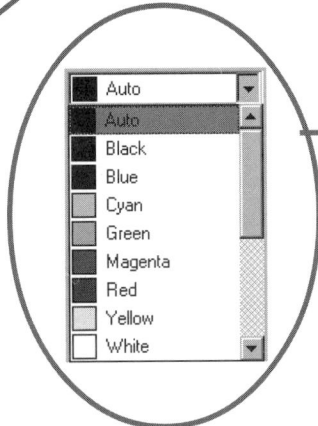

Choose the colors of borders from this drop-down list box (see opposite)

Click this tab to get back to borders options

Shading options are shown when this tab is clicked

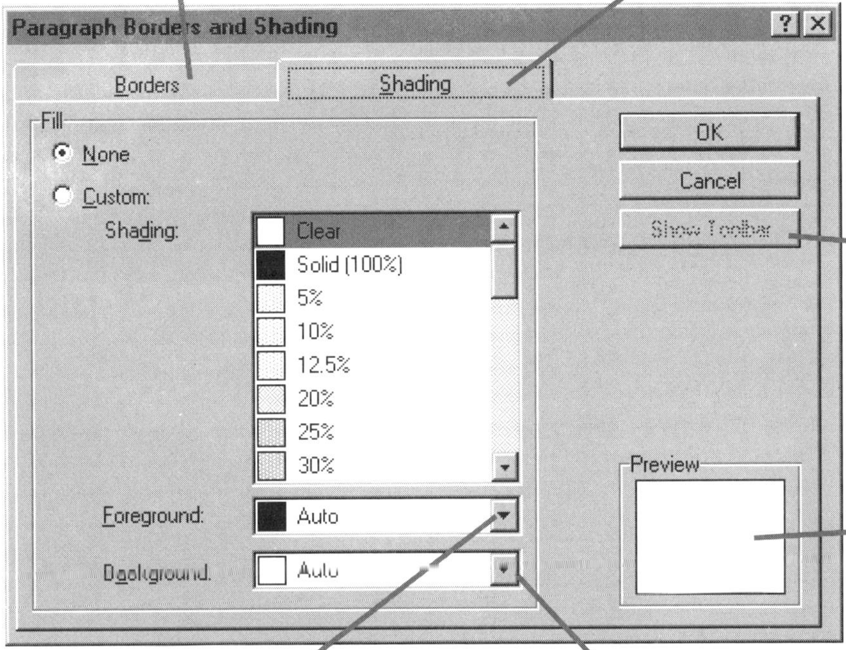

You can display the Borders toolbar (if it's not already displayed) by clicking this button

Preview shows effects of the shading options you select

Select the foreground color (that is, the color of the dots or lines) in the selected shading pattern from this drop-down list box

Select the background color of the shading pattern from this drop-down list box

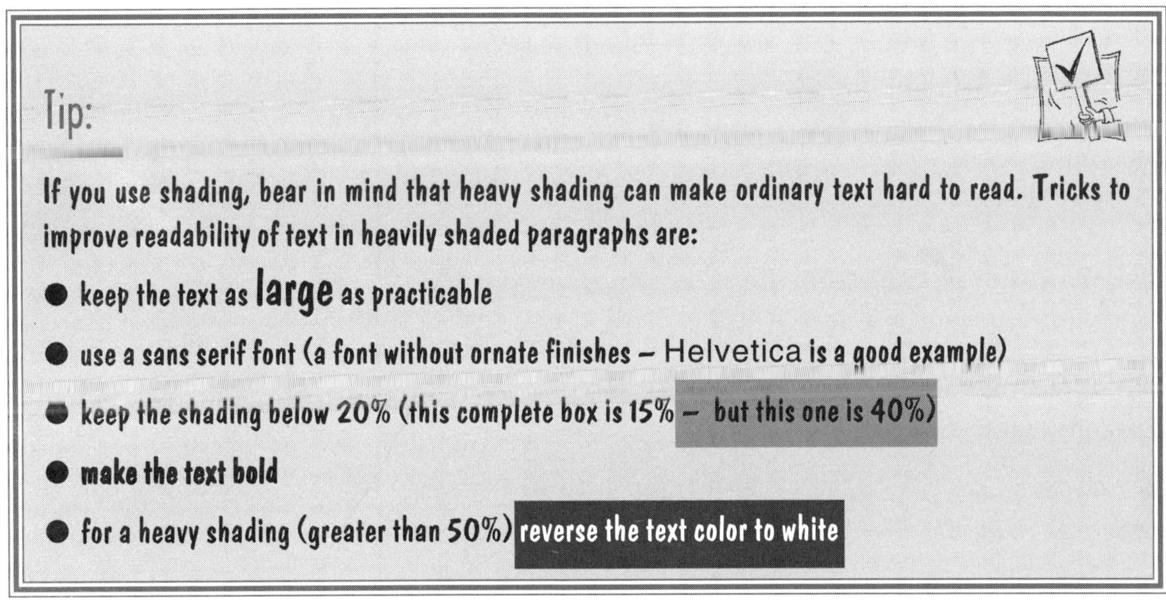

Tip:

If you use shading, bear in mind that heavy shading can make ordinary text hard to read. Tricks to improve readability of text in heavily shaded paragraphs are:

- **keep the text as large as practicable**
- **use a sans serif font (a font without ornate finishes – Helvetica is a good example)**
- **keep the shading below 20% (this complete box is 15% – but this one is 40%)**
- **make the text bold**
- **for a heavy shading (greater than 50%) reverse the text color to white**

Summary for Section 3

- Both character and paragraph formatting are useful — apply them to selected text by all means — but automatic formatting (using Word styles — covered in Section 6) is even more useful.

- Formatting — whether character formats, paragraph formats, or styles — is the key to producing good-looking effective documents.

- Character and paragraph formats are quickly applied by clicking buttons on the Formatting toolbar — keyboard shortcuts, however, are often even quicker.

- If you apply a format to the insertion point, the format continues as you type until you change it again.

- If a format already exists in your document, and you want to use it again, use the Format Painter button on the Standard toolbar to paint the format.

- Paragraph formats are all stored in a paragraph's paragraph marker ¶.

- Don't bother setting tabs *before* you enter text — let Word's default tabs do the work for you until you've typed in the text you want to be tabulated. After you've typed it in, select the text then set and adjust your tabs appropriately.

- Set and adjust tabs from the ruler wherever possible — this is by far the quickest way.

- Use borders and shading to emphasize points in your document.

- Borders (and shading) extend right around the text block — to each indent. If you want the border around *just* the text, bring the indents in to those positions.

4 Sections and pages

About sections 74
Setting up a document 76
Margins 77
Headers and footers 80
Line numbers 84
Columns 86
Summary for Section 4 90

About sections

Sometimes when you are working on a document, you need to split it up into smaller parts, without splitting it up into totally different documents. These smaller parts are called *sections*.

You only need to create sections if you want to change the appearance of parts of your document in certain ways. The changes you can make within a document which require sections to be created include:

- a different page size
- different margins (page 77)
- a different number of columns (page 86)
- a different header or footer (page 80)
- different line numberings (page 84).

In normal view (and in page layout view if the Show/Hide ¶ button ¶ on the Standard toolbar is clicked), a section end is displayed as shown below.

Take note:

You only need to split your document up into sections if *part* of your document needs to have one or more of these changes applied. If the *whole* document needs to have the change applied there's no need to use sections at all.

A section break, indicated by a dotted line. This does not print.

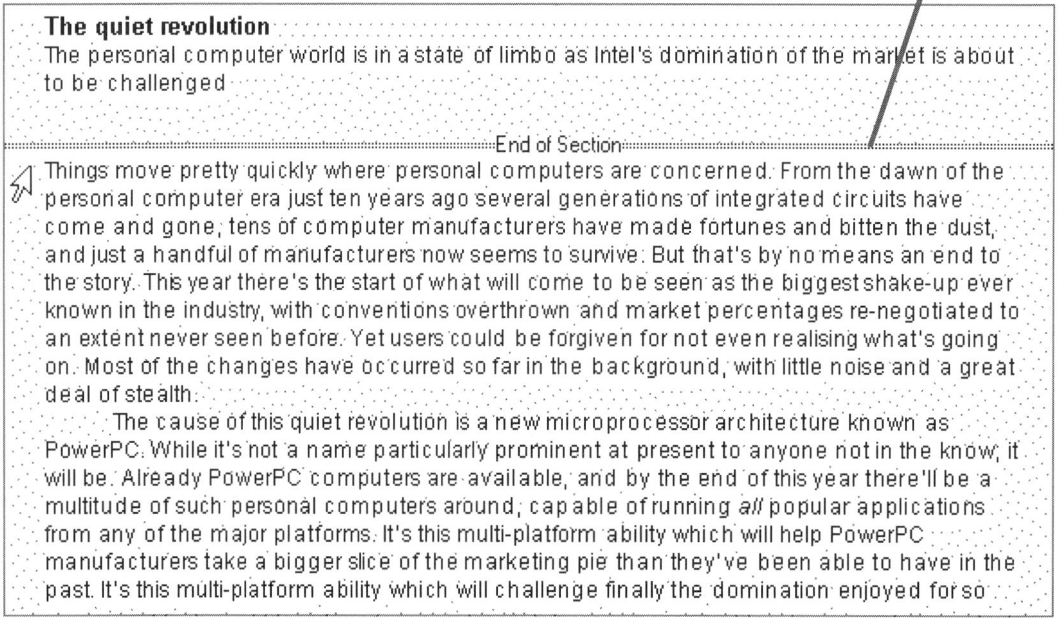

The quiet revolution
The personal computer world is in a state of limbo as Intel's domination of the market is about to be challenged

End of Section

Things move pretty quickly where personal computers are concerned. From the dawn of the personal computer era just ten years ago several generations of integrated circuits have come and gone, tens of computer manufacturers have made fortunes and bitten the dust, and just a handful of manufacturers now seems to survive. But that's by no means an end to the story. This year there's the start of what will come to be seen as the biggest shake-up ever known in the industry, with conventions overthrown and market percentages re-negotiated to an extent never seen before. Yet users could be forgiven for not even realising what's going on. Most of the changes have occurred so far in the background, with little noise and a great deal of stealth.

The cause of this quiet revolution is a new microprocessor architecture known as PowerPC. While it's not a name particularly prominent at present to anyone not in the know, it will be. Already PowerPC computers are available, and by the end of this year there'll be a multitude of such personal computers around, capable of running *all* popular applications from any of the major platforms. It's this multi-platform ability which will help PowerPC manufacturers take a bigger slice of the marketing pie than they've been able to have in the past. It's this multi-platform ability which will challenge finally the domination enjoyed for so

Basic steps:

1 Position the insertion point in your document where you want the new section to be, then choose **Insert↳Break**, or type [Alt]+[I] then [B], to call up the **Break** dialog box.

2 Click the button corresponding to the section break you want:

- **Next Page** — the section break causes the document to force following text to appear at the top of the next page
- **Even Page** — following text is forced to the top of the next even page of the document
- **Odd page** — following text is forced to the top of the next odd page of the document
- **Continuous** — following text occurs straight under the section break, wherever it occurs on a page

3 Click **OK**.

Effectively, the changes listed are parameters you apply much like character and paragraph formats, except they affect the whole section (not just a few characters or paragraphs). Every time you want to change one or more of these parameters in just *part* of your document, you need a new section.

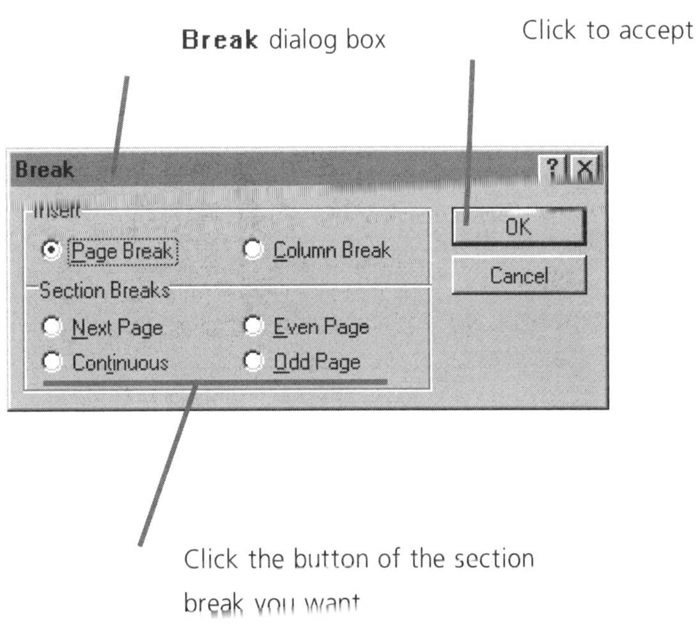
Break dialog box
Click to accept
Break
Insert
Page Break
Column Break
Section Breaks
Next Page
Even Page
Continuous
Odd Page
OK
Cancel
Click the button of the section break you want

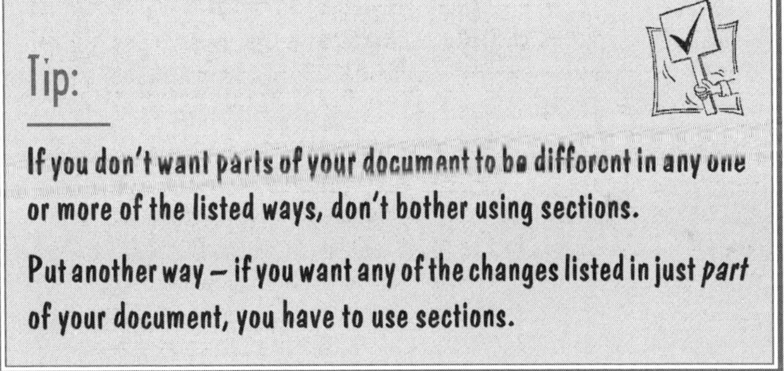
Tip:

If you don't want parts of your document to be different in any one or more of the listed ways, don't bother using sections.

Put another way – if you want any of the changes listed in just *part* of your document, you have to use sections.

Setting up a document

Basic steps:

Apart from character and paragraph formats, a document has other parameters you can format. Where these are contained within a section (or selected sections) of a document, they affect just that section (or sections). Where the document contains no section breaks (that is, the document comprises just one section), or where all sections of a document are selected before formatting, the whole document is affected.

Most of these parameters are adjusted from the **Page Setup** dialog box, although other methods are sometimes available.

1. Choose **File→Page Setup**, or type Alt+F then U, to call up the **Page Setup** dialog box.
2. Click tabs to see the different controls available to adjust parameters.
3. If you make any changes to parameters, click **OK** to accept changes, or **Cancel** to ignore them.

1 **Page Setup** dialog box

2 Tabs allow different controls to be adjusted. Click tabs to bring those controls to the front in the dialog box

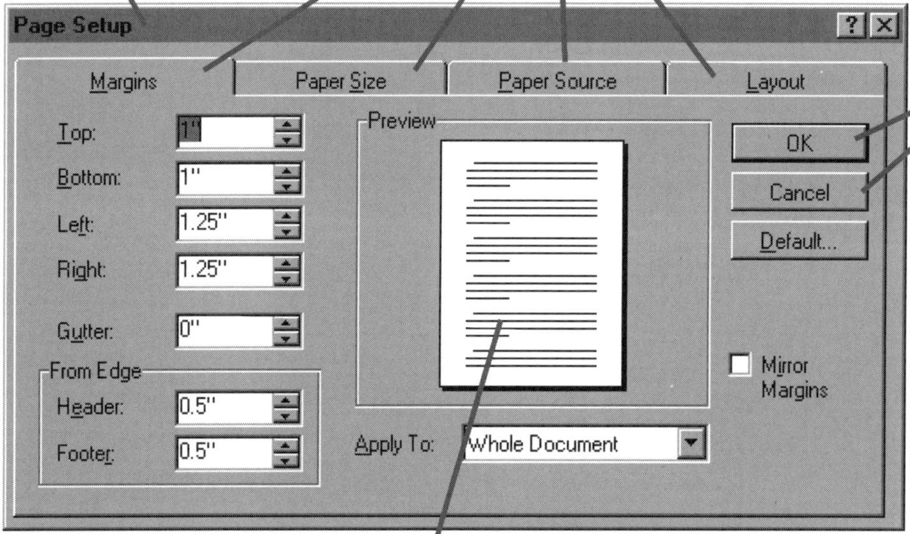

3 Accept or ignore your changes

Page Setup
Margins
Paper Size
Paper Source
Layout
Top: 1"
Bottom: 1"
Left: 1.25"
Right: 1.25"
Gutter: 0"
From Edge
Header: 0.5"
Footer: 0.5"
Preview
Apply To: Whole Document
OK
Cancel
Default...
Mirror Margins

Preview of your document's overall appearance with parameters as you set them in the dialog box

Margins

Margins are imaginary guides on a document page, outside of which text isn't normally situated. By default, Word creates margins for any new document — usually of 1 inch (2.54 cm) from top and bottom of the page, and 1.25 inches (3.17 cm) from left and right page edge.

You can change margins, either for a whole document or for a section, from the **Page Setup** dialog box.

Tip:

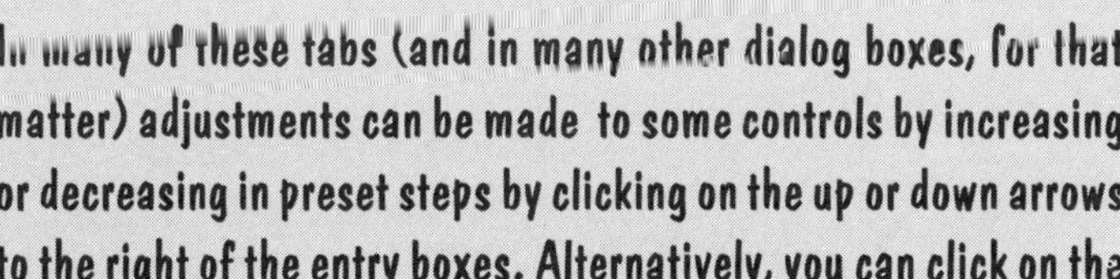
In many of these tabs (and in many other dialog boxes, for that matter) adjustments can be made to some controls by increasing or decreasing in preset steps by clicking on the up or down arrows to the right of the entry boxes. Alternatively, you can click on the entry box you want to change, then enter the exact value you want.

Basic steps:

1. Choose **File↳Page Setup**, or type Alt+F then U, to call up the **Page Setup** dialog box.
2. Click the **Margins** tab if it's not already at the front (see opposite).
3. Adjust margin dimensions as desired.

Tip:

You can specify that the margin changes be applied to just the section you are in, from the current point on (Word places a section break at the insertion point and changes apply to the section following it), or the whole document, from the drop-down list box on the **Margins** tab of the **Page Setup** dialog box.

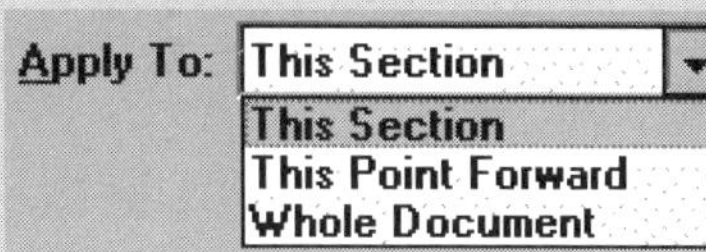
Apply To:
This Section
This Section
This Point Forward
Whole Document

Margins (contd)

Basic steps:

Some of the controls of the **Margins** tab of the **Page Setup** dialog box allow you to control how pages are printed for double-sided purposes (that is, for the likes of books and reports).

1. If the document is to be double-sided, check the **Mirror Margins** check box.
2. Change the **Inside** and **Outside** margins measurements to suit your requirements.
3. If the you plan to bind your document with a ring or similar method, enter a value in the **Gutter** entry box — this gives space inside the inside margins to allow for the binding.

If **Mirror Margins** check box is checked, these entry boxes change to show **Inside** and **Outside** margin measurements

Preview always shows the effects of entries and controls

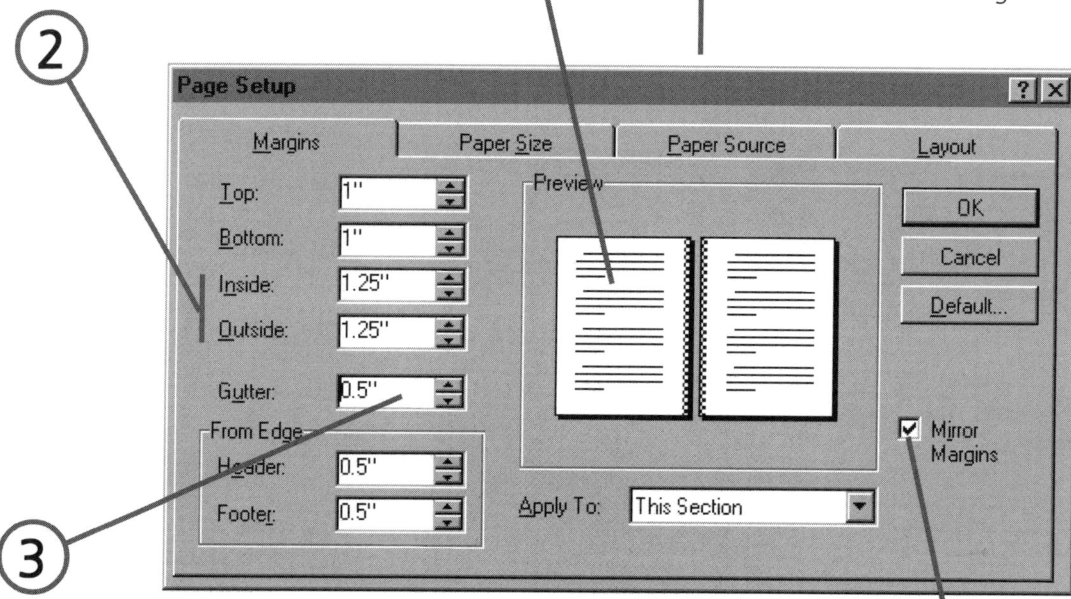
2
Page Setup
Margins
Paper Size
Paper Source
Layout
Top:
1"
Bottom:
1"
Inside:
1.25"
Outside:
1.25"
Gutter:
0.5"
From Edge
Header:
0.5"
Footer:
0.5"
Preview
Apply To:
This Section
OK
Cancel
Default...
Mirror Margins
3

Entering a value here creates an extra space to allow for a binding

Check here for margins which are equal on the insides and equal on the outsides of each left and right hand page

1

Basic steps:

1 Choose **View→Page Layout**, or type Alt+V then P, or (best) click the Page Layout button to view your document in page layout view.

2 Drag your margins to where you want them.

As an alternative to using the Page Setup dialog box, you can adjust margins by dragging margin boundaries in page layout view (or print preview — see page 138). This is probably faster, though you have little accuracy, you can't specify how much of the document you want to apply changes to (current section, current point forward, or the whole document — dragging from the ruler applies changes to just the current section, or whole document if no section break exists), and mirror margin and gutter margin controls aren't available.

Microsoft Word - The quiet revolution.doc

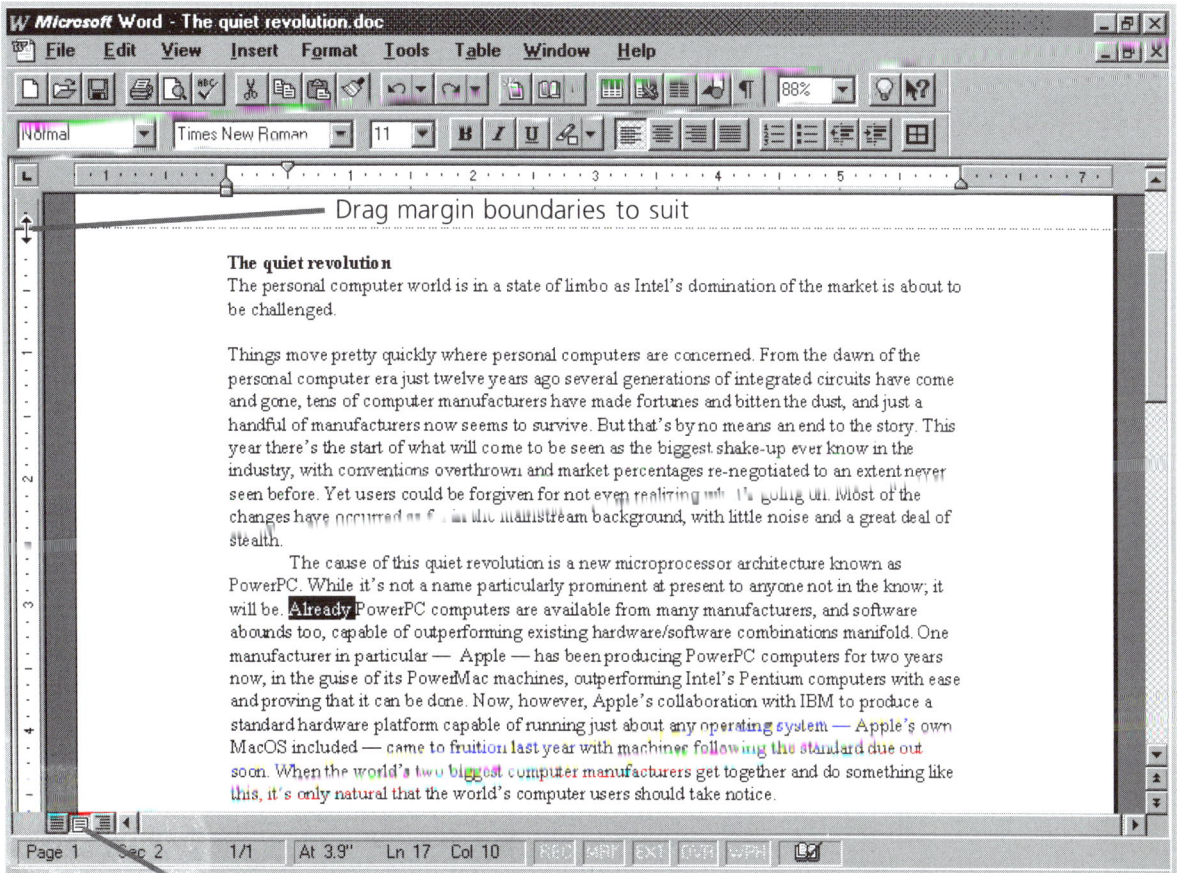

Drag margin boundaries to suit

The quiet revolution
The personal computer world is in a state of limbo as Intel's domination of the market is about to be challenged.

Things move pretty quickly where personal computers are concerned. From the dawn of the personal computer era just twelve years ago several generations of integrated circuits have come and gone, tens of computer manufacturers have made fortunes and bitten the dust, and just a handful of manufacturers now seems to survive. But that's by no means an end to the story. This year there's the start of what will come to be seen as the biggest shake-up ever know in the industry, with conventions overthrown and market percentages re-negotiated to an extent never seen before. Yet users could be forgiven for not even realizing what's going on. Most of the changes have occurred so far in the mainstream background, with little noise and a great deal of stealth.

The cause of this quiet revolution is a new microprocessor architecture known as PowerPC. While it's not a name particularly prominent at present to anyone not in the know; it will be. Already PowerPC computers are available from many manufacturers, and software abounds too, capable of outperforming existing hardware/software combinations manifold. One manufacturer in particular — Apple — has been producing PowerPC computers for two years now, in the guise of its PowerMac machines, outperforming Intel's Pentium computers with ease and proving that it can be done. Now, however, Apple's collaboration with IBM to produce a standard hardware platform capable of running just about any operating system — Apple's own MacOS included — came to fruition last year with machines following the standard due out soon. When the world's two biggest computer manufacturers get together and do something like this, it's only natural that the world's computer users should take notice.

Page 1 Sec 2 1/1 At 3.9" Ln 17 Col 10

Click here if document is not already in page layout view

Headers and footers

A header is a heading (often called a running head) which appears at the top of each page in a document or section of a document. A footer is at the bottom of each page. You can put text or graphical items in either and you can format them in the usual ways.

Basic steps:

1. To create either a header or a footer choose **View↳Header and Footer**, or type [Alt]+[V] then [H]. The document changes to page layout view and displays the header entry box and the Header and Footer toolbar.

Header entry box — type in what you want and format it

Header and footer toolbar

Jump between the header and footer by clicking here

Click to get back to normal view

Document text is displayed but grayed out

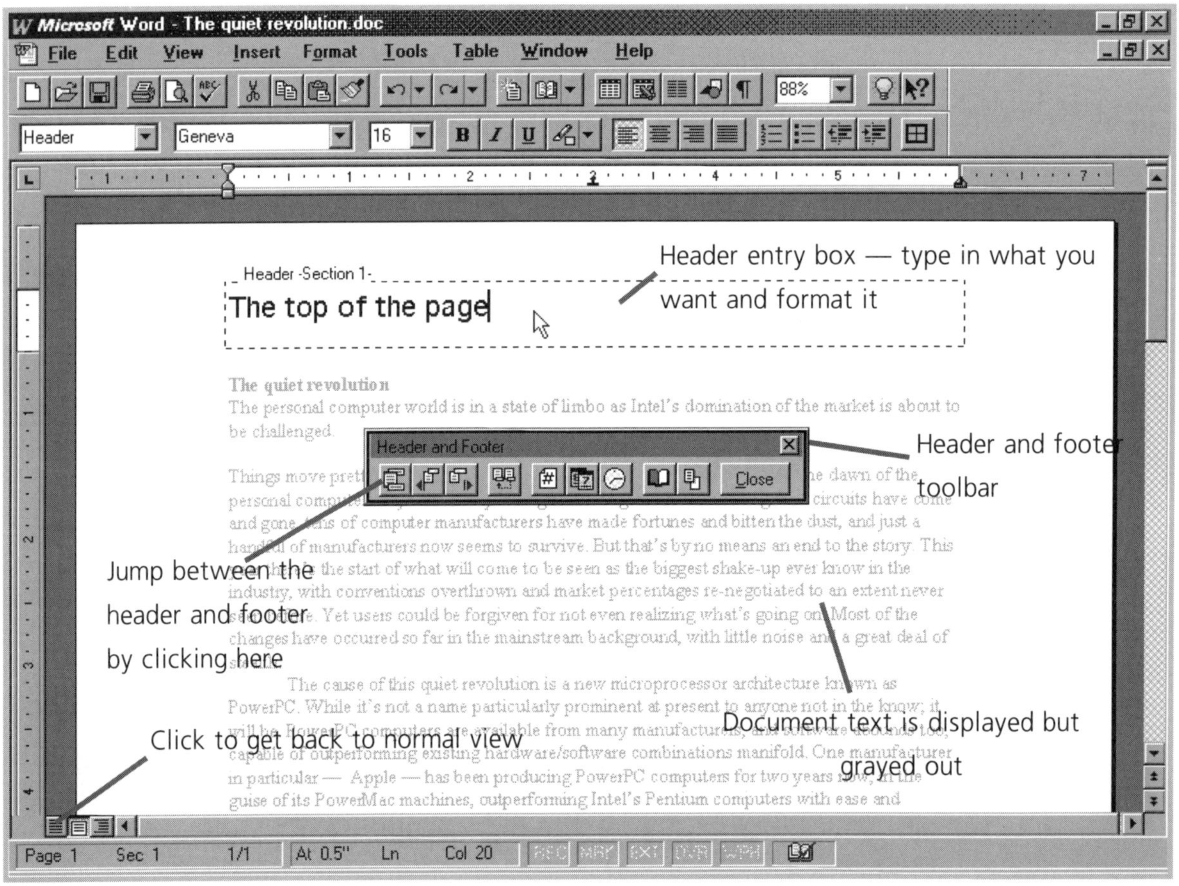

Tip:

Your document's text is displayed gray when in Headers and Footers view. Double-click anywhere in the text, however, and the text becomes active (sending the headers and footers to a grayed background outline). You can switch between the two by double-clicking each in this way.

Tip:

Headers and footers apply to individual sections – in other words, you can have different headers and footers for each section if you want.

Double-click a grayed header to make it active

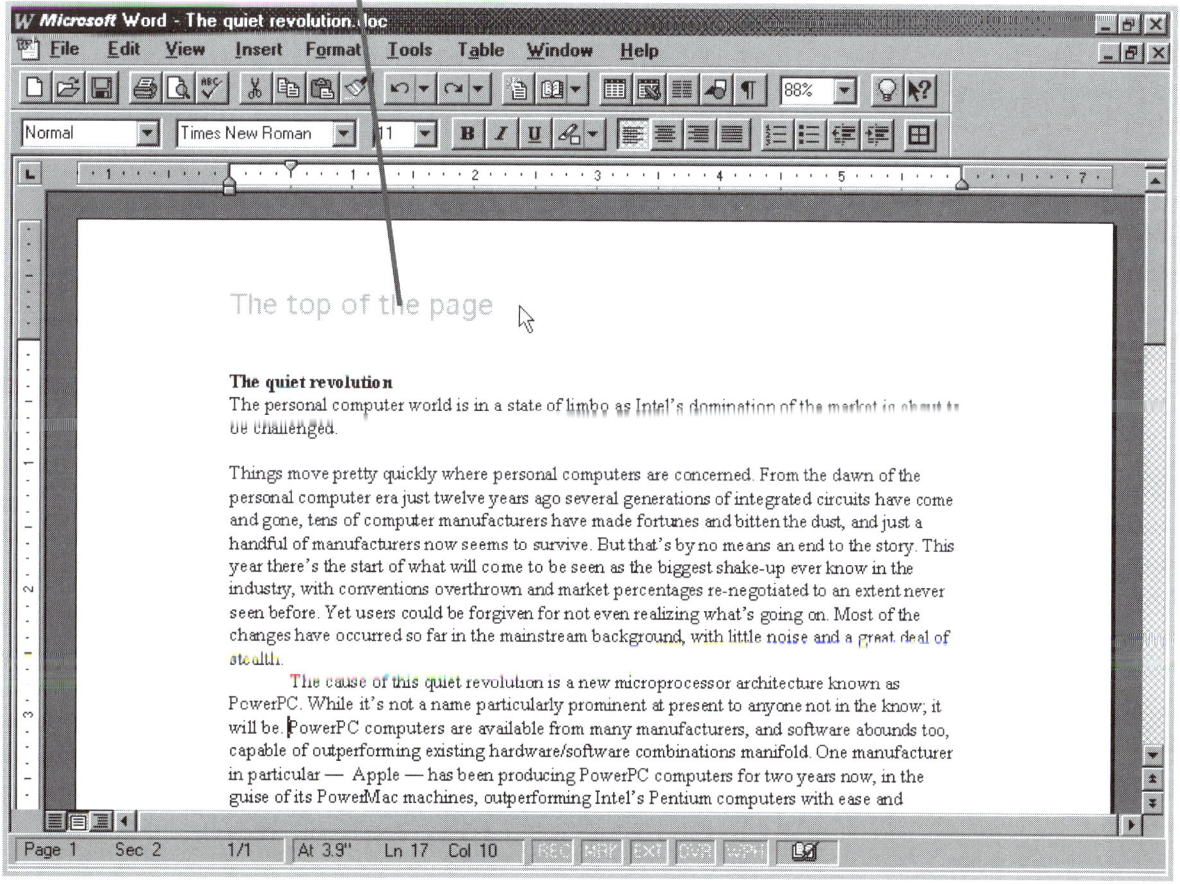

Headers & footers (contd)

The Headers and Footers toolbar has a number of buttons. Use these to access various features and entries you can make into a header or footer.

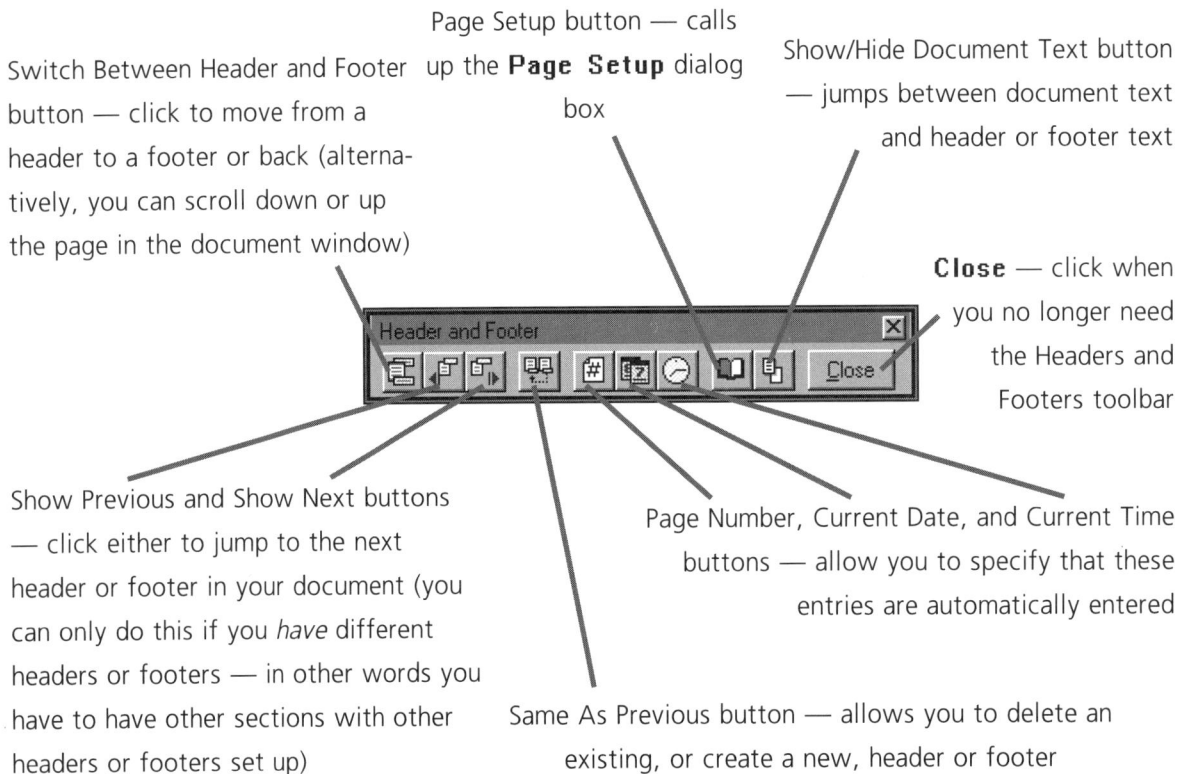

Switch Between Header and Footer button — click to move from a header to a footer or back (alternatively, you can scroll down or up the page in the document window)

Page Setup button — calls up the **Page Setup** dialog box

Show/Hide Document Text button — jumps between document text and header or footer text

Close — click when you no longer need the Headers and Footers toolbar

Show Previous and Show Next buttons — click either to jump to the next header or footer in your document (you can only do this if you *have* different headers or footers — in other words you have to have other sections with other headers or footers set up)

Page Number, Current Date, and Current Time buttons — allow you to specify that these entries are automatically entered

Same As Previous button — allows you to delete an existing, or create a new, header or footer

Tip:

Remember you can format a header or a footer in exactly the same way you format ordinary document text. You can bold, italicize, underline, and so on. You can make it center aligned or right aligned if you want. You are not restricted to just one line of text. You can also use a graphical item.

Also remember that each section you create can have its own header and footer – use this feature to set up a header for each chapter of a large document, for example.

Basic steps:

1 Choose **View↳Page Layout**, or type Alt+V then P, or (best) click the Page Layout button to view your document in page layout view.

2 Drag margin and header (or footer) boundaries to where you want them.

You can adjust the distance from a page edge taken up by a header at the top of your document page (or the footer at the bottom) from the **Page Setup** dialog box (the **From Edge** entries). You can also change margins from here (allowing you to adjust the distance between the header or footer and the document text).

An easier way, however, is to switch to page layout view and drag the various boundaries to suit what you want.

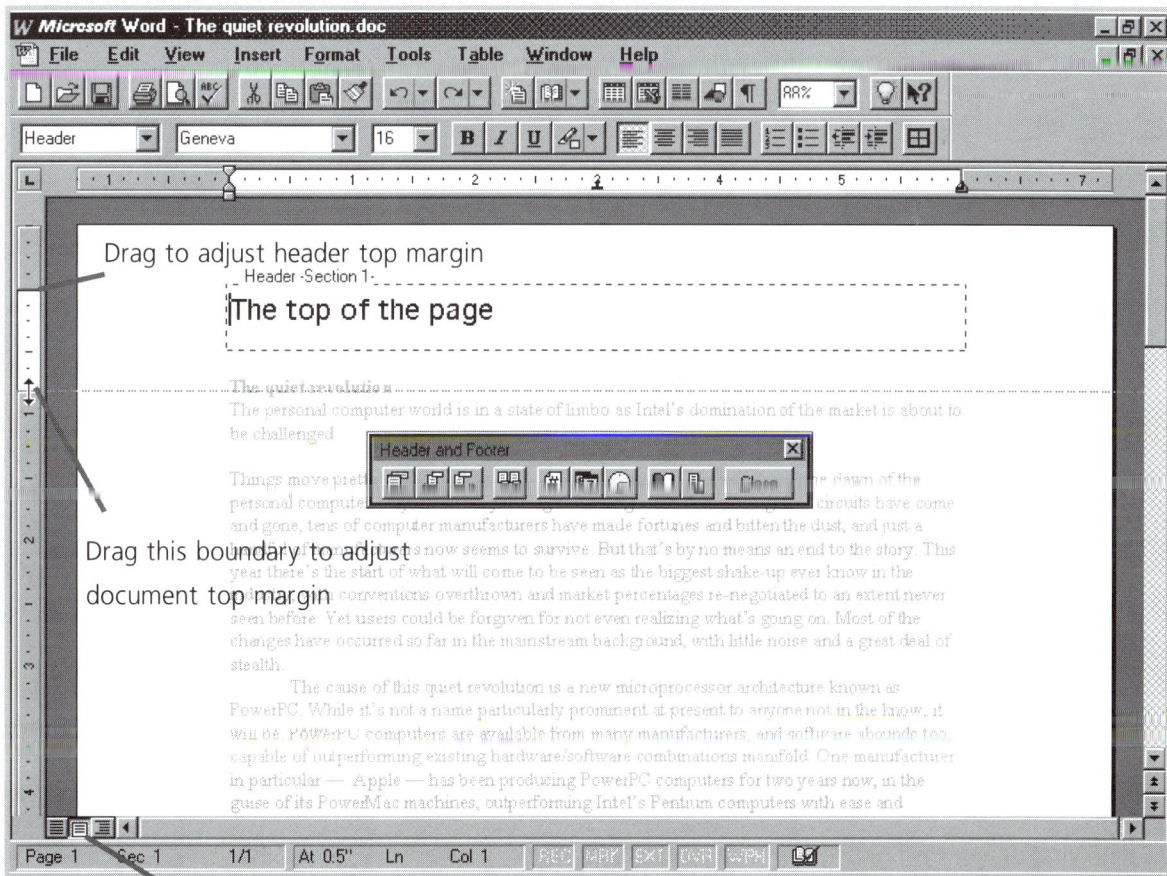

Drag to adjust header top margin

Drag this boundary to adjust document top margin

1 Click to get to page layout view

Line numbers

Basic steps:

Word can display and print line numbers alongside text. This can be useful in technical documentation, and even required in legal literature.

Line numbers are:

- printed in the left margin
- numbered excluding lines in tables, headers, footers and some other parts of a document
- only visible on-screen in page layout view (or print preview — see page 138).

1. Choose **File→Page Setup**, or type Alt+F then U to call up the **Page Setup** dialog box. Click the **Layout** tab if it's not already at the front. Next click the **Line Numbers** button to call up the **Line Numbers** dialog box.
2. Check the **Add Line Numbering** check box to create line numbers.
3. Adjust controls to suit and click **OK** to accept and view line numbers.

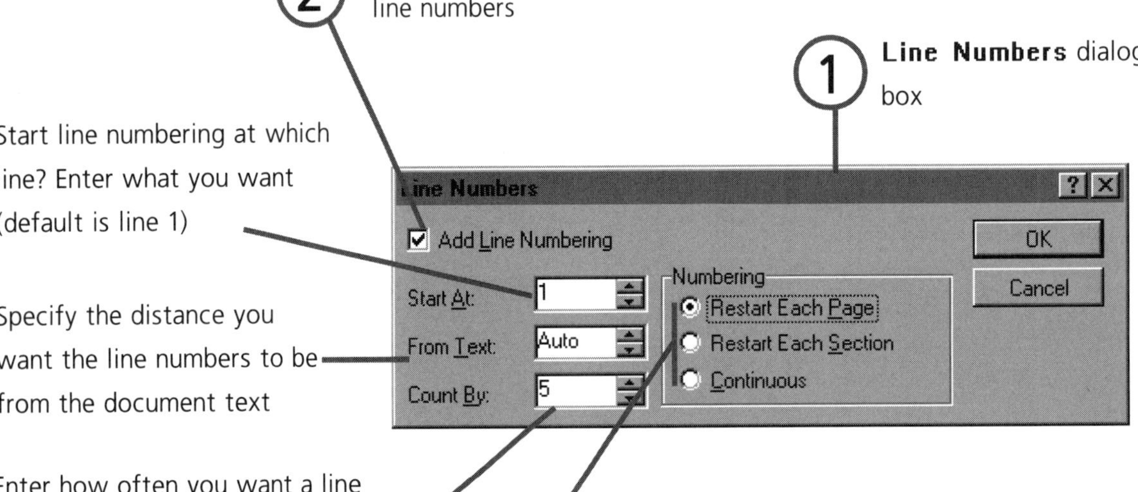
2
Check to create line numbers
1
Line Numbers dialog box
Start line numbering at which line? Enter what you want (default is line 1)
Specify the distance you want the line numbers to be from the document text
Enter how often you want a line number to occur — for example, if you only want a line number every 10 lines — 10, 20, 30 and so on — enter 10
Click a button to specify whether the line numbers restart at the top of each page; restart at the beginning of each section in the document; or are continuous throughout
Line Numbers
Add Line Numbering
Start At:
1
From Text:
Auto
Count By:
5
Numbering
Restart Each Page
Restart Each Section
Continuous
OK
Cancel

3 Line numbers are visible in page layout (or print preview) views only

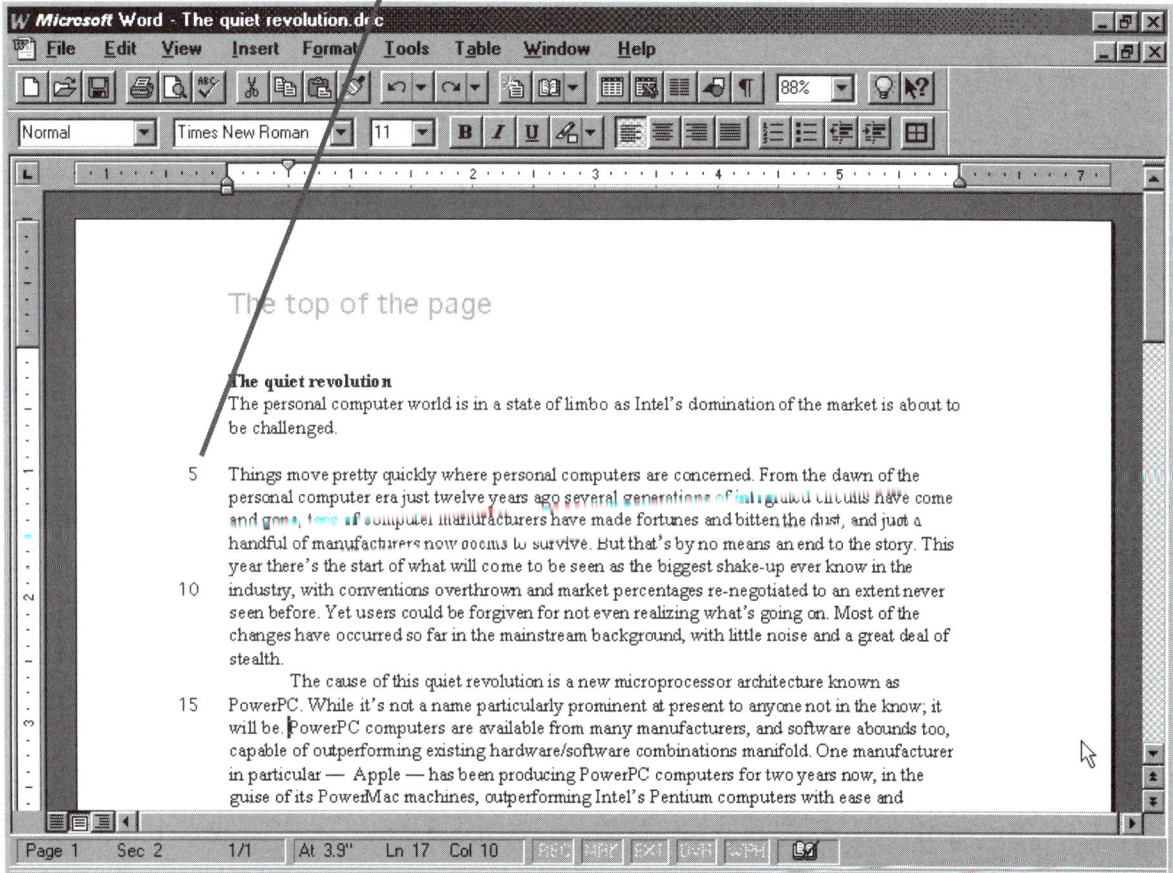

Microsoft Word - The quiet revolution.doc

The top of the page

The quiet revolution

The personal computer world is in a state of limbo as Intel's domination of the market is about to be challenged.

Things move pretty quickly where personal computers are concerned. From the dawn of the personal computer era just twelve years ago several generations of integrated circuits have come and gone, tens of computer manufacturers have made fortunes and bitten the dust, and just a handful of manufacturers now seems to survive. But that's by no means an end to the story. This year there's the start of what will come to be seen as the biggest shake-up ever know in the industry, with conventions overthrown and market percentages re-negotiated to an extent never seen before. Yet users could be forgiven for not even realizing what's going on. Most of the changes have occurred so far in the mainstream background, with little noise and a great deal of stealth.

The cause of this quiet revolution is a new microprocessor architecture known as PowerPC. While it's not a name particularly prominent at present to anyone not in the know; it will be. PowerPC computers are available from many manufacturers, and software abounds too, capable of outperforming existing hardware/software combinations manifold. One manufacturer in particular — Apple — has been producing PowerPC computers for two years now, in the guise of its PowerMac machines, outperforming Intel's Pentium computers with ease and

Page 1 Sec 2 1/1 At 3.9" Ln 17 Col 10

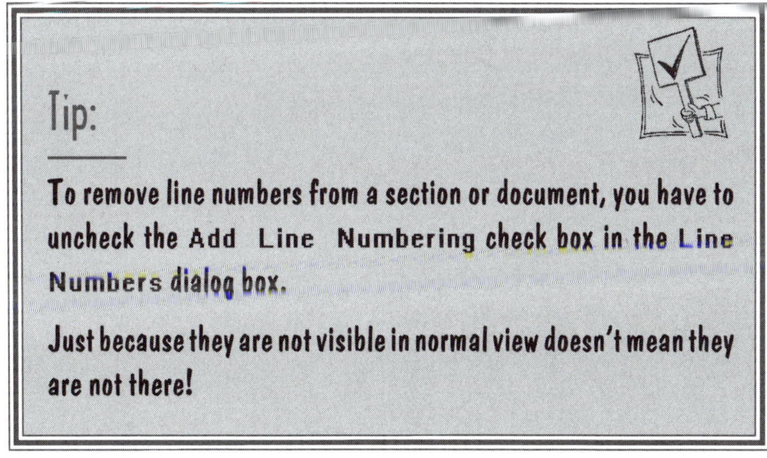
Tip:
To remove line numbers from a section or document, you have to uncheck the Add Line Numbering check box in the Line Numbers dialog box.
Just because they are not visible in normal view doesn't mean they are not there!

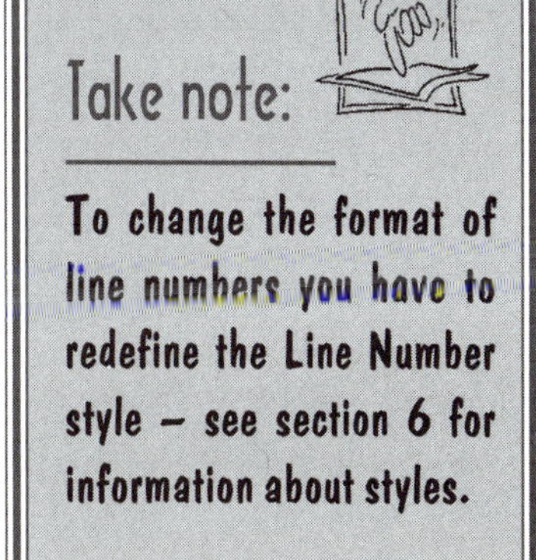
Take note:
To change the format of line numbers you have to redefine the Line Number style – see section 6 for information about styles.

Columns

Generally, text in a Word document is in a single column — that is, a single vertical division down the page. You can, however, create two or more columns of text quite simply, where columns are unattached or where a story flows from the bottom of one column to the top of the next. Columns can be used to create newspaper-style or newsletter-style documents, or books such as this one.

You can create columns in your document from either:

- a button on the Standard toolbar; or
- the **Columns** dialog box.

Basic steps:

USING THE STANDARD TOOLBAR

1. Select the text you want to be formatted into columns, then click the Columns button on the Standard toolbar.
2. Drag across the drop-down window to select the number of columns you want.

Cancel

Click the Columns button to display this drop-down window

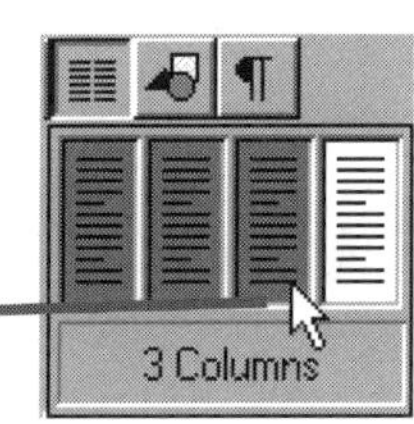
3 Columns

Drag across to select the number of columns you want — let go of the mouse button to accept

Take note:

You can only see columns you create in page layout view or print preview view (see page 138)! In normal view, text is simply displayed at the width of a *single* column – so if your text is across two columns on the page, normally viewed text will only be a half page wide.

Basic steps:

FROM THE COLUMNS DIALOG BOX

1 Select the text you want to be formatted into columns, then choose **Format→Columns** to call up the **Columns** dialog box.

2 Choose the number of columns you want.

3 Change column widths and other controls to suit your requirements.

Tip:

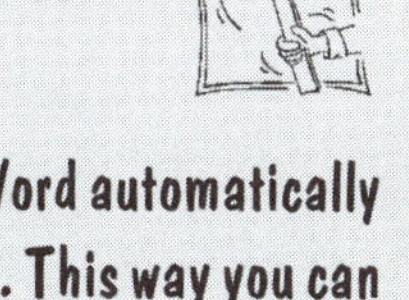

If you select text then format it into columns, Word automatically inserts section breaks before and after the text. This way you can have different numbers of columns in different parts of the document – columns are section parameters, remember.

If you simply position the insertion point in your document before formatting into columns (that is, you *don't* select any text), the whole section (the whole *document* if no section breaks are present in the document) is formatted.

1 **Columns** dialog box

2 Click to select the number of columns from these buttons, or enter the number in the lower box

3 Adjust column widths

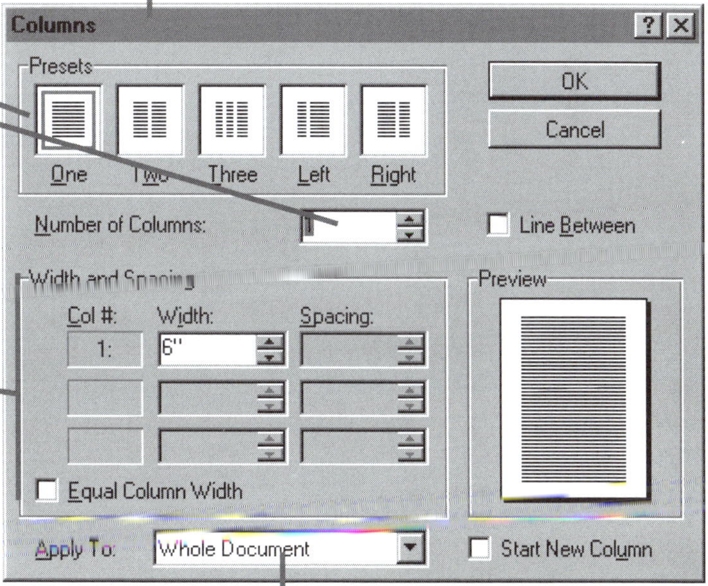

Specify which part of document to apply columns to (whole document, current section, or from this point on)

Columns (contd)

If you want to format your section or document into even-width columns, the quickest method is with the Columns button on the Standard toolbar.

On the other hand, if you want *uneven* columns you have to use the **Columns** dialog box. The **Columns** dialog box also gives some other controls unavailable with the Columns button:

- the spacing between columns
- whether a line between columns is displayed
- whether the columns apply to the whole document, the current section, or from the current point on.

Tip:

If you want multi-column text underneath single column text, first enter text without any column formatting. Next, select the text to be multi-column formatted and format it. Word automatically creates section breaks before and after the multi-column formatted section.

Click here to give two columns of unequal width — measurements in the width entry boxes are automatically adjusted

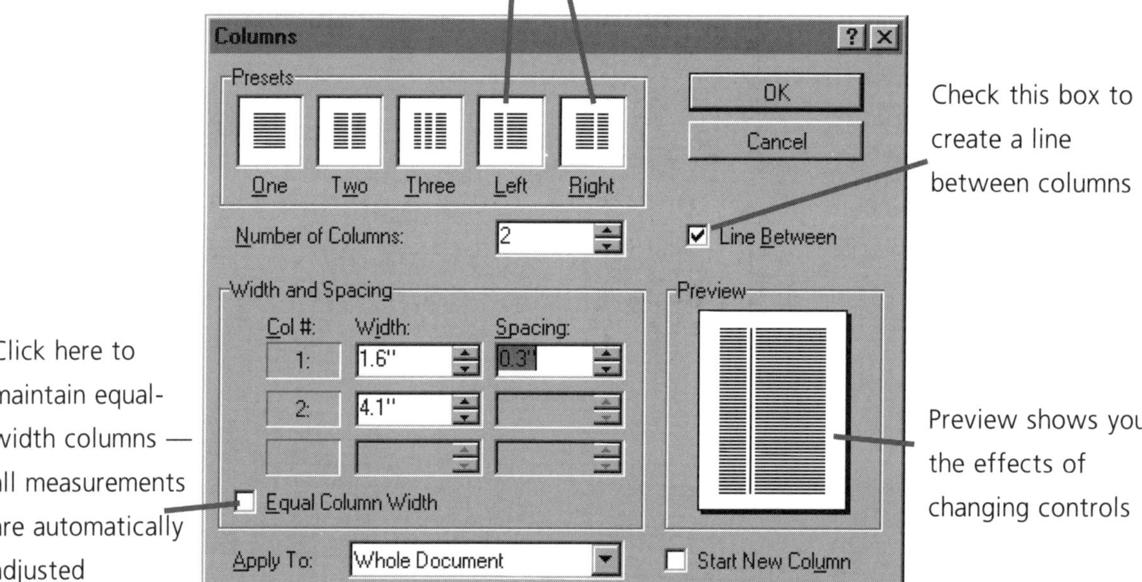
Columns
Presets
One
Two
Three
Left
Right
OK
Cancel
Number of Columns:
2
Line Between
Width and Spacing
Col #:
Width:
Spacing:
1:
1.6"
0.3"
2:
4.1"
Equal Column Width
Preview
Apply To:
Whole Document
Start New Column
Check this box to create a line between columns
Click here to maintain equal-width columns — all measurements are automatically adjusted
Preview shows you the effects of changing controls

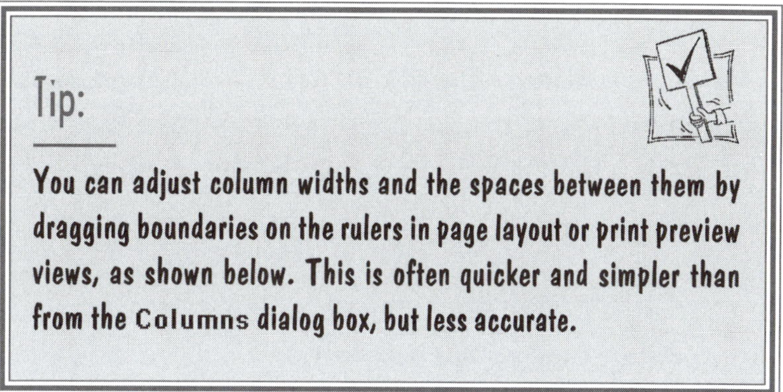

Tip:

You can adjust column widths and the spaces between them by dragging boundaries on the rulers in page layout or print preview views, as shown below. This is often quicker and simpler than from the **Columns** dialog box, but less accurate.

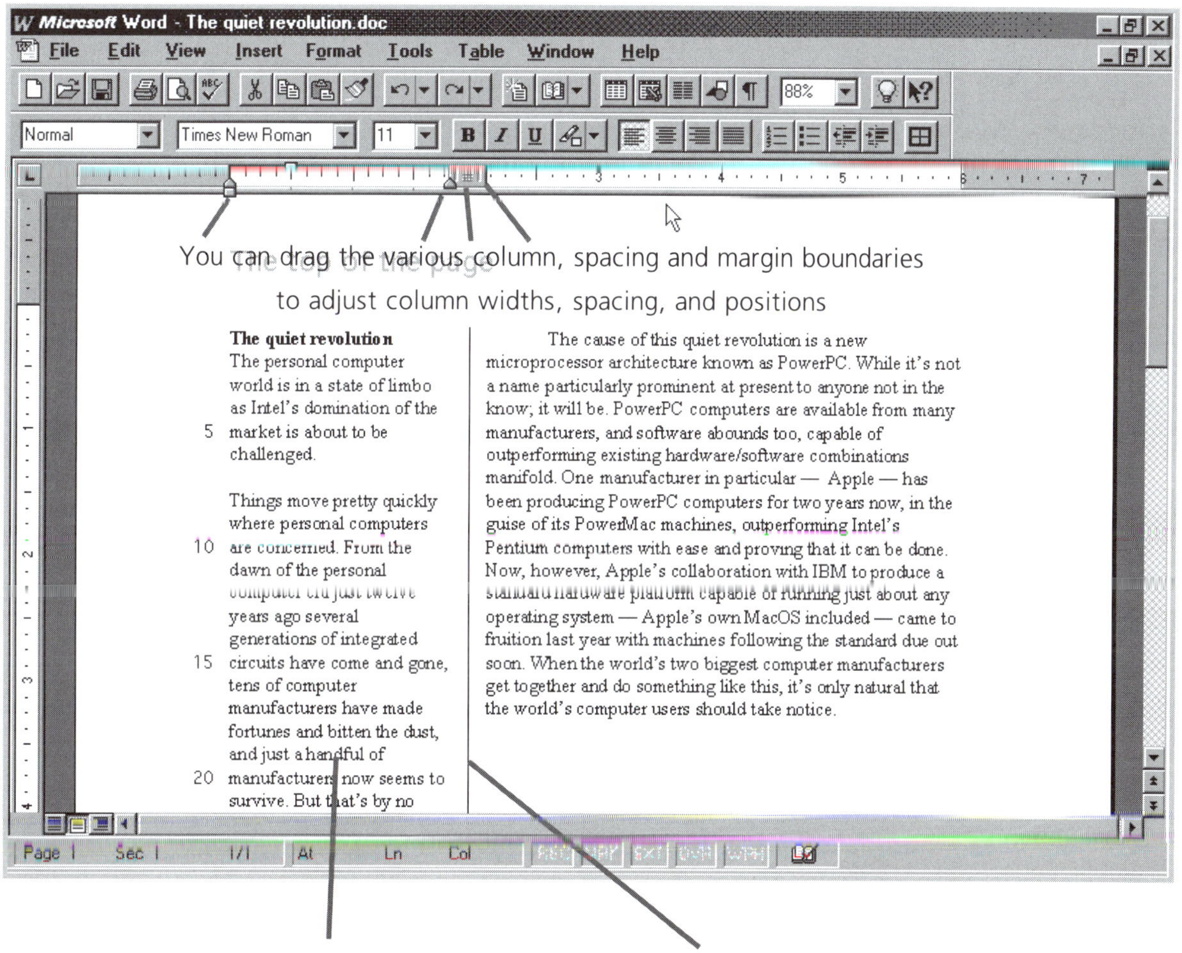

You can drag the various column, spacing and margin boundaries to adjust column widths, spacing, and positions

This document was set up using the controls as entered in the **Columns** dialog box shown opposite

Line between columns

Summary for Section 4

- Use a section where you need to change certain parameters for only *part* of your document. The parameters for which a section has to be created include:
  - ❑ a different page size
  - ❑ different margins
  - ❑ a different number of columns
  - ❑ a different header or footer
  - ❑ different line numberings.
- If you change any of these parameters for *the whole document*, don't use a section.
- Create margins, headers and footers, and columns from dialog boxes (as this is most exact), but remember you can adjust them and their spacings by dragging boundaries in page layout (or print preview) view.

5 Text control

Finding text 92

Replacing 94

Spelling 96

AutoCorrect 100

AutoText 102

Outlining 104

Tables 108

Table conversions 111

Table formatting 112

Counting your words 113

Graphics 114

Summary for Section 5 116

Finding text

Although it probably sounds odd, one of the main jobs a word processor is asked to do in everyday life is to find text. You'd think a word processor had enough coping with all it's asked to do with text without having to actually find the stuff for you too, wouldn't you?

Problem is, in long documents it's not always easy for us to locate specific instances of small pieces of text. Let's say you have worked for weeks and weeks on your latest novel, and you decide that little bit around half way through about your heroine's need for money needs expanding somewhat. What do you do? You could scroll through the book, screen by screen, trying to find it, but that could take hours — you wrote it weeks ago remember — and you have no idea exactly where it is.

Let Word do the job for you.

Keep in mind, though, that text in Word doesn't just comprise the individual letters you type in at the keyboard. As we've seen in other sections, text can be formatted with bold, italic, and other character formats. It can have paragraph formats applied to it. It can be sectioned and have columns, line numbers, different margins, and so on.

The **Find** command in Word can find any format which you care to apply to text, so is extremely powerful. You can even ask Word to check for words which *sound* similar.

Basic steps:

1. Choose **Edit→Find**, or type Alt+E then F, or type Ctrl+F. This calls up the **Find** dialog box.
2. In the **Find What** entry box, type in the text you want to locate.
3. Specify the controls you want to control the search.
4. Click the **Find Next** button to start the search.

Tip:

When Word finds your text it leaves the Find dialog box open for further searches. Just click (again) the Find Next button to get Word to look again for your selected text. If the dialog box is in your way you can move it around by dragging its title bar, and close it when you've finished.

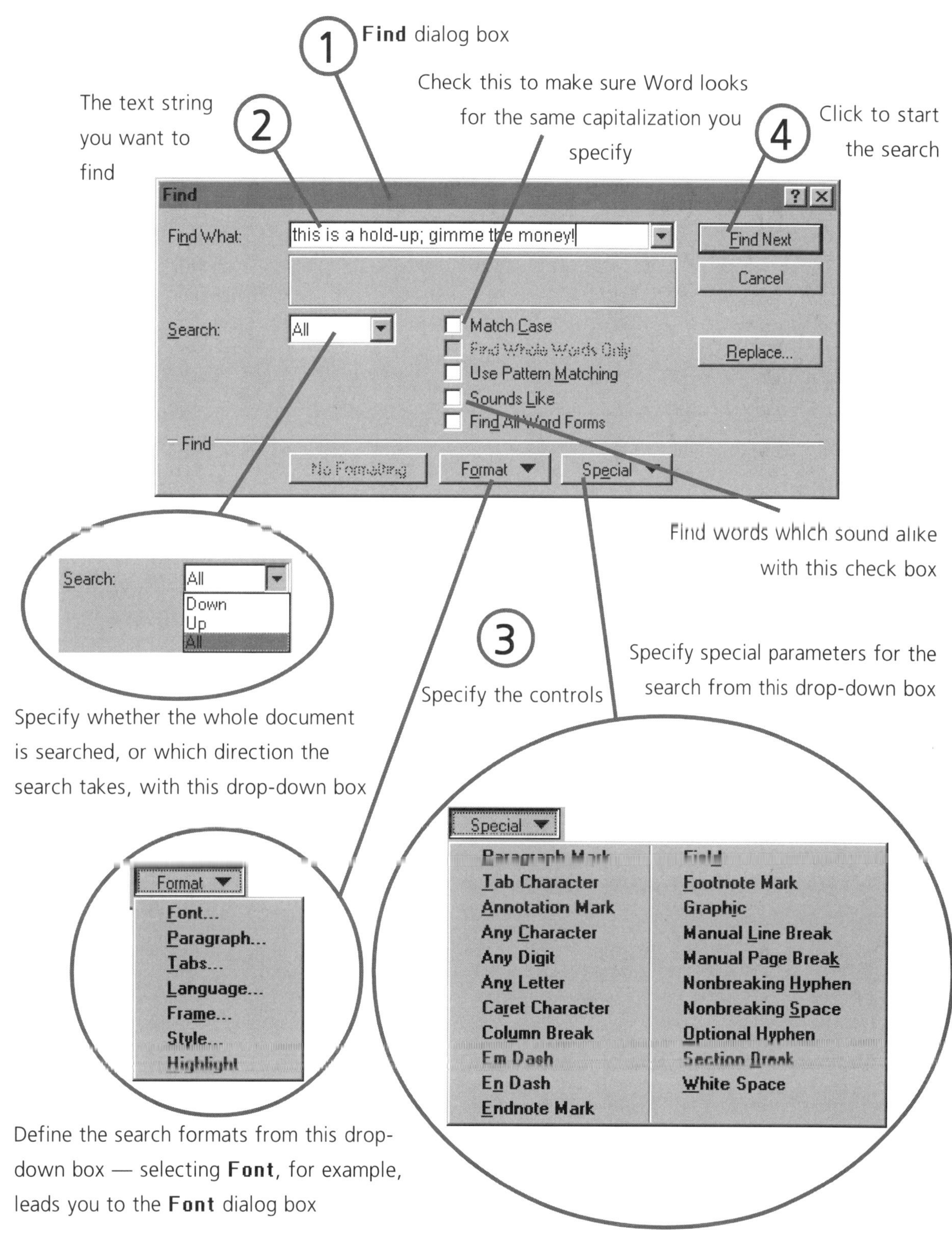
1
Find dialog box
The text string you want to find
2
Check this to make sure Word looks for the same capitalization you specify
Click to start the search
4
Find
Find What:
this is a hold-up; gimme the money!
Find Next
Cancel
Search:
All
Match Case
Find Whole Words Only
Use Pattern Matching
Sounds Like
Find All Word Forms
Replace...
Find
No Formatting
Format
Special
Find words which sound alike with this check box
Search:
All
Down
Up
All
3
Specify special parameters for the search from this drop-down box
Specify the controls
Specify whether the whole document is searched, or which direction the search takes, with this drop-down box
Special
Paragraph Mark
Tab Character
Annotation Mark
Any Character
Any Digit
Any Letter
Caret Character
Column Break
Em Dash
En Dash
Endnote Mark
Field
Footnote Mark
Graphic
Manual Line Break
Manual Page Break
Nonbreaking Hyphen
Nonbreaking Space
Optional Hyphen
Section Break
White Space
Format
Font...
Paragraph...
Tabs...
Language...
Frame...
Style...
Highlight
Define the search formats from this drop-down box — selecting Font, for example, leads you to the Font dialog box

Replacing

In the **Find** dialog box you may have noticed a button marked **Replace**. Clicking this leads you to the **Replace** dialog box (or you can call up the dialog box directly). This lets you find text in the same way we've seen, then replaces the instances of text with a different text string. Say your heroine's expression of admiration isn't quite what you want. No problem — get Word to replace it.

Take note:

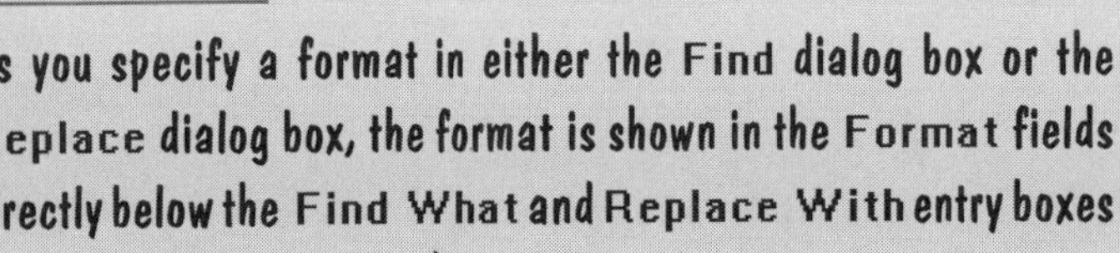
As you specify a format in either the Find dialog box or the Replace dialog box, the format is shown in the Format fields directly below the Find What and Replace With entry boxes (see opposite for example).

Basic steps:

1. Choose **Edit↳Replace**, or type Alt+E then E, or type Ctrl+H, or (as we've seen) click the **Replace** button in the **Find** dialog box. This calls up the **Replace** dialog box.
2. Enter the text string to look for.
3. Type in the text string to replace it.
4. Specify the controls (see page 93 for details).

Tip:

While Word will happily find and replace text strings for you (formatted or unformatted) it is equally at home finding and replacing just formats (without any text string associated with them).

So, for example, you can find instances of text which are underlined (a typical typists' method of emphasizing text) and replace them all with italicized text (*the usual typographers' emphasis method*) by specifying the formats. Remember not to enter any text in either of the Find What or Replace With entry boxes.

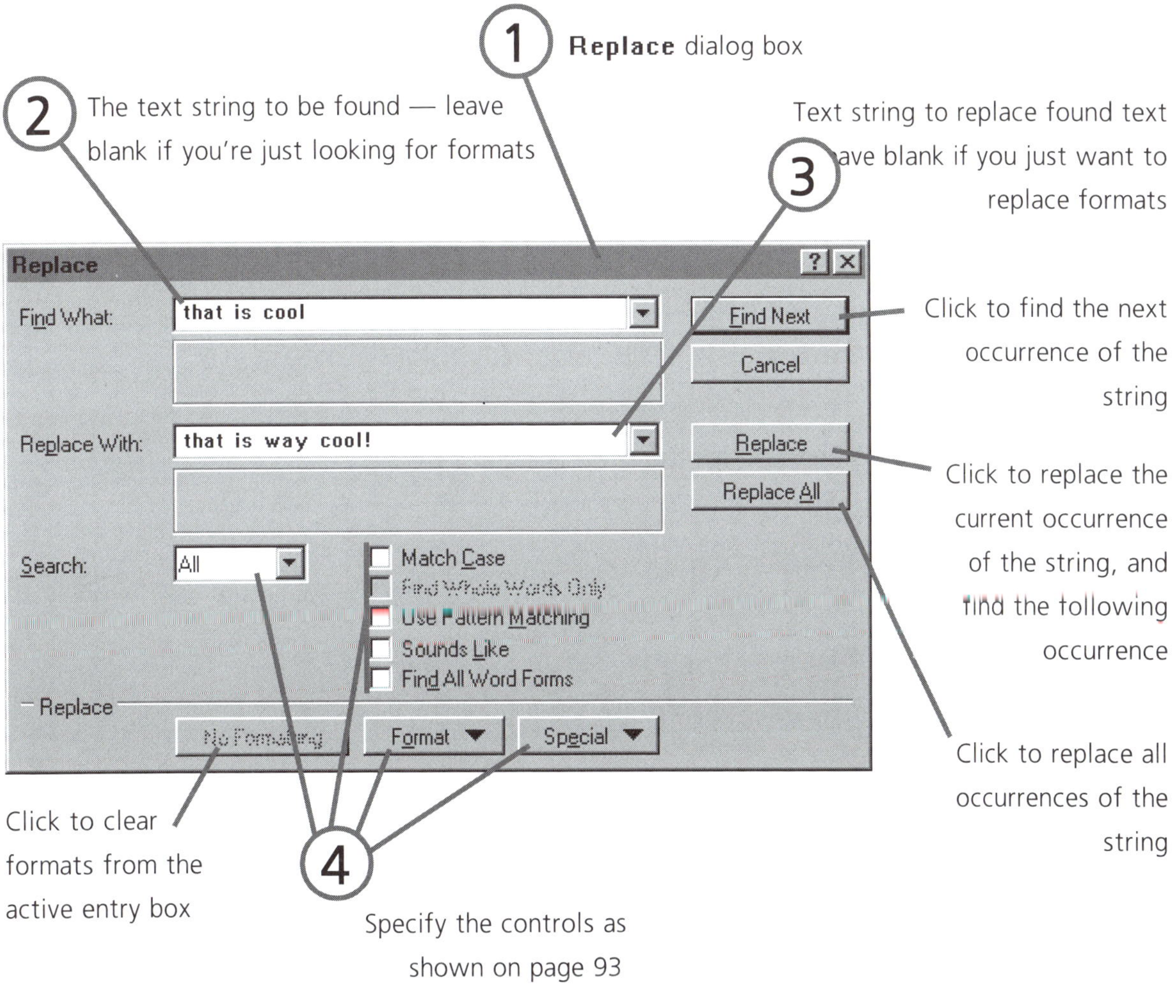

1 **Replace** dialog box

2 The text string to be found — leave blank if you're just looking for formats

3 Text string to replace found text — leave blank if you just want to replace formats

Click to find the next occurrence of the string

Click to replace the current occurrence of the string, and find the following occurrence

Click to replace all occurrences of the string

Click to clear formats from the active entry box

4 Specify the controls as shown on page 93

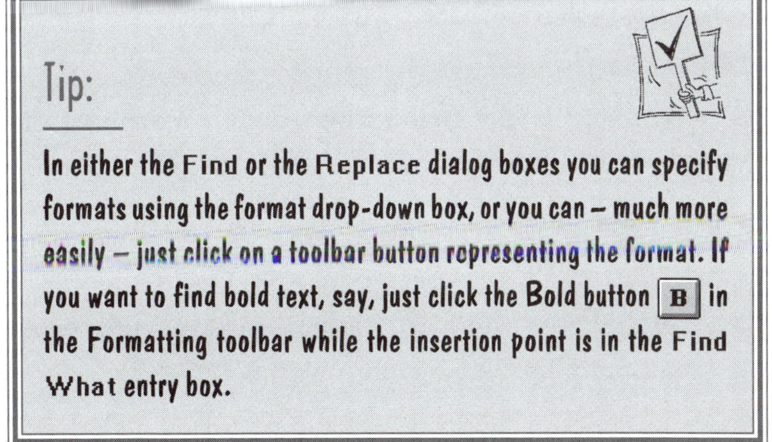
Tip:

In either the Find or the Replace dialog boxes you can specify formats using the format drop-down box, or you can – much more easily – just click on a toolbar button representing the format. If you want to find bold text, say, just click the Bold button B in the Formatting toolbar while the insertion point is in the Find What entry box.

Spelling

One of Word's most useful tools is a spelling checker which looks through your document and compares each word with the words in an electronic dictionary. If Word finds a word in the dictionary, it assumes that word is spelled correctly.

Using Word's spelling checker you can rapidly check even the longest of documents — far more quickly than you could *read* through the document, at least.

Under default conditions the spell check works automatically, telling you of your mistakes in two ways:

- highlighting the words it considers misspelled with a wavy red underline
- changing the spelling button on the status bar from its normal [button] to — [button] complete with a cross.

MAKING USE OF WORD'S SPELLING CHECKER

Your course of action following notification of a spelling error depends on

- whether you want to change the word at all (maybe it's a person's name, or a scientific word which is actually spelled correctly but Word hasn't recognized it)
- whether you want to add the word to Word's dictionary, so it won't be flagged the next time you type it in
- whether you want to correct the spelling of a misspelled word
- whether you want to have the word corrected automatically by Word from now on.

Basic steps:

IF THE WORD IS CORRECT

1 Click the underlined word with your right mouse button.

2 Choose **Ignore All** from the drop-down menu — the underlined highlighting is removed from the word (and any other entries of the word).

Tip:

If you type a word regularly which Word incorrectly assumes is misspelled, add it to Word's dictionary. From the drop-down menu displayed on the next page, choose Add. From now on, Word recognizes the word and ignores it.

1 Click a correctly spelled word that is underline highlighted, with your right mouse button

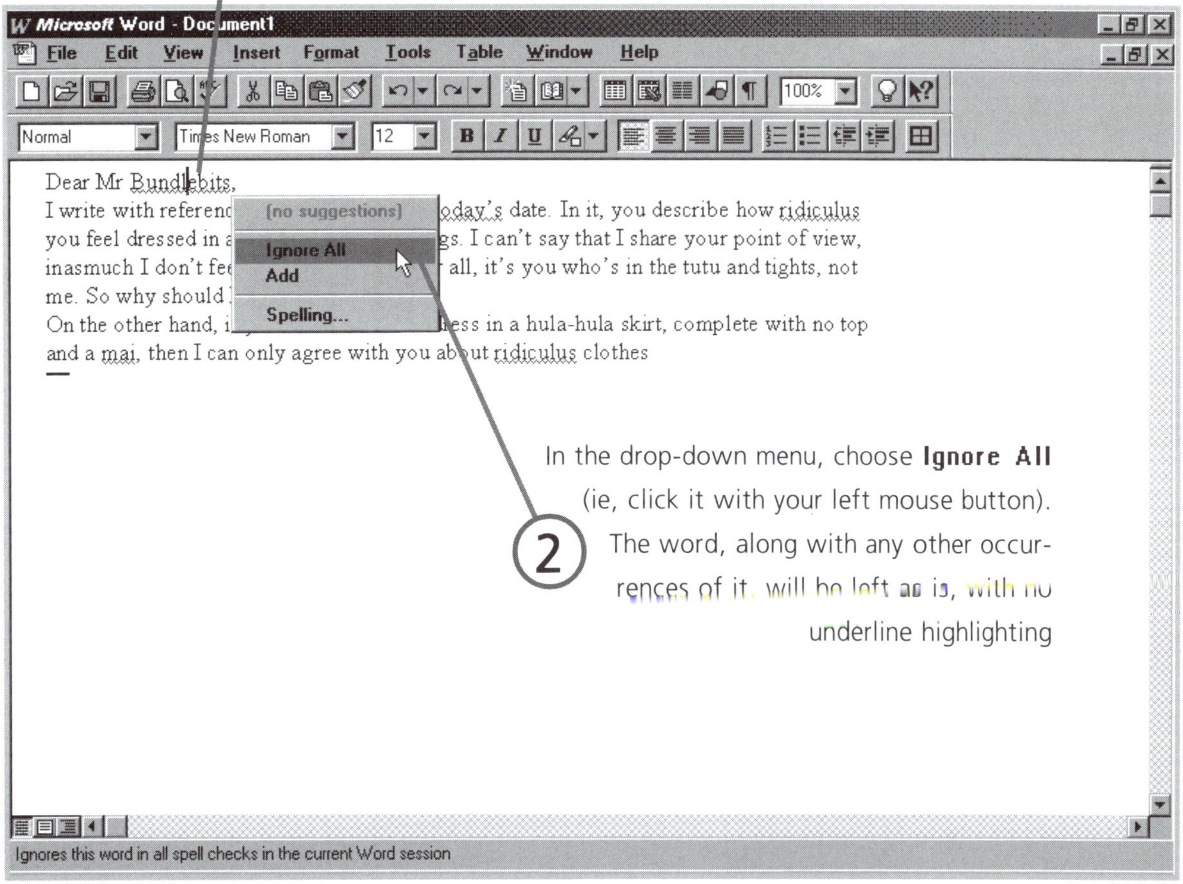

2 In the drop-down menu, choose **Ignore All** (ie, click it with your left mouse button). The word, along with any other occurrences of it, will be left as is, with no underline highlighting

Take note:

While Word's spelling checker is an extremely useful tool, you must remember that it only compares words in your document with the words in an electronic list called a dictionary. If the words in your document are misspelled in context but in fact make properly spelled words out of context, Word *still* assumes they are spelled correctly. Thus, Word thinks *with complements* (instead of *with compliments*) is OK. Remember the anonymous ode:

I have a spelling checker – it came with my pea see
It plainly marques four my revue mistakes eye cannot sea
I've run this poem threw it, I'm shore your pleased too no
Its let a perfect inn it's weigh – my checquer told me sew

Spelling (contd)

Basic steps:

Tip:

You can have Word correct your bad spelling on the fly with AutoCorrect. If there's a word in particular you regularly misspell, click on it with your right mouse button and choose `Spelling` from the drop-down menu. In the resultant dialog box type or choose the correct spelling and click `AutoCorrect`. From now on Word will correct it for you immediately as you type it incorrectly.

IF THE WORD IS INCORRECT

1. Click the underlined word with your right mouse button.
2. Choose the correct spelling of the word from the drop-down menu.

Microsoft Word - Document1

File Edit View Insert Format Tools Table Window Help

Normal Times New Roman 12 B I U

Dear Mr Bundlebits,
I write with refference to your letter of yestoday's date. In it, you describe how ridiculus
you feel dressed in a t **reference** gs. I can't say that I share your point of view,
inasmuch I don't feel p **reverence** all, it's you who's in the tutu and tights, not
me. So why should I f **referenced**
On the other hand, if y **references** ress in a hula-hula skirt, complete with no top
and a maj, then I can c about ridiculus clothes

Ignore All
Add

Spelling...

Replaces this word by the selected suggestion

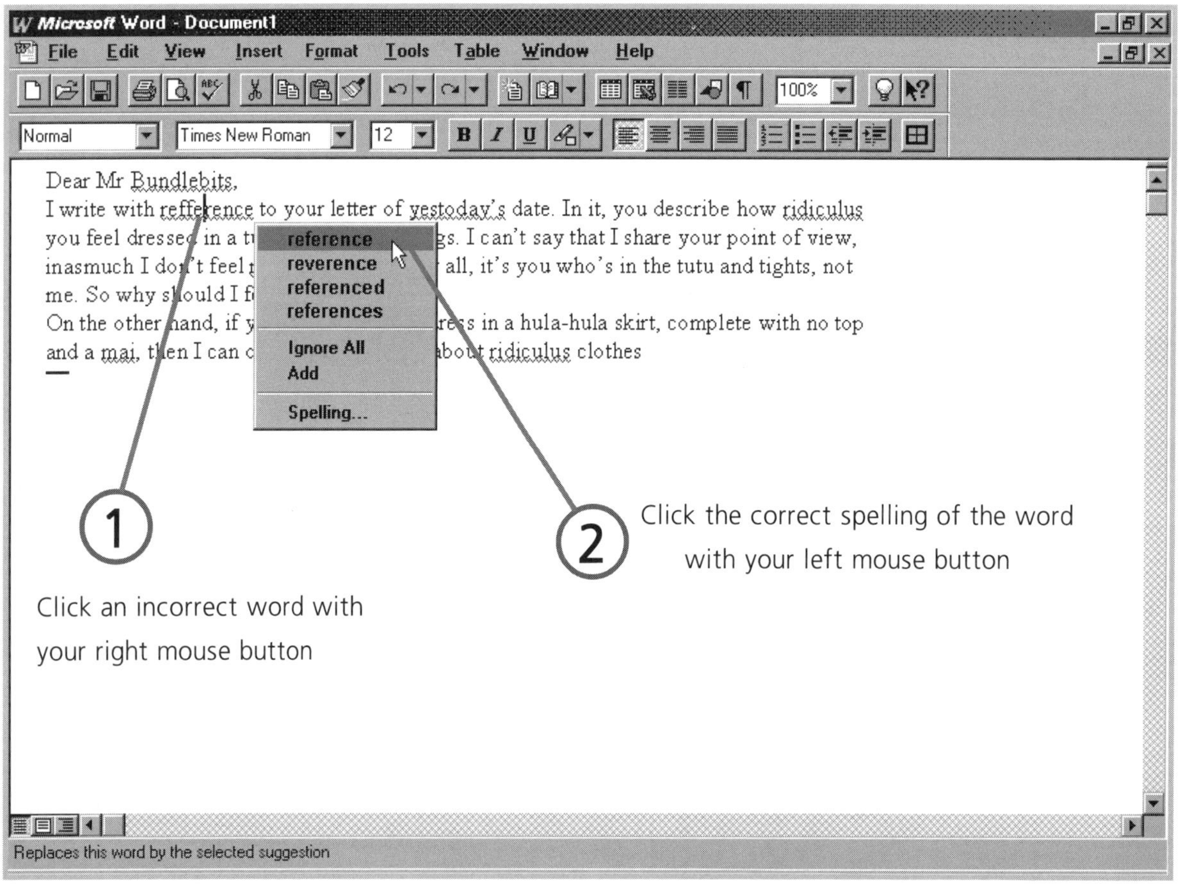

1 Click an incorrect word with your right mouse button

2 Click the correct spelling of the word with your left mouse button

CHANGING SPELLING OPTIONS

1 Choose **Tools→Options** to call up the **Options** dialog box.

2 Click the **Spelling** tab.

3 Change options to suit, then click **OK**.

Word gives you several options to change how it monitors and controls your spelling.

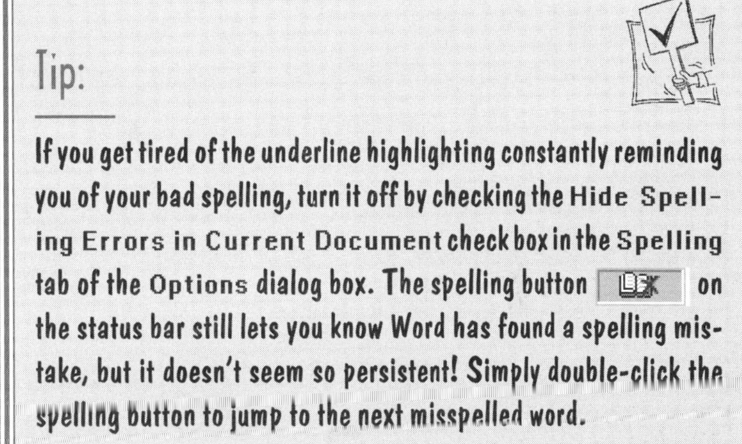

Tip:

If you get tired of the underline highlighting constantly reminding you of your bad spelling, turn it off by checking the Hide Spelling Errors in Current Document check box in the Spelling tab of the Options dialog box. The spelling button on the status bar still lets you know Word has found a spelling mistake, but it doesn't seem so persistent! Simply double-click the spelling button to jump to the next misspelled word.

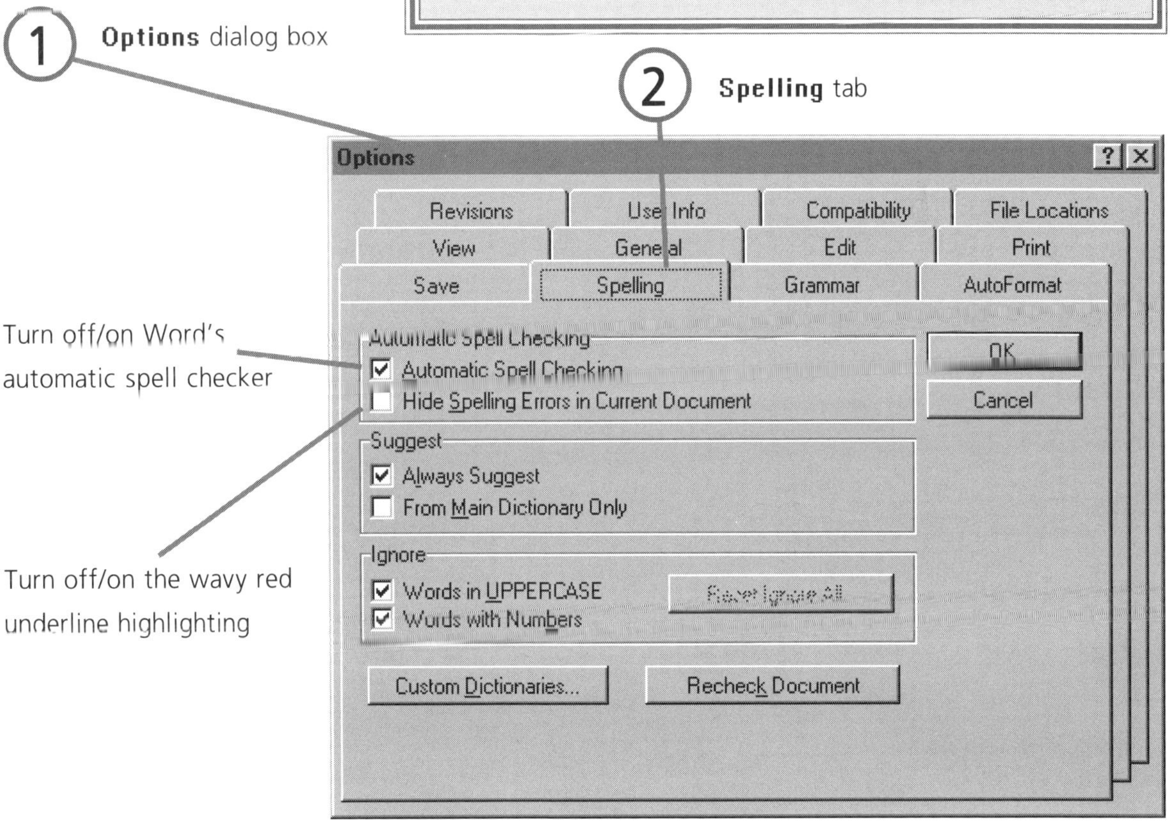

1 **Options** dialog box

2 **Spelling** tab

Turn off/on Word's automatic spell checker

Turn off/on the wavy red underline highlighting

AutoCorrect

If you make the same spelling mistake regularly — say you always type *anf* instead of *and* (the author's problem; well, one of his problems, anyway) — Word's AutoCorrect feature is a boon.

To use AutoCorrect you simply have to specify which mistakes you make, and the correct spelling. Then whenever you make the mistake it is replaced automatically with the correct word.

Basic steps:

1. Call up the **AutoCorrect** dialog box by choosing **Tools→AutoCorrect**, or type [Alt]+[T] then [A].
2. Type the spelling mistake you often make into the **Replace** entry box, and the proper spelling in the **With** entry box.
3. Click **Add** to add the word to the AutoCorrect list.

AutoCorrect dialog box

1

Other controls

Check to turn AutoCorrect on — uncheck to turn it off

Click to accept

AutoCorrect

Correct TWo INitial CApitals

Capitalize First Letter of Sentences

Capitalize Names of Days

Correct accidental usage of cAPS LOCK Key

Replace Text as You Type

Replace: With: Plain Text Formatted Text

Replace	With
anf	and

anbd	and
andthe	and the
appeares	appears
applyed	applied
aren;t	aren't
arguement	argument

OK

Cancel

Exceptions...

Add

Delete

Click to add your entries to the AutoCorrect list

Mistake you often make, and proper spelling

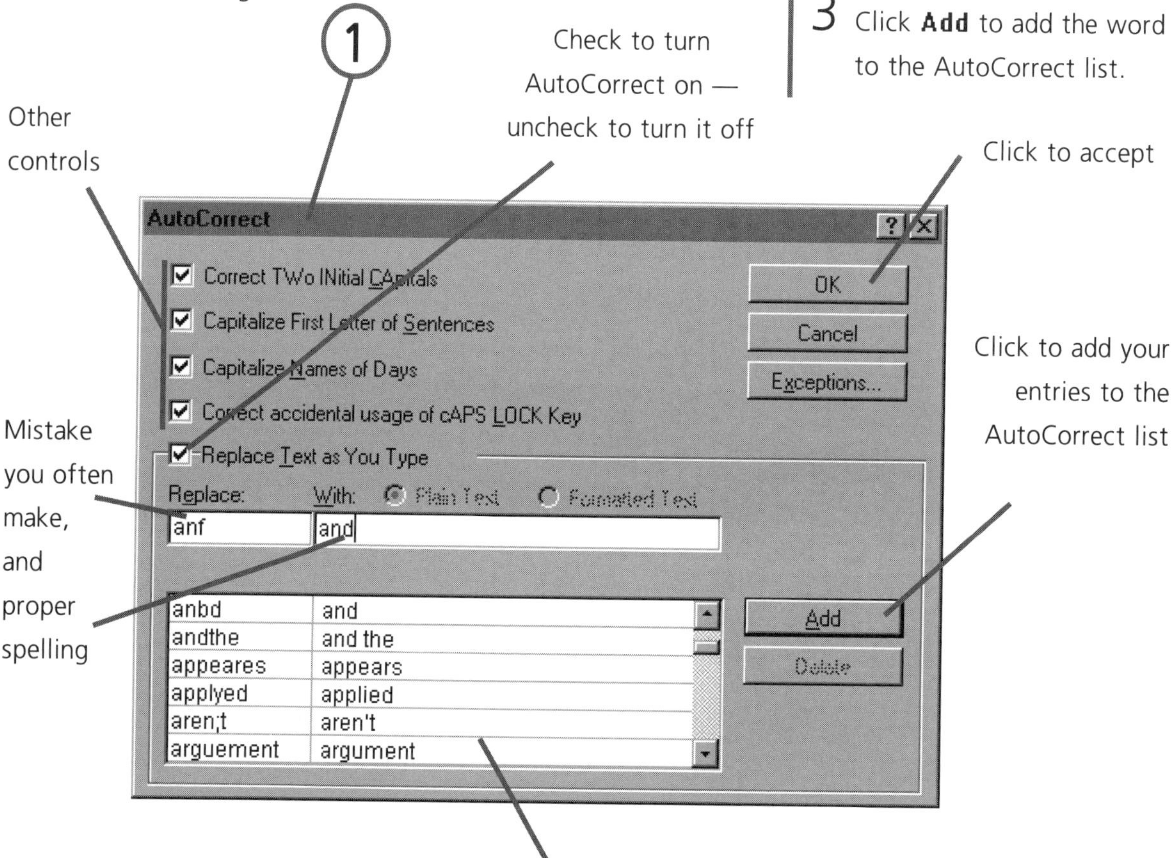

The AutoCorrect list — scroll through it to view, edit, and delete entries

Tip:

Remember that you can create an AutoCorrect entry directly from the drop-down menu as you click an underline, highlighted word with your right mouse button..

If you find that Word is finding the same spelling error repeatedly, follow the tip on page 98 to enter it automatically into the AutoCorrect list .

Tip:

AutoCorrect can be used to insert chunks of text into a document when you type a simple keyword. For example, a phrase like *Yours sincerely,* at the end of a letter can have a keyword such as *ys*. As you type *ys* and hit the Enter or ↵ key, Word automatically replaces it with the longer phrase.

Phrases up to 255 characters (including spaces and punctuation) are possible, so a considerable amount of *boilerplate text* (as it's known in the computer business) can be accessed using AutoCorrect. For longer boilerplate text, and items you access less frequently, use Word's AutoText feature instead of AutoCorrect (see next page).

Tip:

Not only text can be replaced by AutoCorrect entries. Graphics can be included; as can all formatting such as bolding, sections, borders and shades, and so on.

Put your company letterhead into an AutoCorrect entry, and make light work of typing letters.

Take note:

Word detects when you have finished a word – hence knows when to replace it, if it has an AutoCorrect entry – when an end-of-word specifier (usually a space) occurs.

So if the spelling error is followed by another letter, Word doesn't recognize the mistake and cannot correct it with AutoCorrect.

AutoText

Basic steps:

Word can greatly speedup the entering of text you regularly use with AutoText.

AutoCorrect, of course (see previous pages), allows you to do this as an automatic — on-the-fly as-you-type — feature. If you don't want it to occur automatically but instead want manual control over automatic insertion of entries, use AutoText.

To use an AutoText entry in your documents, you first have to create it.

CREATING AN ENTRY

1 Type in the text you want as an AutoText entry anywhere in a document. Select the text, then choose **Edit↳AutoText**. This calls up the **AutoText** dialog box.

2 Enter a new name for the entry (if the default name isn't suitable).

3 Click **Add** to accept the new entry.

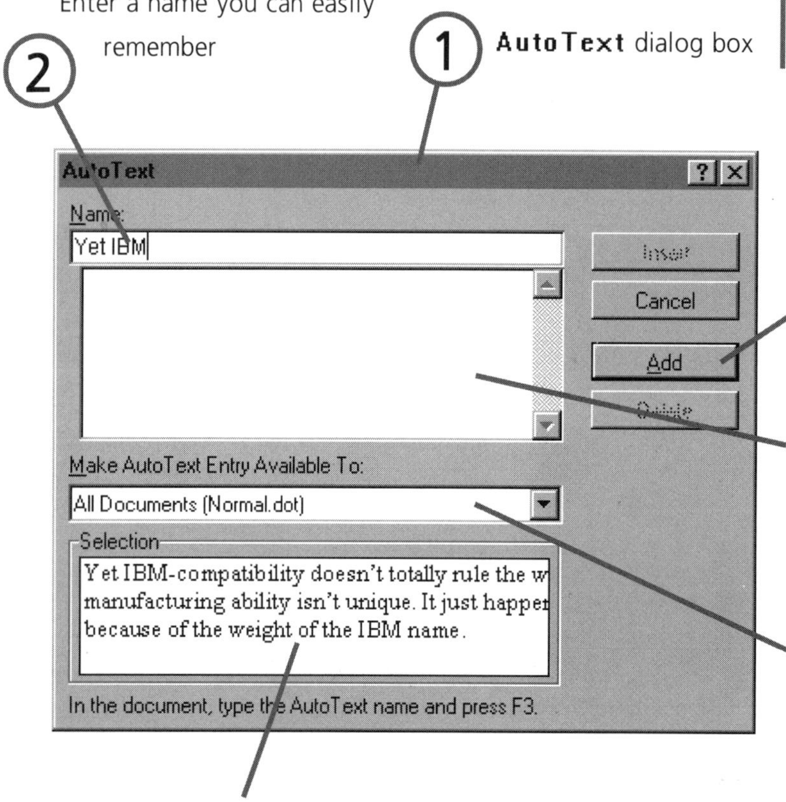

Enter a name you can easily remember
2
1
AutoText dialog box
AutoText
Name:
Yet IBM
Insert
Cancel
Add
Delete
Make AutoText Entry Available To:
All Documents (Normal.dot)
Selection
Yet IBM-compatibility doesn't totally rule the w
manufacturing ability isn't unique. It just happe
because of the weight of the IBM name.
In the document, type the AutoText name and press F3.
3
Click to accept
List box of AutoText entries (currently empty, as this is the first AutoText entry)
You can specify the template the entry is available to (see page 132)
Preview of selected text

Using an entry

1 When you want to insert an AutoText entry into your document, type in the entry name you previously gave it.

2 Hit [F3]. The entry is inserted into the document.

Once your entry is created, you can use it wherever and whenever you want in your documents.

When you want to insert an AutoText entry, simply type in the entry name...

I shall give you these with my complements. Take them home and keep them. Add other complimentary things to them to make them whole.
Yet IBM

...then press [F3]

I shall give you these with my complements. Take them home and keep them. Add other complimentary things to them to make them whole.
Yet IBM-compatibility doesn't totally rule the world. Its combination of hardware, software and manufacturing ability isn't unique. It just happened to create the biggest personal computer type simply because of the weight of the IBM name.

Tip:

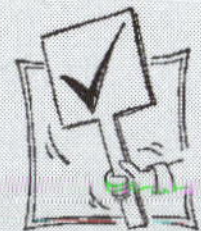

As with AutoCorrect, the entries you create for AutoText can include graphical items and text formatting. Like AutoCorrect entries, too, you can use AutoText to insert boilerplate text into your documents.

In fact, the only *real* difference between AutoText and AutoCorrect as far as the ordinary user – you – is concerned, is how the entries are inserted into your documents.

AutoCorrect entries are inserted automatically, as soon as the entry name is typed.

AutoText entries are inserted semi-automatically – *you* have to specify that the entry name be replaced with the entry.

They each have their uses.

Outlining

Basic steps:

We saw an outline view back on page 18. Outlining is another way of looking at your Word documents and, what's more important, is the best way of controlling how the various text parts within a document are organized and arranged.

The easiest way to see how outlining works is with an example. Let's say you've been working long and hard at a chapter of your book. It's a long chapter and technically quite involved — so involved that you're sure there's a problem somewhere, but you're not exactly sure *where*.

1 Choose **View→Outline**, or type [Alt]+[V] then [O], or (best) click the Outline button at the lower left corner of the document window. Your document is displayed in outline view.

A document in outline view (1)

W Microsoft Word - Document1

File Edit View Insert Format Tools Table Window Help

Normal Arial 18

1 2 3 4 5 6 7 8 All

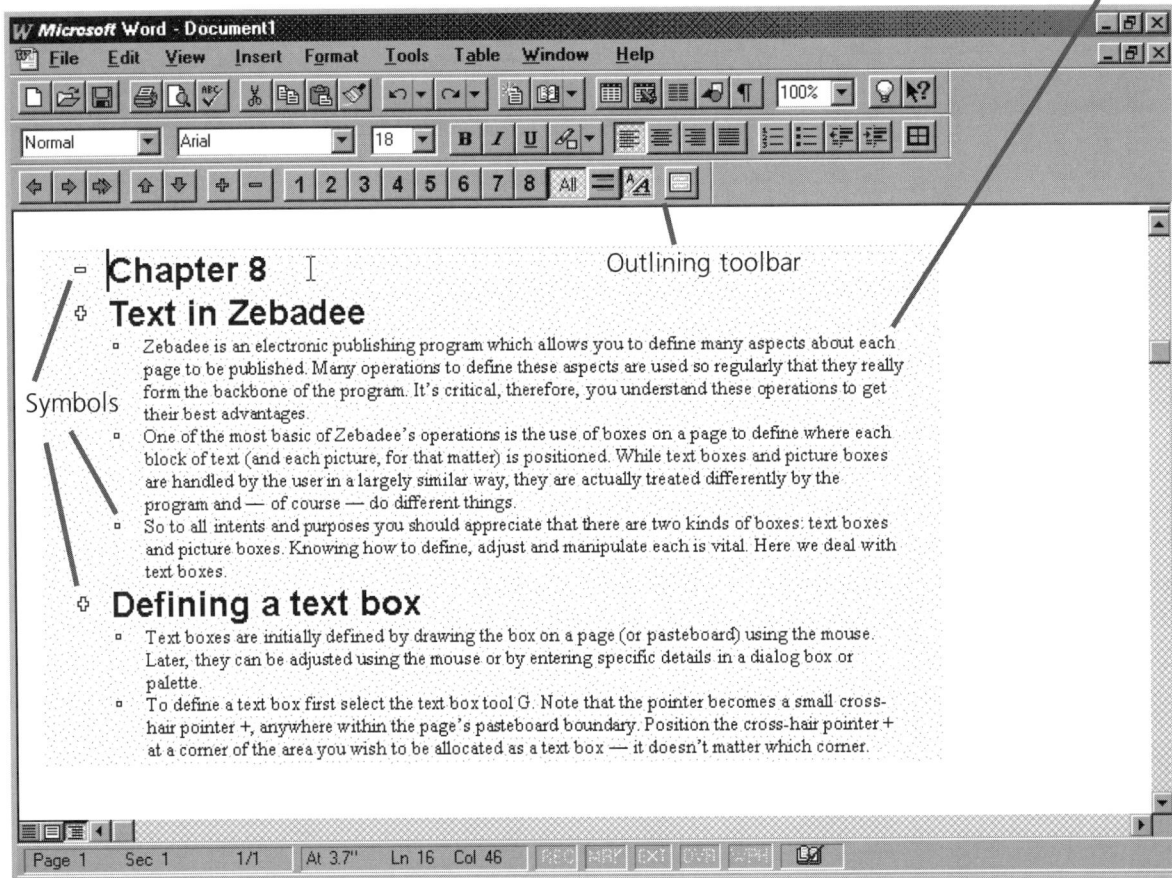

Outlining toolbar

Symbols

Chapter 8

Text in Zebadee

Zebadee is an electronic publishing program which allows you to define many aspects about each page to be published. Many operations to define these aspects are used so regularly that they really form the backbone of the program. It's critical, therefore, you understand these operations to get their best advantages.

One of the most basic of Zebadee's operations is the use of boxes on a page to define where each block of text (and each picture, for that matter) is positioned. While text boxes and picture boxes are handled by the user in a largely similar way, they are actually treated differently by the program and — of course — do different things.

So to all intents and purposes you should appreciate that there are two kinds of boxes: text boxes and picture boxes. Knowing how to define, adjust and manipulate each is vital. Here we deal with text boxes.

Defining a text box

Text boxes are initially defined by drawing the box on a page (or pasteboard) using the mouse. Later, they can be adjusted using the mouse or by entering specific details in a dialog box or palette.

To define a text box first select the text box tool G. Note that the pointer becomes a small cross-hair pointer +, anywhere within the page's pasteboard boundary. Position the cross-hair pointer + at a corner of the area you wish to be allocated as a text box — it doesn't matter which corner.

Page 1 Sec 1 1/1 At 3.7" Ln 16 Col 46 REC MRK EXT OVR WPH

Outline symbols

In outline view, your document is displayed with its headings and body text displayed with various symbols to their left. The symbols indicate what is associated with the various parts of a document.

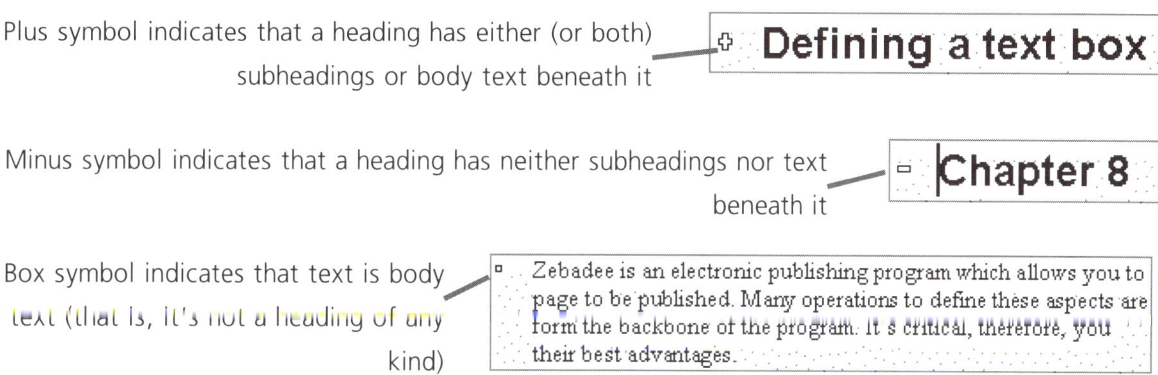

Plus symbol indicates that a heading has either (or both) subheadings or body text beneath it
Defining a text box
Minus symbol indicates that a heading has neither subheadings nor text beneath it
Chapter 8
Box symbol indicates that text is body text (that is, it's not a heading of any kind)
Zebadee is an electronic publishing program which allows you to
page to be published. Many operations to define these aspects are
form the backbone of the program. It's critical, therefore, you
their best advantages.

Outlining toolbar

Along with outline view comes the Outlining toolbar, with its new buttons.

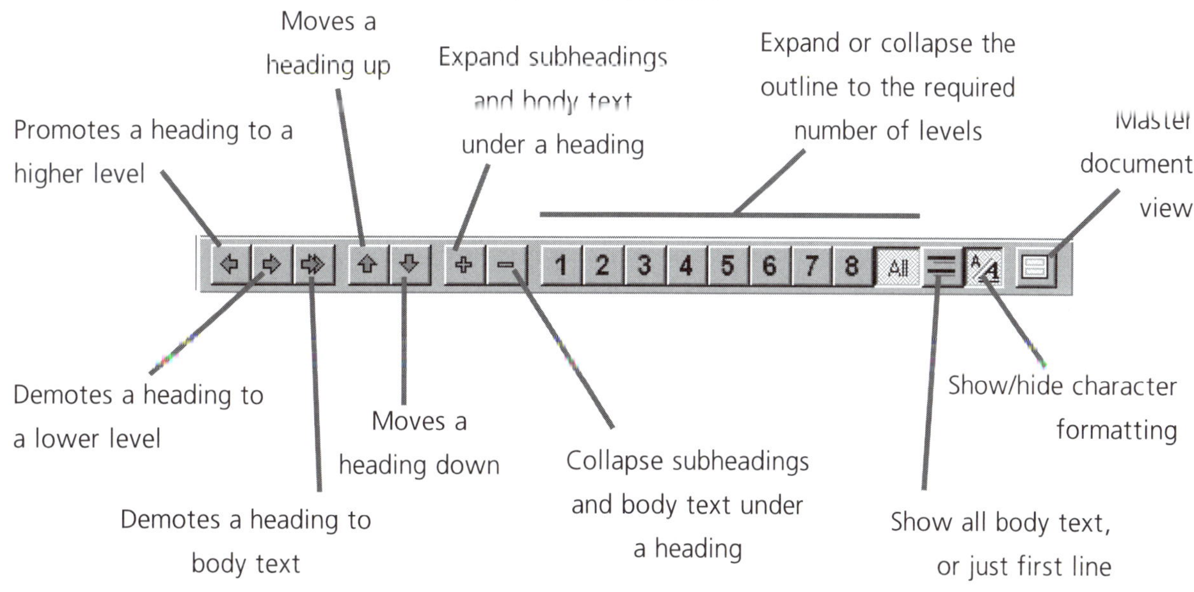

Moves a heading up
Expand subheadings and body text under a heading
Expand or collapse the outline to the required number of levels
Promotes a heading to a higher level
document view
1 2 3 4 5 6 7 8 All
Demotes a heading to a lower level
Moves a heading down
Collapse subheadings and body text under a heading
Show/hide character formatting
Demotes a heading to body text
Show all body text, or just first line

Outlining (contd)

In essence, outlining allows you to:

- get an overall view of your document — to various degrees of complexity
- easily move headings around (while their associated subheadings and body text parts move automatically with them).

Another example can show you.

Basic steps:

1 Click the Show/hide character formatting button and the Expand/collapse to level 1 button on the Outlining toolbar.

Now all character formatting has gone, and only the first level headings are displayed.

Document with character formatting hidden and levels collapsed to level 1

Microsoft Word - Document1
File Edit View Insert Format Tools Table Window Help
Normal Arial 18
Chapter 8
Text in Zebadee
Defining a text box
Adjusting a text box
Text features
Importing text
Editing text
Page 1 Sec 1 1/1 At 3.7" Ln 16 Col 46

Expand/collapse to level 1 button

Show/hide character formatting button

If body text is present under a heading, a grayed line indicates this

Now only the first level headings are displayed (but *all* the associated subheading and body text is still there — it's just not visible, leaving your outlined document uncluttered)

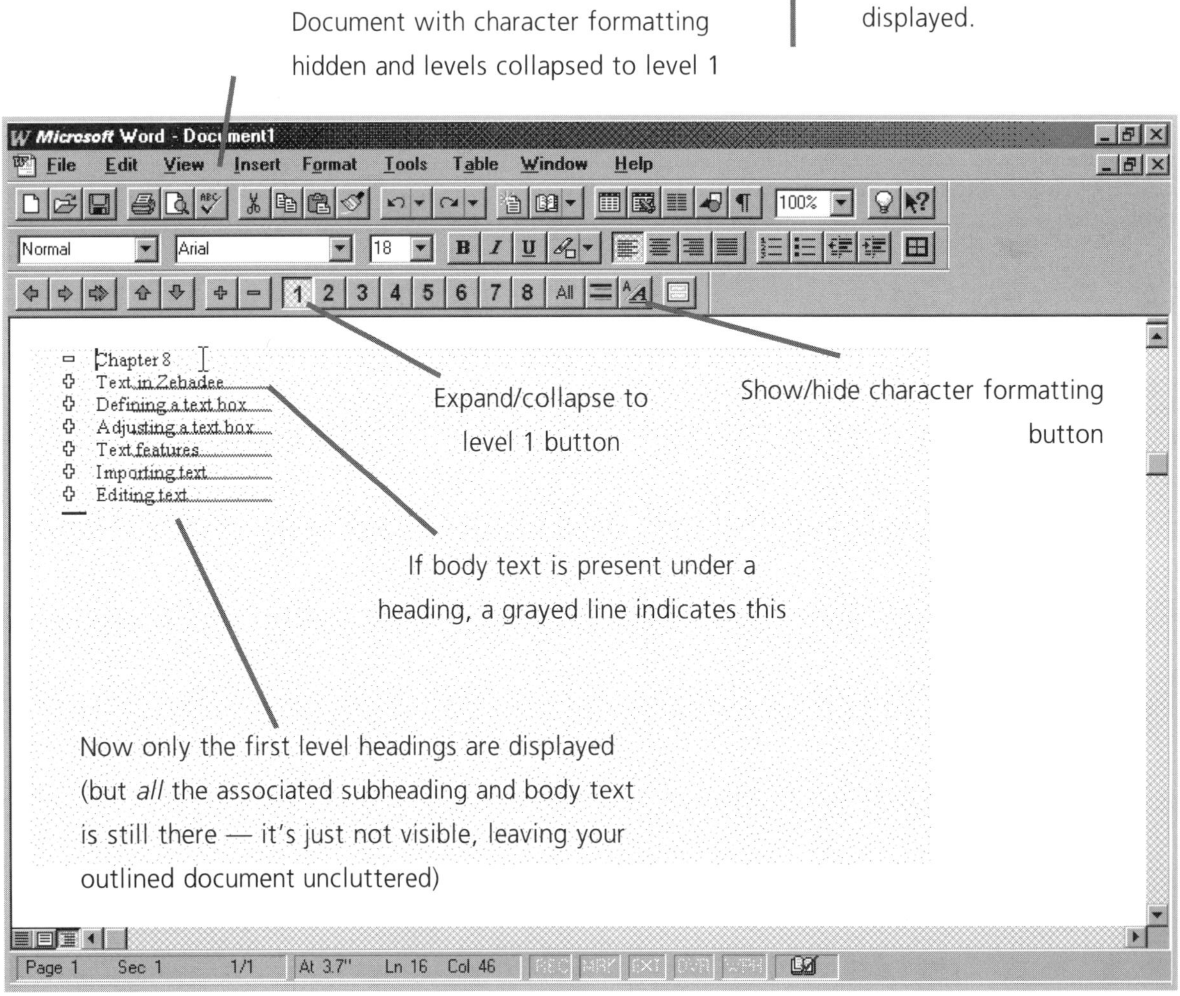

2 Select the headings *Defining a text box*, and *Adjusting a text box*. Now click the Demote heading button on the Outlining toolbar.

3 Select the heading *Editing text*, then click the Move heading up button .

From this position, let's now say you realize that:

- the level 1 headings *Defining a text box*, and *Adjusting a text box* really *should* be level 2 headings
- the heading *Editing text* should be before the heading *Importing text*.

With outlining, that's easily done.

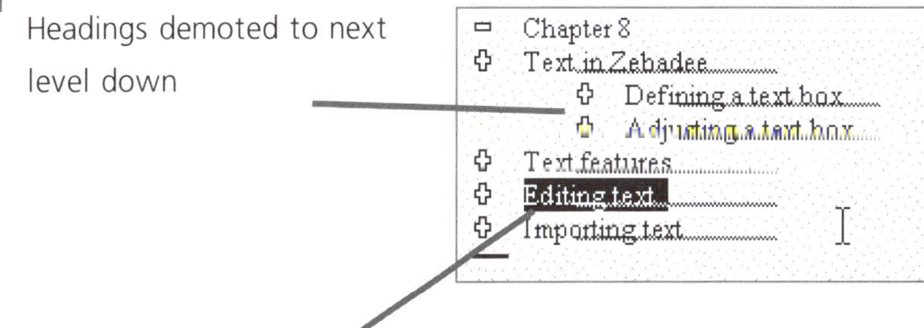
Chapter 8
Text in Zebadee
Defining a text box
Adjusting a text box
Text features
Editing text
Importing text

Headings demoted to next level down

Heading moved up

Take note:

Remember that in outline view it may *look* as though your text has disappeared but it hasn't – if you expand the outline again your text will come back (phew!)

Tip:

You can drag headings, subheadings, and body text around, too, in whatever state of expansion or collapse they are – just like drag-and-drop editing, except more powerful. Much more powerful!

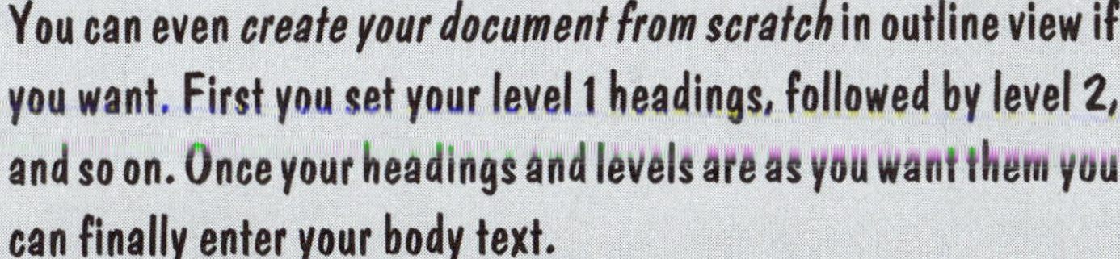

Tip:

You can even *create your document from scratch* in outline view if you want. First you set your level 1 headings, followed by level 2, and so on. Once your headings and levels are as you want them you can finally enter your body text.

Writing a document in this manner means your document can be logically structured.

Tables

Basic steps:

Earlier in the book we saw how to produce a simple table using tab stops. This is fine for just that — simple tables — but for anything more complex than just a couple of rows and columns things can be made much easier with Word's built in table feature.

Tables are made up of a collection of *cells*, in rows and columns. Word displays a table in *gridlines* (dotted lines around all the cells of a table) which are not printed and are merely provided on-screen for guidance.

You can add text or graphical elements to cells of a Word table, and you can format text in any character or paragraph format as usual.

You create a table in one of two ways:

- from the **Insert Table** dialog box
- with the Table button on the Standard toolbar.

INSERT TABLE DIALOG BOX

1 Position the insertion point where you want to create a table, then choose **Table↳Insert Table**, or type [Alt]+[A] then [I]. This calls up the **Insert Table** dialog box.

2 Enter the numbers of columns and rows you want.

3 Click **OK** to create the table — Word displays the empty table as dotted gridlines.

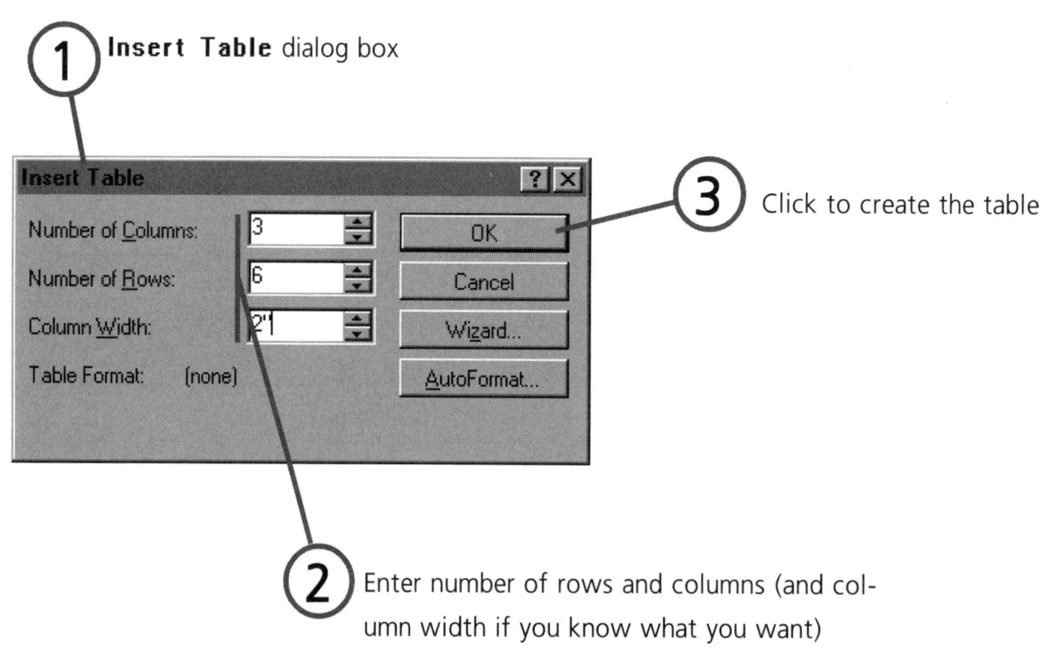
1 Insert Table dialog box
Insert Table
Number of Columns:
3
Number of Rows:
6
Column Width:
2"
Table Format:
(none)
OK
Cancel
Wizard...
AutoFormat...
3 Click to create the table
2 Enter number of rows and columns (and column width if you know what you want)

INSERT TABLE BUTTON

1 Position the insertion point where you want to create a table, then click the Insert Table button on the Standard toolbar.

2 Drag across the drop-down grid to select the number of columns and rows you want, then let go of the mouse button.

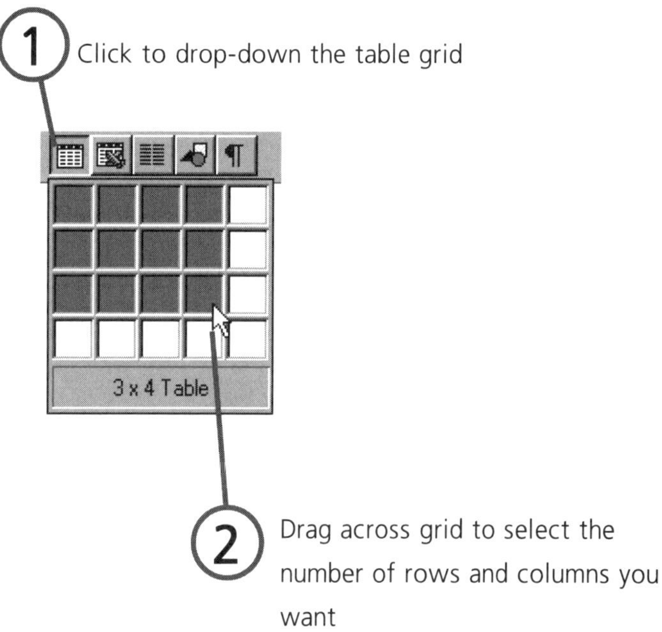
1 Click to drop-down the table grid
3 x 4 Table
2 Drag across grid to select the number of rows and columns you want

The insertion point is positioned at the top left cell in the table ready for you to enter text. You move around in a table by clicking the mouse in another cell, tabbing with the Tab key, or pressing the ↑↓←→ keys in the direction you want to move.

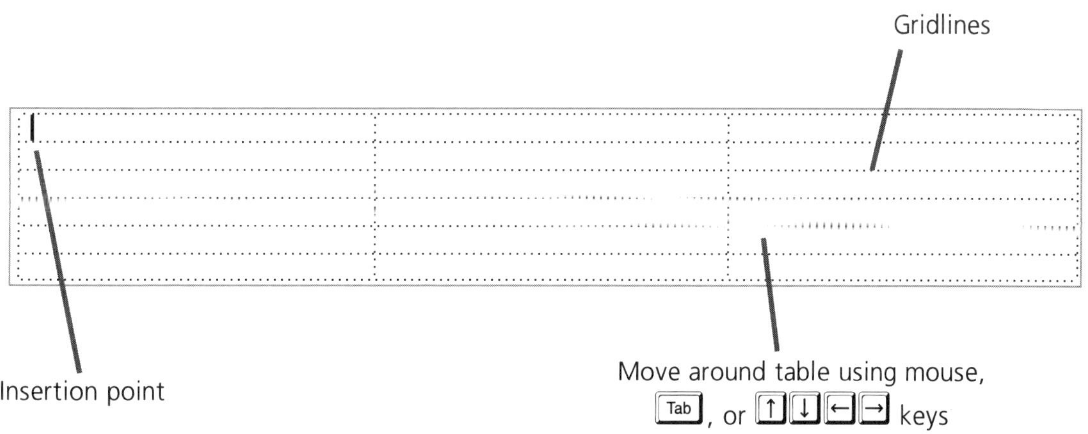
Gridlines
Insertion point
Move around table using mouse, Tab, or ↑↓←→ keys

Tables (contd)

Once you've created a table you can change it to fit your needs. You can drag column widths and indents from the document ruler (bottom) and you can drag a column gridline left or right directly from the table.

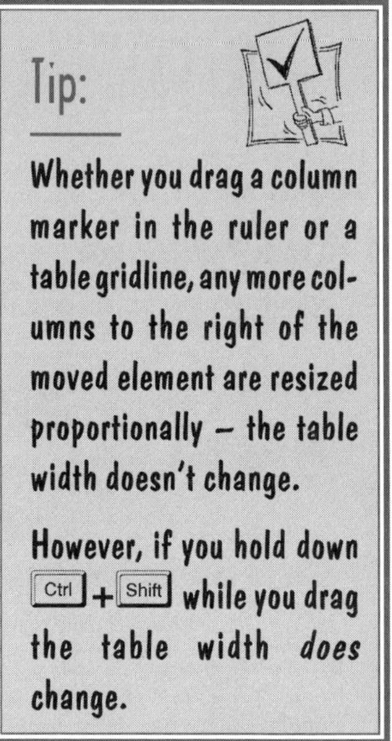

Tip:

Whether you drag a column marker in the ruler or a table gridline, any more columns to the right of the moved element are resized proportionally – the table width doesn't change.

However, if you hold down Ctrl + Shift while you drag the table width *does* change.

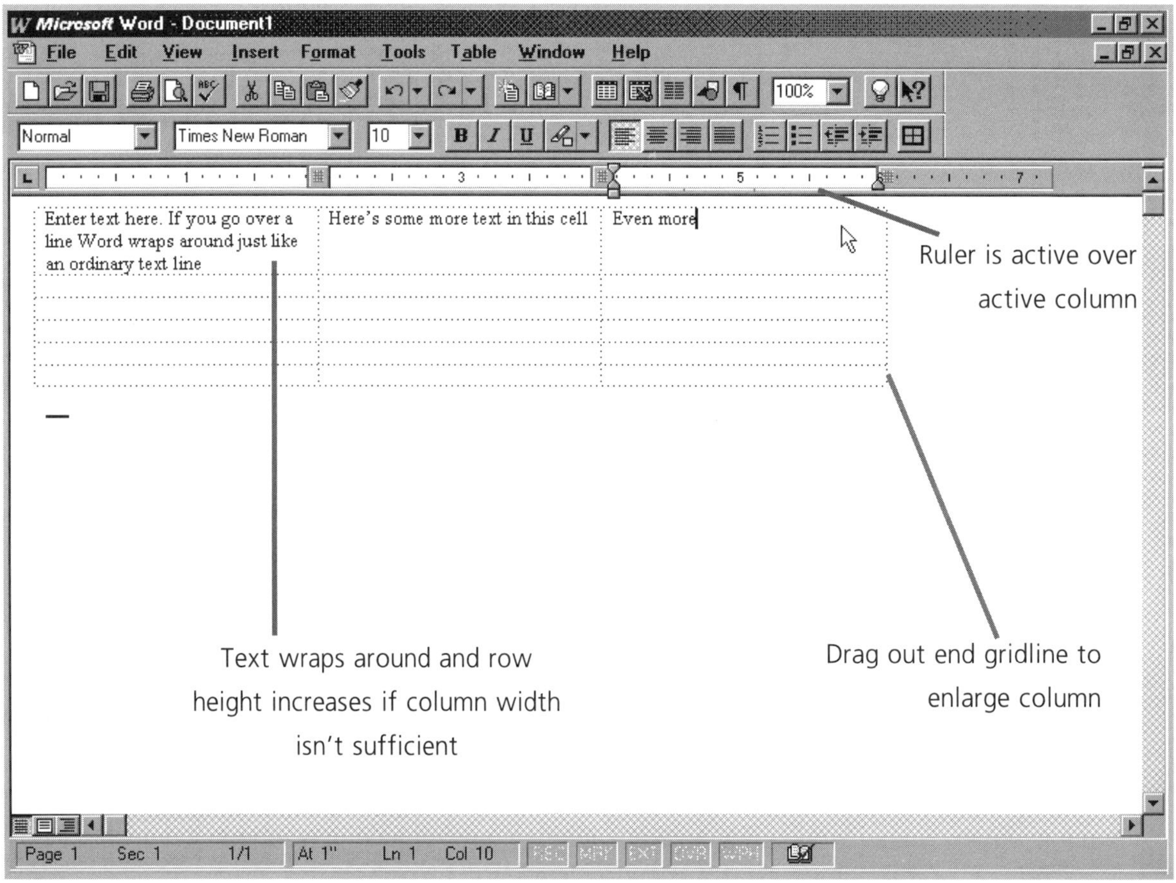

Ruler is active over active column

Text wraps around and row height increases if column width isn't sufficient

Drag out end gridline to enlarge column

Table conversions

Basic steps:

Even if you've already entered text you can still convert it into a Word table. Simply make sure there are separators which Word recognizes — commas or tabs between the items of text you want in each cell, and paragraph marks between each row — in the text.

1 Select the text you want to convert to a table.

2 Click the Insert Table button on the Standard toolbar — that text is converted into a table.

Select the text you want to convert into a table — make sure it has adequate separators (1)

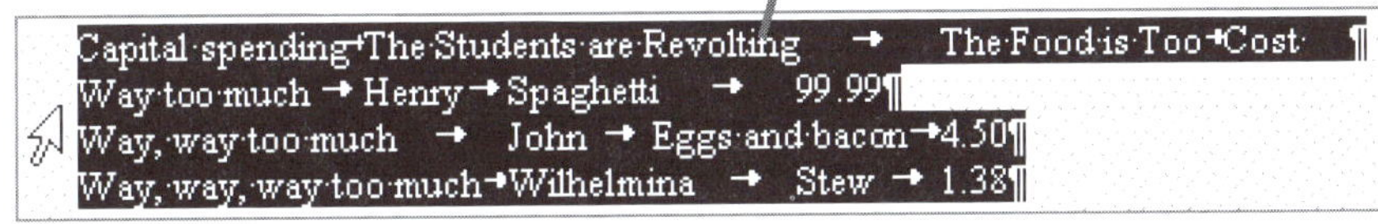
Capital·spending→The·Students·are·Revolting → The·Food·is·Too→Cost· ¶
Way·too·much → Henry → Spaghetti → 99.99¶
Way,·way·too·much → John → Eggs·and·bacon→4.50¶
Way,·way,·way·too·much→Wilhelmina → Stew → 1.38¶

Capital·spending¤	The·Students·are·Revolting¤	The·Food·is·Too¤	Cost·¤
Way·too·much¤	Henry¤	Spaghetti¤	99.99¤
Way,·way·too·much¤	John¤	Eggs·and·bacon¤	4.50¤
Way,·way,·way·too·much¤	Wilhelmina¤	Stew¤	1.38¤

(2) Converted into a table

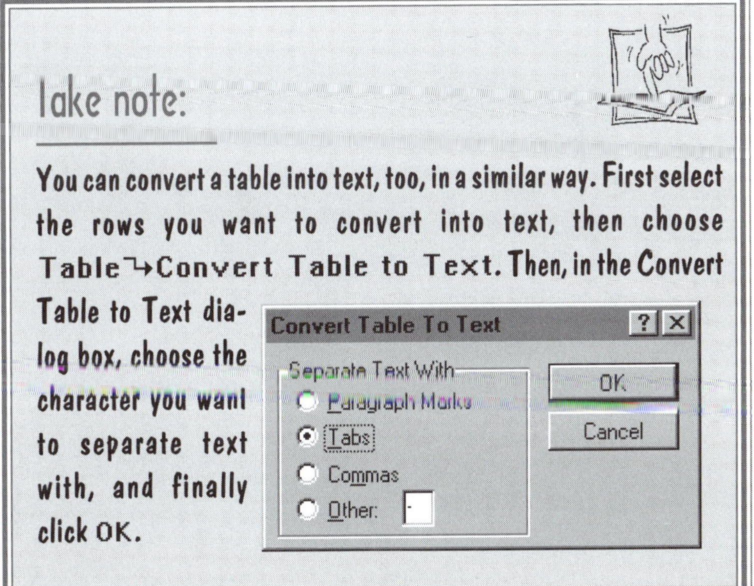

Take note:

You can convert a table into text, too, in a similar way. First select the rows you want to convert into text, then choose Table→Convert Table to Text. Then, in the Convert Table to Text dialog box, choose the character you want to separate text with, and finally click OK.

Convert Table To Text
Separate Text With
Paragraph Marks
Tabs
Commas
Other:
OK
Cancel

Table formatting

Basic steps:

Once you've created a table, you can format it in all the usual ways. However, Word gives you several suggested options to format it automatically, which are both faster and (probably) better than doing it manually.

1 Select the table and choose **Table↳Table AutoFormat**, or type [Alt]+[A] then [F], to call up the **Table AutoFormat** dialog box.

2 From the list of formats select one you want.

3 Click **OK** to accept this format onto your table.

1 **Table AutoFormat** dialog box

2 Scroll through list to select a table format

3 Click to accept your selected format

Preview gives an example of format

Other controls over formatting

Capital spending	The Students are Revolting	The Food is Too	Cost
Way too much	Henry	Spaghetti	99.99
Way, way too much	John	Eggs and bacon	4.50
Way, way, way too much	Wilhelmina	Stew	1.38

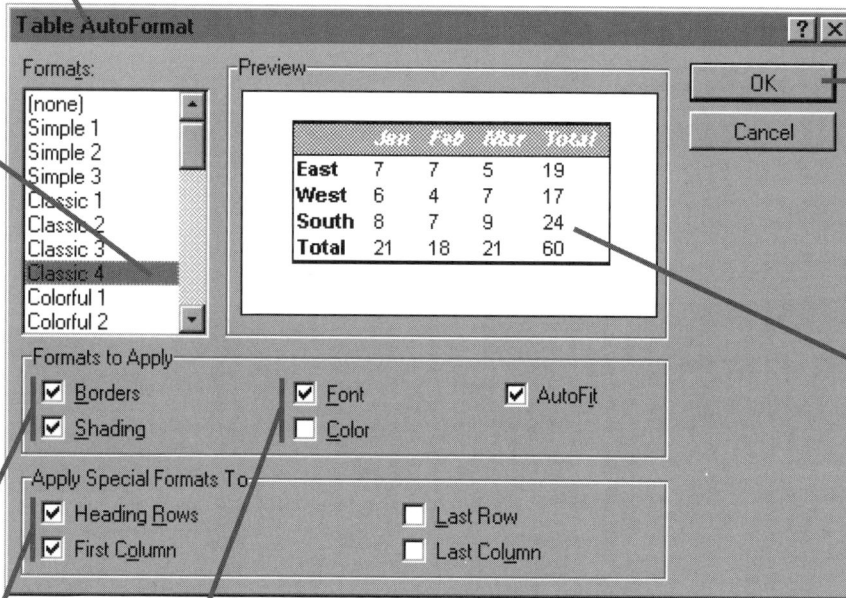

The table on the previous page, formatted with the Classic 4 format above

Counting your words

Basic steps:

When all your text has been entered into a document, it's often necessary to count the total number of words in it. Most publishers need a word count, for example, to give some idea of how long a document is, therefore a rough estimate of how many pages it'll fill in the finished publication.

Word can do much more than just count the words in a document, however.

1 Choose **Tools→Word Count**, or type [Alt]+[T] then [W], to call up the **Word Count** dialog box.

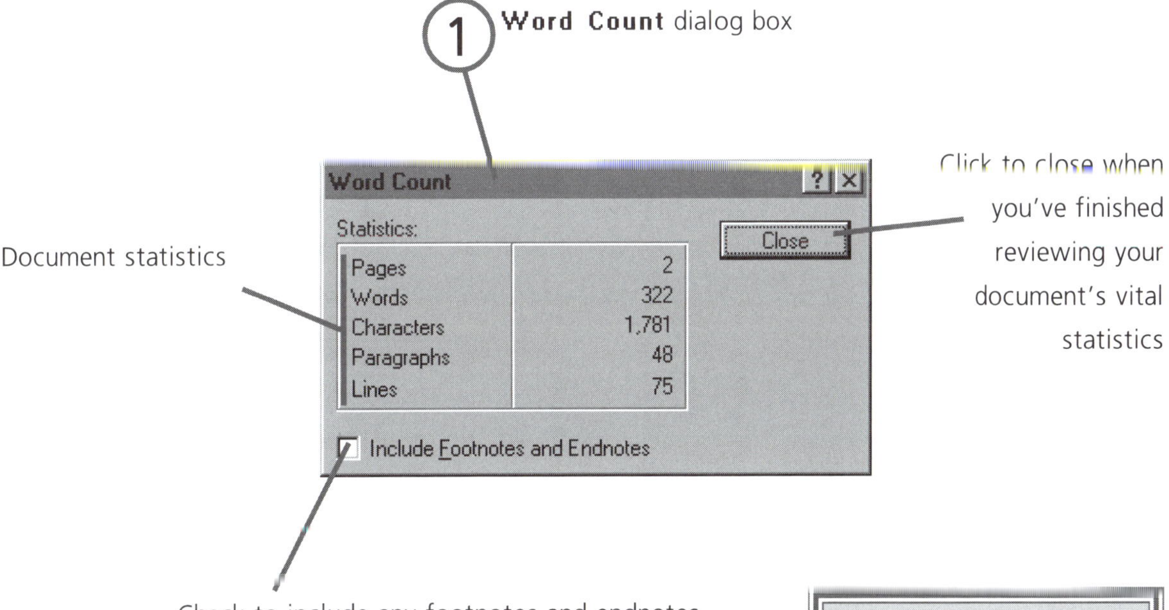

1 **Word Count** dialog box
Document statistics
Word Count
Statistics:
Pages 2
Words 322
Characters 1,781
Paragraphs 48
Lines 75
Include Footnotes and Endnotes
Close
Click to close when you've finished reviewing your document's vital statistics
Check to include any footnotes and endnotes in the word count

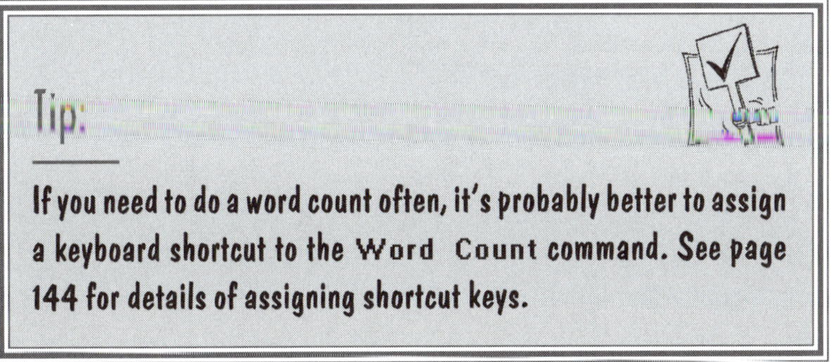

Tip:

If you need to do a word count often, it's probably better to assign a keyboard shortcut to the Word Count command. See page 144 for details of assigning shortcut keys.

Tip:

If you select text prior to calling up the Word Count dialog box, only the selected text (pages, words, characters, paragraphs, and lines) is included.

Graphics

You can import a graphic created in another application into a Word document. Once imported, any graphic can be edited in several ways.

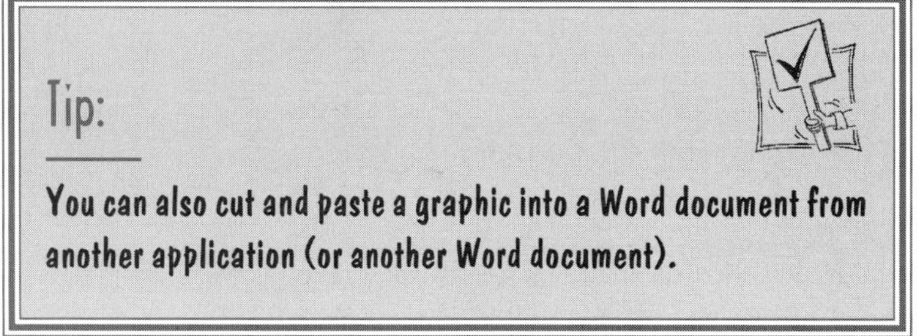

Tip:

You can also cut and paste a graphic into a Word document from another application (or another Word document).

Basic steps:

IMPORTING A GRAPHIC

1 Position the insertion point where you want the graphic to be placed. Choose **Insert→Picture**, or type [Alt]+[I] then [P].

2 Locate the graphic you want in the **Insert Picture** dialog box and click **OK**. The graphic is imported to your document.

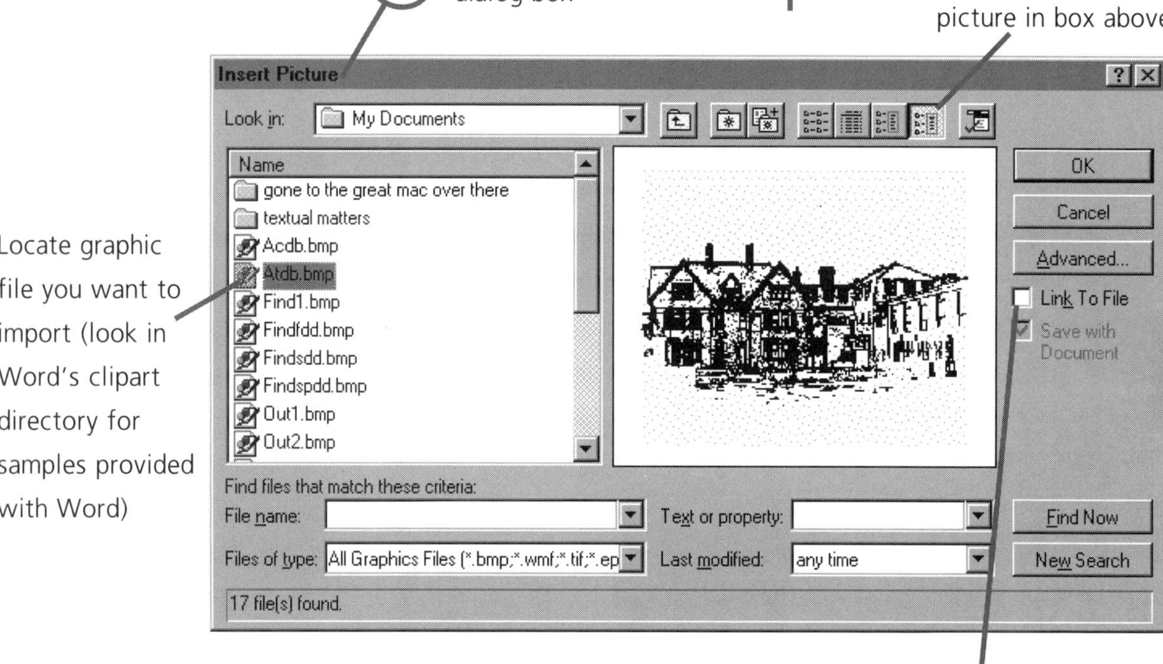

1 **Insert Picture** dialog box
Check to preview picture in box above
Locate graphic file you want to import (look in Word's clipart directory for samples provided with Word)
Insert Picture
Look in: My Documents
Name
gone to the great mac over there
textual matters
Acdb.bmp
Atdb.bmp
Find1.bmp
Findfdd.bmp
Findsdd.bmp
Findspdd.bmp
Out1.bmp
Out2.bmp
OK
Cancel
Advanced...
Link To File
Save with Document
Find files that match these criteria:
File name:
Text or property:
Find Now
Files of type: All Graphics Files (*.bmp;*.wmf;*.tif;*.ep
Last modified: any time
New Search
17 file(s) found.

You can create a link to a graphic file by checking here, so that the file itself is not imported (only its screen representation and details of the link). This keeps your Word document file size down, while Word refers to the link as it prints the document.

Basic steps:

EDITING A GRAPHIC

1 Click a graphic in a Word document.

2 Drag any of the box handles to adjust the size or shape.

Select a graphic by clicking on it

As you let go of the mouse button, the graphic resizes itself

Drag a box handle to resize a graphic. Dragging a corner handle resizes the graphic proportionally. Dragging a middle handle resizes it disproportionately.

Take note:

Word uses special files called graphics filters to let it import graphics files. While Windows bitmaps (with the extension *.bmp*), Windows metafiles (*.wmf*), and tag image file format files (*.tif*) are imported directly, you need filters (available from Microsoft) to import any other graphics file formats.

Tip:

You can effectively box a graphic by creating a border around it using the Borders toolbar. Shading, too, can be used to a good effect (see page 66 for details of creating borders and shading).

Summary for Section 5

- Use Word's powerful find and replace commands to search for and change text or even just formatting within your documents.
- Word's spell checker can locate instances of misspelled words, but remember that a word may be spelled correctly but still be out of context.
- Create custom dictionaries if you regularly use technical jargon.
- Word's on-line thesaurus can assist you in employing supplementary asseverations (OK — it finds new words!).
- Check your grammar to weed out those misspelled out-of-context words the spelling checker can't detect.
- Use AutoCorrect to correct spelling mistakes you regularly make, and automatically insert phrases at your abbreviated prompt.
- Use AutoText to insert phrases at your manual prompt.
- Remember that outlining helps you to organize your documents logically, and can be a boon when writing, too.
- Tables in Word can be most effectively created with the **Table** command.
- You can import certain graphics files into your Word documents, then edit them in various ways.

6 Automatic formatting

Styles 118
Character and paragraph styles 121
Creating styles 122
More about styles 128
About templates 132
Creating a template 134
Summary for Section 6 136

Styles

Styles are the first method of automatic formatting. They are *extremely* important, because:

- their use makes it easy to define the formats which any particular paragraph has applied to it
- styles are groups of formats gathered together under one label (all the formats considered in Section 3 — and some others — can be gathered together and given just a single style name)
- if you apply a style to selected text *all* that text has the same formats applied to it simultaneously
- all you need to do to apply a style to selected text is choose that style from a drop-down list — the text is formatted with all the individual formats by this one action
- you can use styles instantly, because any Word document has default styles already built in.

Basic steps:

1 Enter some text into a new Word document. Don't bother applying any character or paragraph formats yet. Make sure you type in a few paragraphs and make the top paragraph and some others single-line ones — say headings or subheadings.

2 Select the top heading of the document (you can click anywhere in the first paragraph) then click the Style drop-down list box of the Formatting toolbar.

Report into the oxidation of ferrous materials under load conditions
Oxidation defined
Under most circumstances, ferrous materials have iron in them. Iron is a substance which combines with oxygen under certain conditions, forming a chemical compound called an oxide.
Oxides are often of no concern — aluminum oxide for example is actually of some benefit in aluminum substances because it creates a hard barrier against physical damage to the rest of the material.
Ferrous oxide, on the other hand, *is* of concern. Ferrous oxide, aka iron oxide, aka rust is of particular importance because:
it is unsightly
it is weaker than its non-oxidised counterpart.
Load conditions
Under certain conditions ferrous oxidation occurs more rapidly than under other conditions. There are two critical conditions which, when applied together to ferrous materials, make the likelihood of oxidation much greater. These two conditions are:
application of moisture in the form of water or water vapour
application of oxygen in the form of gas.
It is reasonably safe to say that if either of these conditions can be prevented then ferrous oxidation does not occur.

2 Select the top paragraph of the entered text — you don't need to select the *whole* paragraph, you only need to click *in* it

1 Enter unformatted text into your document

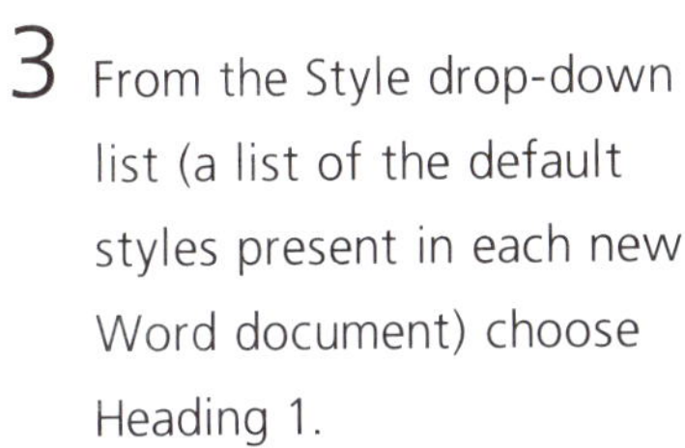

3 From the Style drop-down list (a list of the default styles present in each new Word document) choose Heading 1.

4 View the results of this style change.

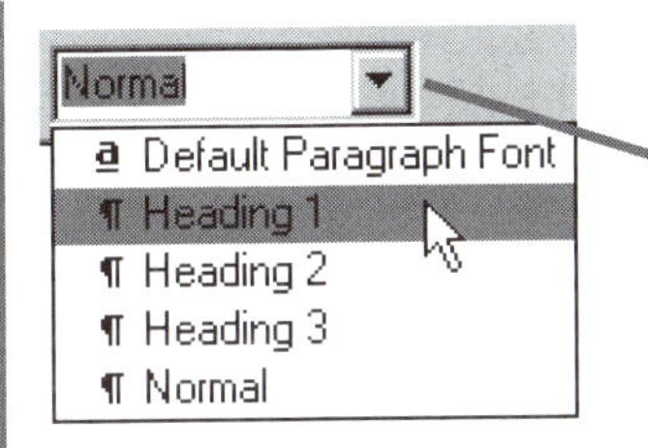

Normal
Default Paragraph Font
Heading 1
Heading 2
Heading 3
Normal

3 The Style drop-down list box. Default styles for Word documents are listed

Note how the whole paragraph has been formatted with the formats contained within the Heading 1 style

4 The style applied to the top paragraph — the document's heading

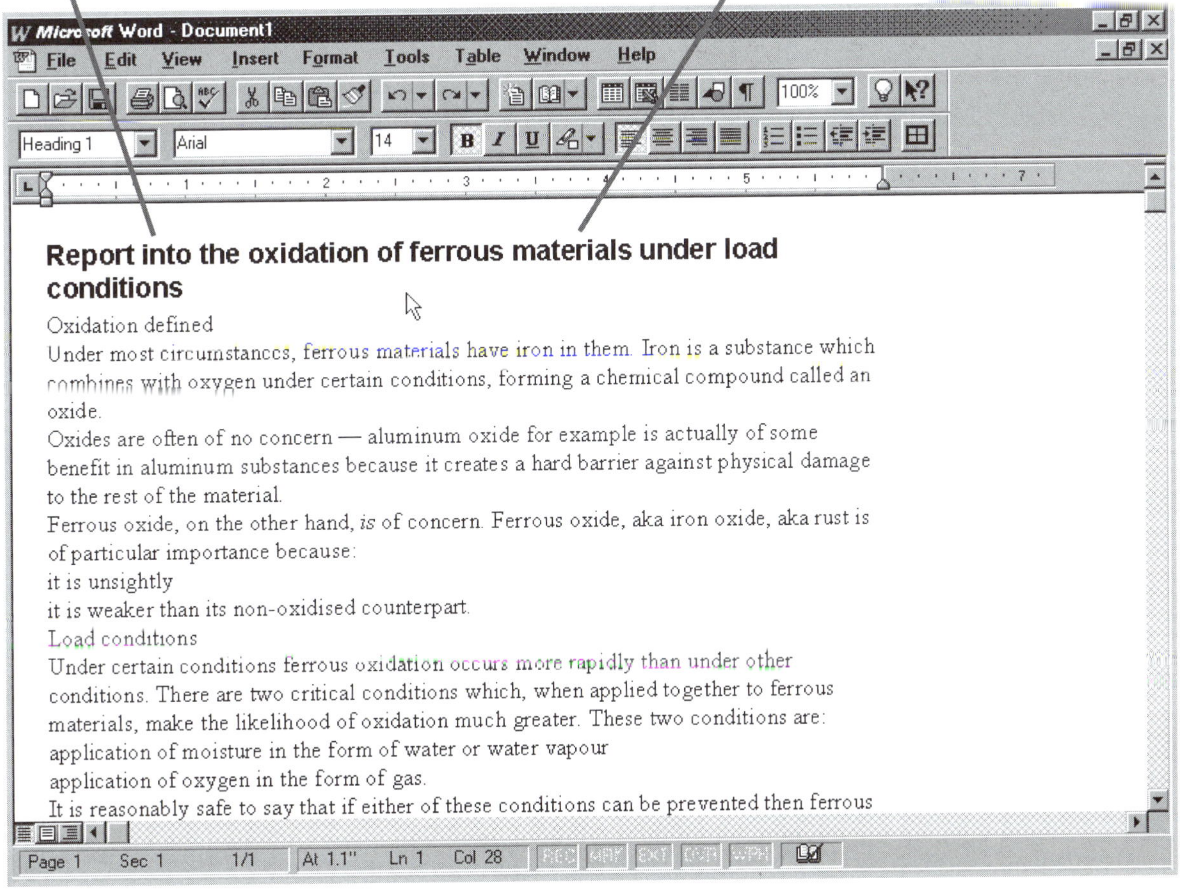

Microsoft Word - Document1

File Edit View Insert Format Tools Table Window Help

Heading 1 | Arial | 14 | 100%

Report into the oxidation of ferrous materials under load conditions

Oxidation defined

Under most circumstances, ferrous materials have iron in them. Iron is a substance which combines with oxygen under certain conditions, forming a chemical compound called an oxide.

Oxides are often of no concern — aluminum oxide for example is actually of some benefit in aluminum substances because it creates a hard barrier against physical damage to the rest of the material.

Ferrous oxide, on the other hand, *is* of concern. Ferrous oxide, aka iron oxide, aka rust is of particular importance because:

it is unsightly

it is weaker than its non-oxidised counterpart.

Load conditions

Under certain conditions ferrous oxidation occurs more rapidly than under other conditions. There are two critical conditions which, when applied together to ferrous materials, make the likelihood of oxidation much greater. These two conditions are:

application of moisture in the form of water or water vapour

application of oxygen in the form of gas.

It is reasonably safe to say that if either of these conditions can be prevented then ferrous

Page 1 Sec 1 1/1 At 1.1" Ln 1 Col 28

Styles (contd)

Basic steps:

5 Continue applying styles in the same way, trying out the other heading styles available.

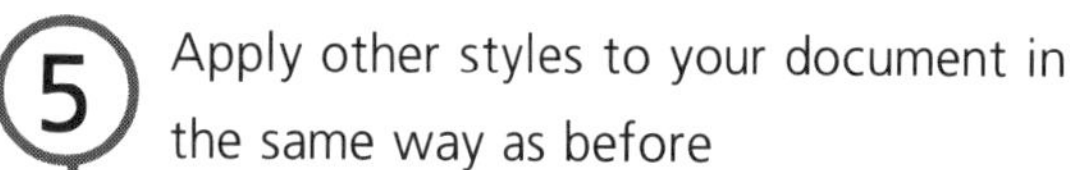
5
Apply other styles to your document in the same way as before

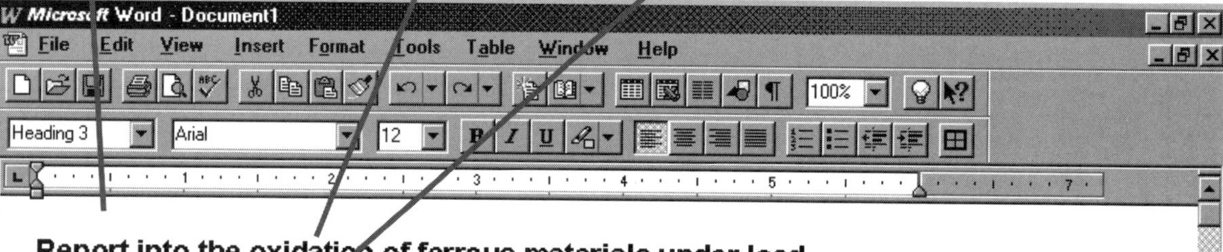
Heading 1
Heading 2
Microsoft Word - Document1
File Edit View Insert Format Tools Table Window Help
100%
Heading 3
Arial
12

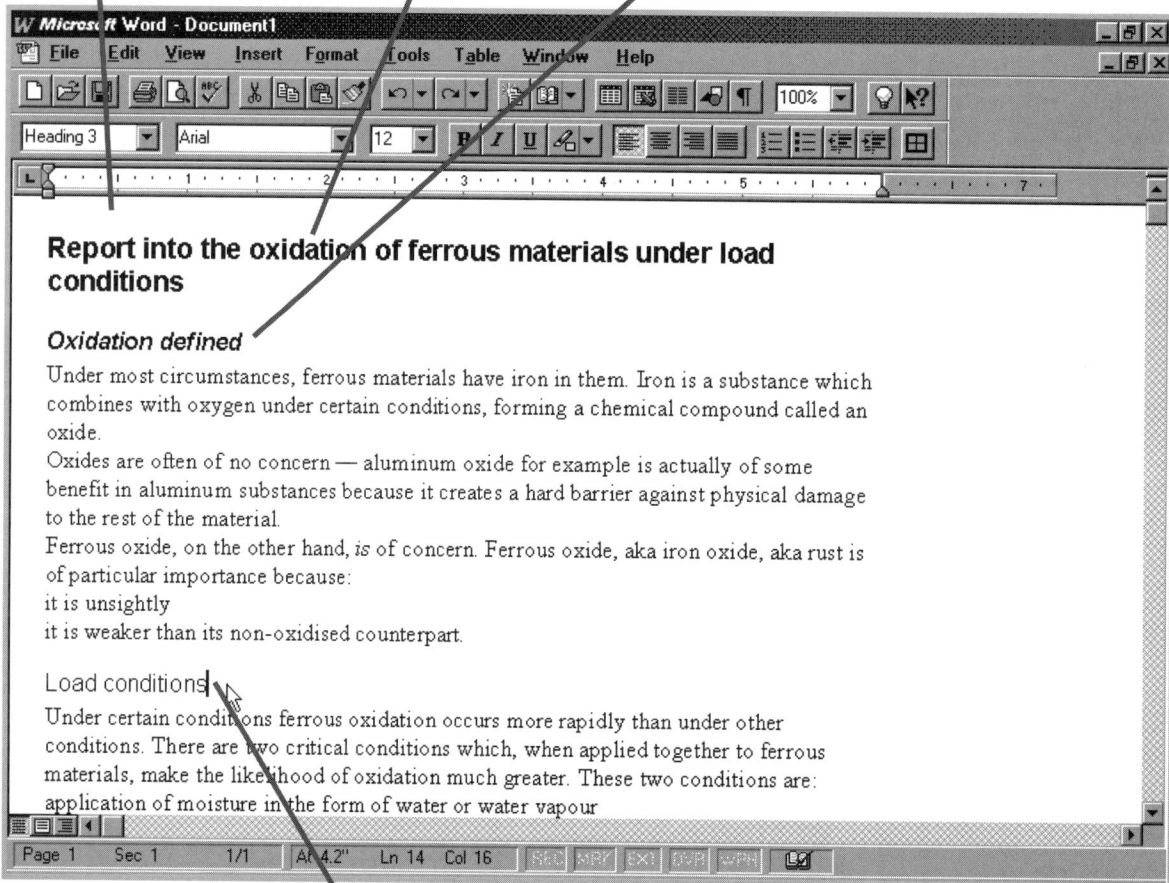

Report into the oxidation of ferrous materials under load conditions

Oxidation defined

Under most circumstances, ferrous materials have iron in them. Iron is a substance which combines with oxygen under certain conditions, forming a chemical compound called an oxide.
Oxides are often of no concern — aluminum oxide for example is actually of some benefit in aluminum substances because it creates a hard barrier against physical damage to the rest of the material.
Ferrous oxide, on the other hand, *is* of concern. Ferrous oxide, aka iron oxide, aka rust is of particular importance because:
it is unsightly
it is weaker than its non-oxidised counterpart.

Load conditions

Under certain conditions ferrous oxidation occurs more rapidly than under other conditions. There are two critical conditions which, when applied together to ferrous materials, make the likelihood of oxidation much greater. These two conditions are:
application of moisture in the form of water or water vapour

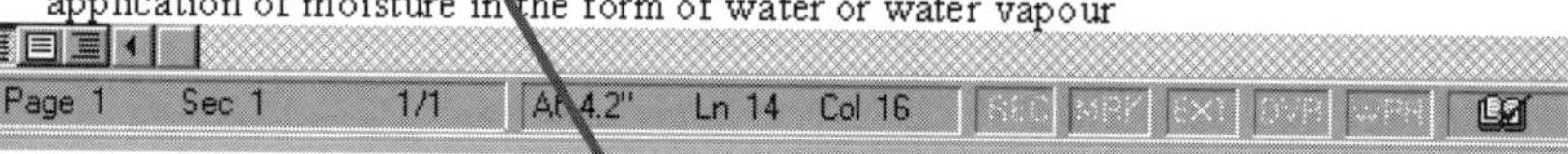
Page 1 Sec 1 1/1 At 4.2" Ln 14 Col 16
Heading 3

Character and paragraph styles

There are two types of styles:

- character styles
- paragraph styles.

They are identified by their appearance in the Styles drop-down list of the Formatting toolbar. They work in essentially the same way (that is, you select the text to be stylized, then select the style) but what they do to the selected text differs.

Character styles are displayed with a character symbol before them. When you apply a character style to text, only selected text (that is, *not* the whole paragraph — unless the whole paragraph is selected!) has the formats applied.

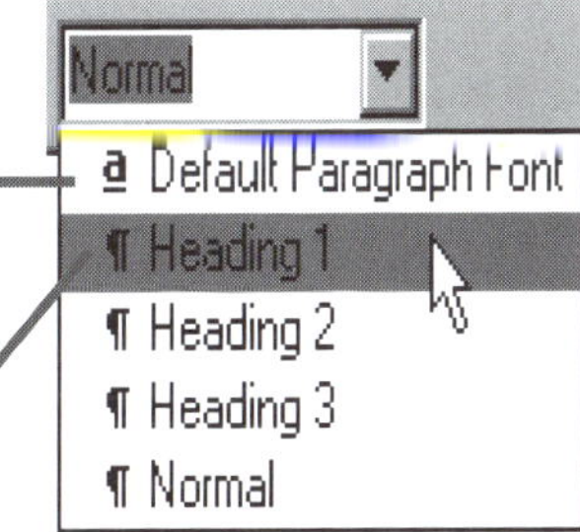
Normal
a Default Paragraph Font
¶ Heading 1
¶ Heading 2
¶ Heading 3
¶ Normal

Paragraph styles are displayed with a paragraph symbol before them. When you apply a paragraph font to selected text, the *whole* paragraph has the formats applied.

Take note:

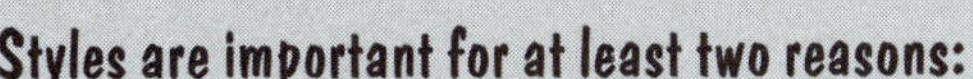

Styles are important for at least two reasons:

- **because they speed up the way you can format a document. Rather than formatting each selection of text with individual character and paragraph formats (which can take some time if you have quite a few formats to apply) you can apply *all* the formats in one operation.**
- **because the formats you apply as a style are always the same, there is no chance that you have forgotten any particular formats – if you apply each format individually you will probably forget some of them – all text with a particular style applied is identical in formats.**

Creating styles

Basic steps:

There are three main ways you can create your own paragraph style:

- apply formats to your own sample text until it is the way you want it, then create the style from those formats (for most people, this is ideal)
- adapt another style
- copy styles from other documents to your own.

1 To create a style from your own sample text, apply formats to your text until it is the way you want it (look again at Section 3 if you're a bit hazy about formatting).

2 Select the text you want to make a style of.

1 Apply different formats to text until it is as you want

2 Select formatted text to make a style

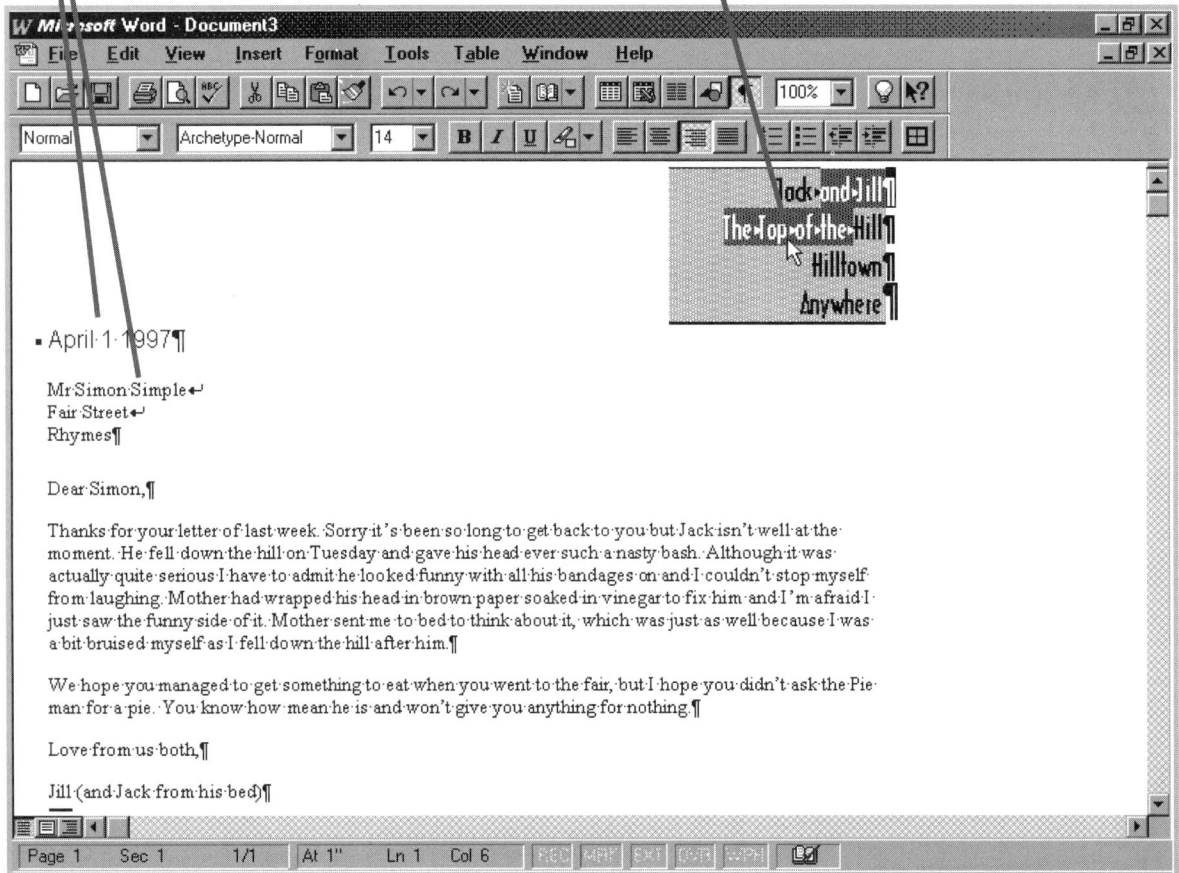

Microsoft Word - Document3

File Edit View Insert Format Tools Table Window Help

Normal | Archetype-Normal | 14 | 100%

Jack and Jill¶
The Top of the Hill¶
Hilltown¶
Anywhere¶

April 1 1997¶

Mr Simon Simple↵
Fair Street↵
Rhymes¶

Dear Simon,¶

Thanks for your letter of last week. Sorry it's been so long to get back to you but Jack isn't well at the moment. He fell down the hill on Tuesday and gave his head ever such a nasty bash. Although it was actually quite serious I have to admit he looked funny with all his bandages on and I couldn't stop myself from laughing. Mother had wrapped his head in brown paper soaked in vinegar to fix him and I'm afraid I just saw the funny side of it. Mother sent me to bed to think about it, which was just as well because I was a bit bruised myself as I fell down the hill after him.¶

We hope you managed to get something to eat when you went to the fair, but I hope you didn't ask the Pie man for a pie. You know how mean he is and won't give you anything for nothing.¶

Love from us both,¶

Jill (and Jack from his bed)¶

Page 1 Sec 1 1/1 At 1" Ln 1 Col 6

3 Choose **Format↳Style**, or type [Alt]+[O] then [S], to call up the **Style** dialog box. Click **New** to call up the **New Style** dialog box.

4 Enter a name for your style.

5 Check the **Add to Template** check box, then click **OK**, then click **Close** in the **Style** dialog box.

If you repeat this procedure for all the different styles within your document, when you have finished you will end up with a number of styles which have been added to Word (in the Normal template, actually), and which will be present whenever you open a new document using that template.

Next time you want to produce a similar looking document the styles are already there to use. Simply enter your text in the new document, select the text to be formatted with any particular style, then apply the style from the Formatting toolbar's Style button drop-down list. The text is formatted as you defined.

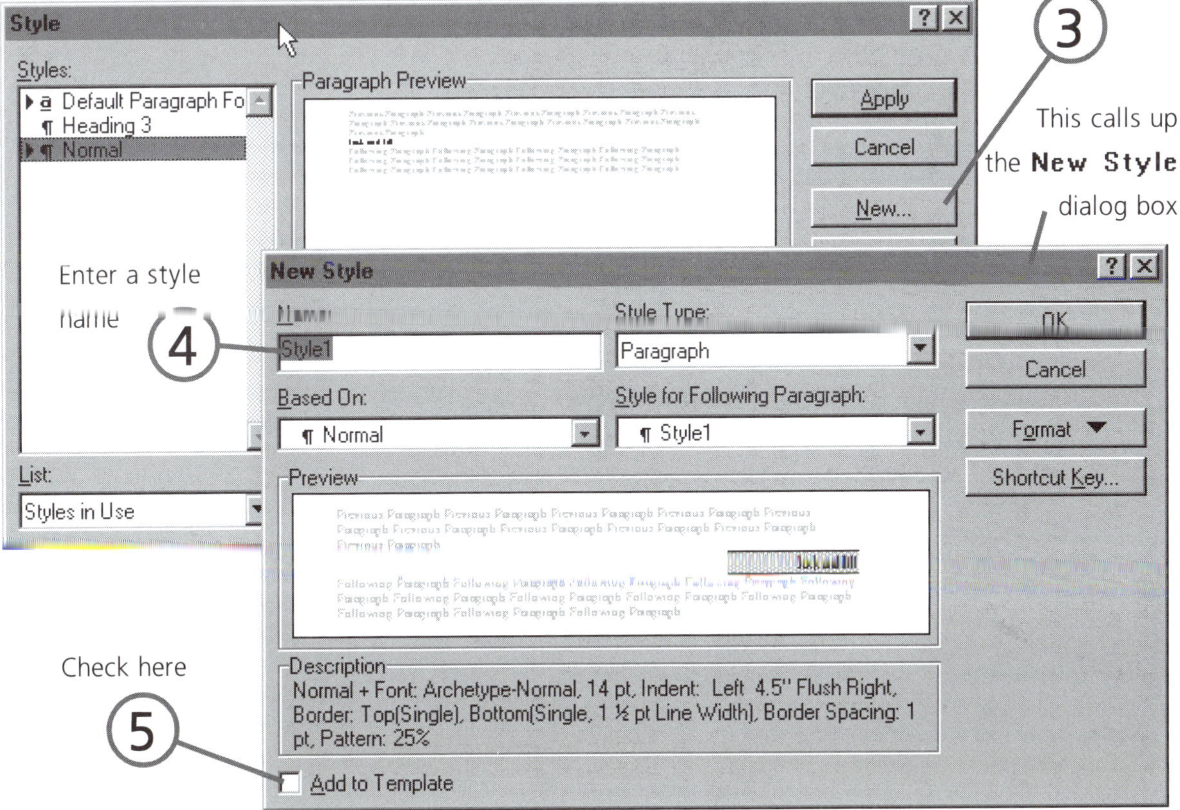

Click **New** in the **Style** dialog box
3
This calls up the **New Style** dialog box
Enter a style name
4
Check here
5
Style
Styles:
Default Paragraph Fo
Heading 3
Normal
Paragraph Preview
Apply
Cancel
New...
List:
Styles in Use
New Style
Name:
Style1
Style Type:
Paragraph
Based On:
Normal
Style for Following Paragraph:
Style1
OK
Cancel
Format
Shortcut Key...
Preview
Description
Normal + Font: Archetype-Normal, 14 pt, Indent: Left 4.5" Flush Right, Border: Top(Single), Bottom(Single, 1 ½ pt Line Width), Border Spacing: 1 pt, Pattern: 25%
Add to Template

Creating styles (contd)

One of the beauties of styles is their ability to be modified. What's more, if you modify a style *all* text in a document which has been formatted with that style is modified too. This is extremely useful when you're formatting a document, but it's also a useful method of creating your own styles.

Basic steps:

1 To modify a style, choose **Format↳Style**, or type Alt+O then S, to call up the **Style** dialog box.

2 Select the style you want to modify in the **Styles** entry list, then click **Modify** to call up the **Modify** dialog box.

1 **Style** dialog box

2 Select the style to modify, then click **Modify**

Modify Style dialog box

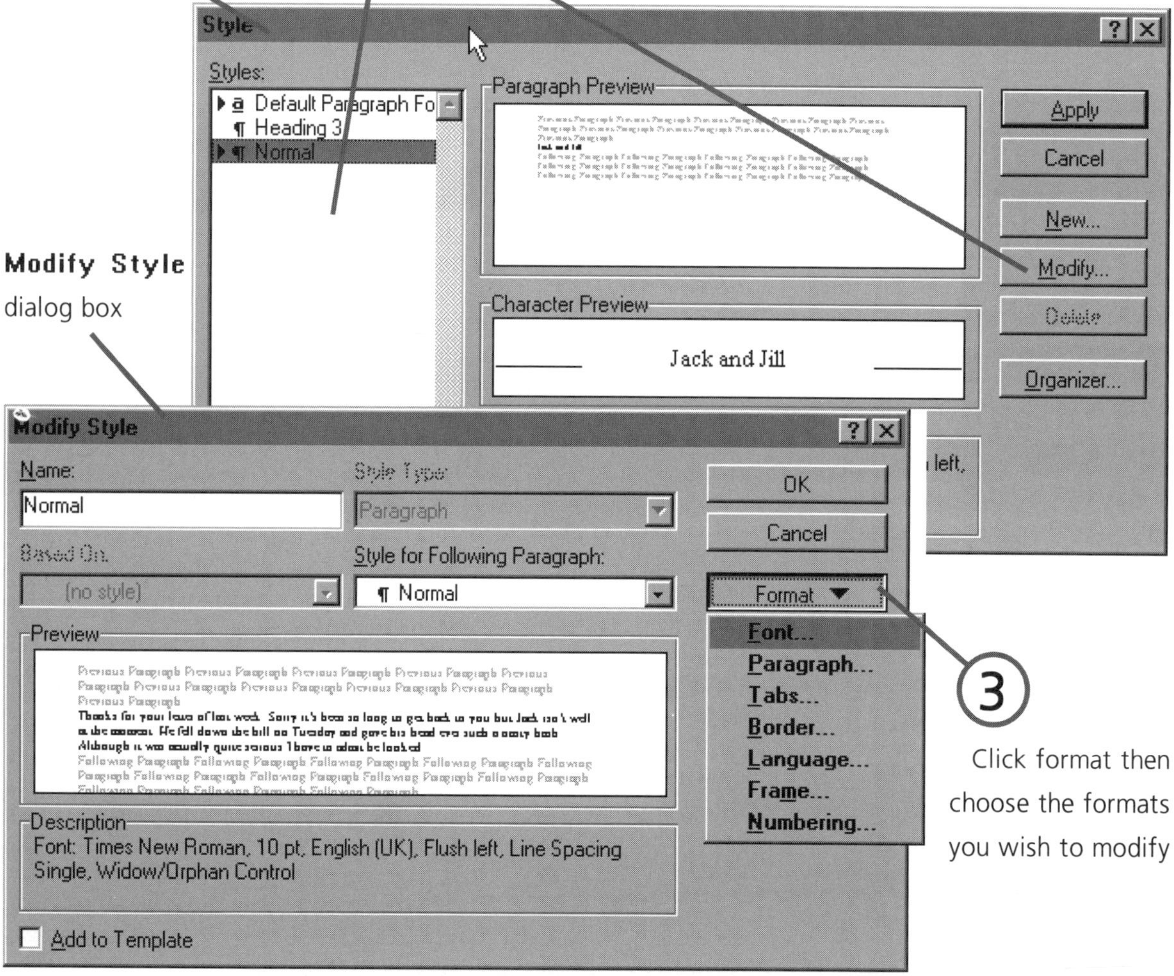

3 Click format then choose the formats you wish to modify

3 Click the **Format** button to drop down a list of formats which you can modify, select the format you want, and adjust it in the resultant dialog box. Repeat this if you want to modify more than one format type.

Take note:

When you click the Format button at step 3, you can modify any of the formats we've seen already (along with some new ones). All the formats available in the drop-down list are assigned to the style – then, when you have finished, all text which is formatted with that style is modified too. In other words, you can make some immense changes to the appearance of your document quite simply just by modifying a style.

Tip:

You can assign keyboard shortcuts to any style – simply modify the style as suggested here, and in the Modify Style dialog box click Shortcut Key, to call up the Customize dialog box with its Keyboard tab active. Enter the shortcut you want assigned to the style and if that shortcut isn't already used for some other function click Assign. Click Close, then OK in the Modify Style dialog box, followed by Close in the Style dialog box.

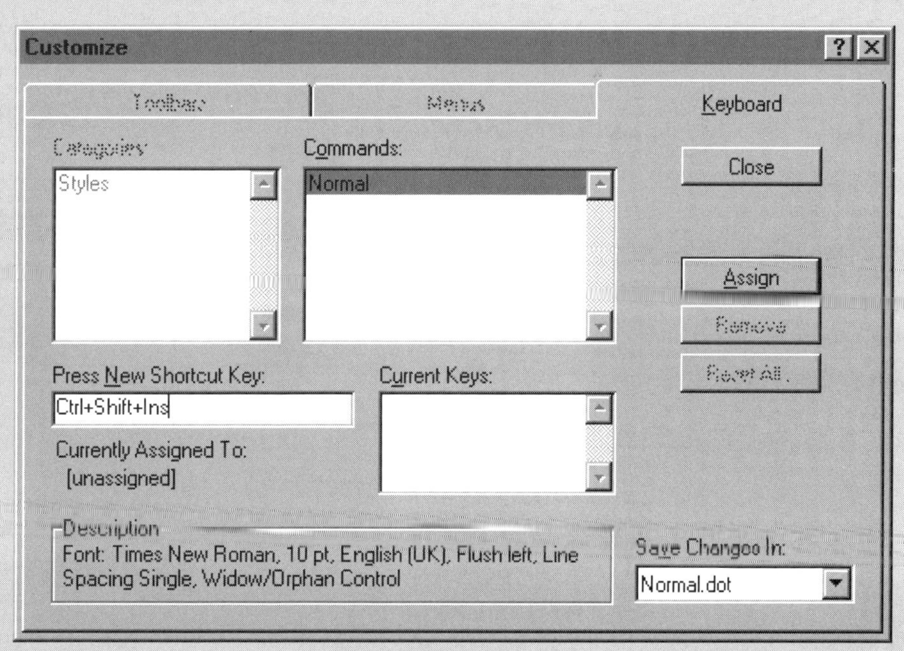
Customize
Toolbars
Menus
Keyboard
Categories:
Styles
Commands:
Normal
Close
Assign
Remove
Reset All...
Press New Shortcut Key:
Ctrl+Shift+Ins
Current Keys:
Currently Assigned To:
[unassigned]
Description
Font: Times New Roman, 10 pt, English (UK), Flush left, Line Spacing Single, Widow/Orphan Control
Save Changes In:
Normal.dot

Now you can apply a style simply by selecting the text and pressing your keyboard shortcut.

Creating styles (contd)

Basic steps:

The last method of creating styles in a document is to copy styles from other documents which have the styles you want. It's the **Organizer** dialog box which allows you to do this, listing styles in two documents side-by-side, so that you can copy styles from one to the other.

The styles to be copied can be in a true Word document, or in a Word template. Word has many default templates which you can use for this purpose, and we'll use one to illustrate how you can do it.

1 To copy one or more styles from one document to another, choose **Format↳Style**, or type Alt+O then S, to call up the **Style** dialog box. Click the **Organizer** button to call up the **Organizer** dialog box.

1 **Organizer** dialog box

2 Click **Close** then **Open File** to call up the **Open** dialog box

3 Select a template

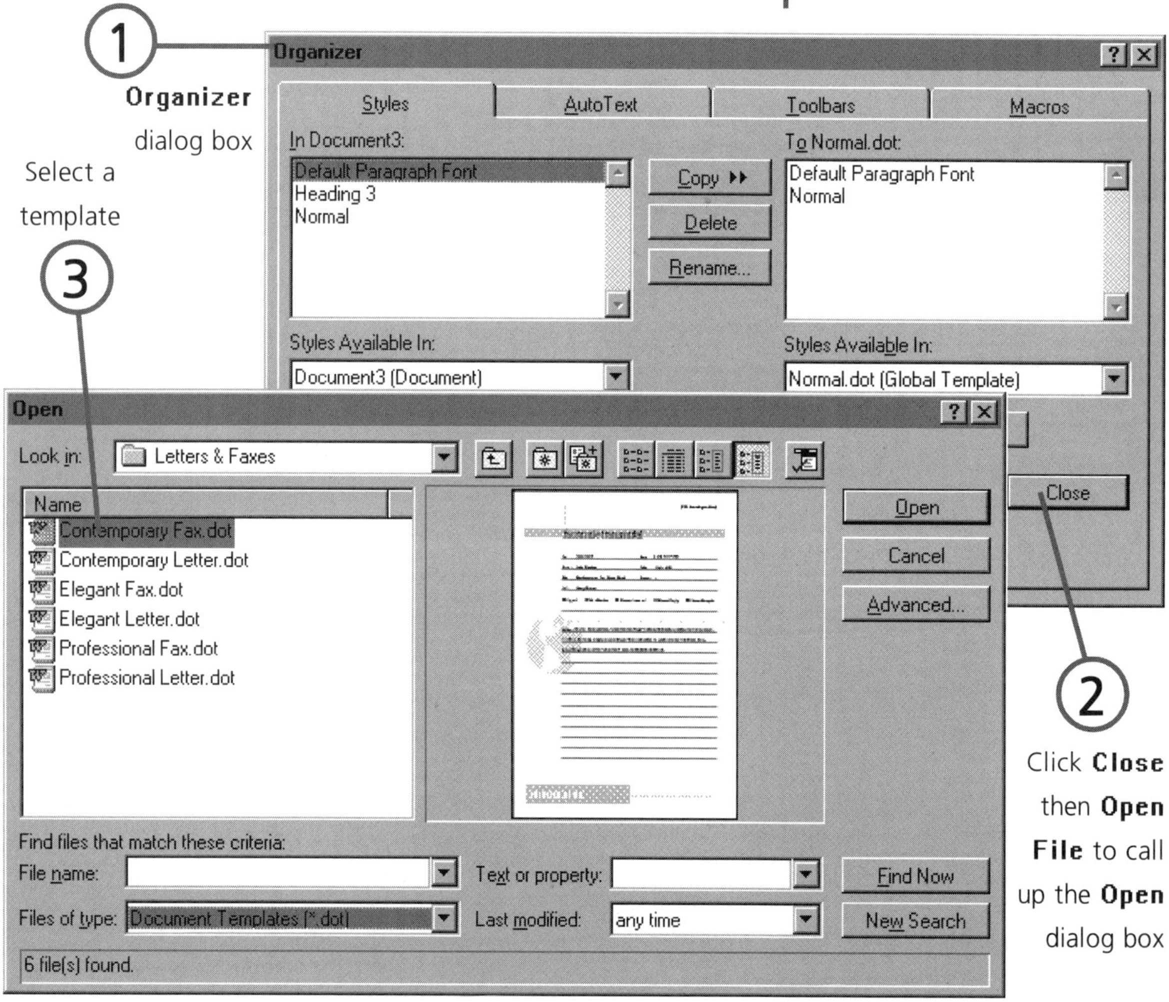

2 Click **Close** on the right side of the dialog box (the button changes to **Open File**) then click **Open File**. This displays a list of available files which you can select. Locate the templates directory in the MSOffice directory on your hard disk and make sure you're listing files of **.dot* type.

3 Select a template in the list and click **Open**. Now the **Organizer** dialog box displays all the styles in the template in a scrollable list.

4 You can select individual styles, or you can select multiple styles by Ctrl + clicking them.

5 Copy them to your own document by clicking **Copy.**

6 Click **Close** to close the **Organizer** dialog box, then try out your new styles in your own document.

Once you've selected some styles, click here to copy them to your document

Select the styles you want in your own document

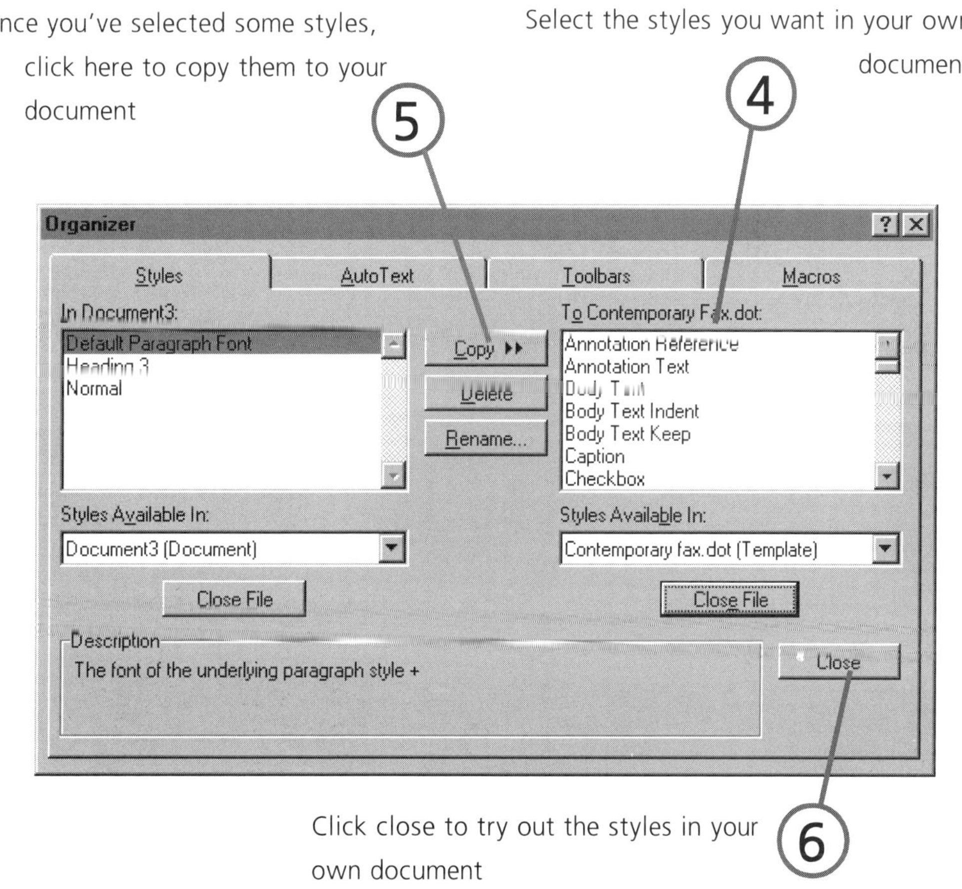

5
4
Organizer
Styles
AutoText
Toolbars
Macros
In Document3:
Default Paragraph Font
Heading 3
Normal
Copy ▸▸
Delete
Rename...
To Contemporary Fax.dot:
Annotation Reference
Annotation Text
Body Text
Body Text Indent
Body Text Keep
Caption
Checkbox
Styles Available In:
Document3 (Document)
Styles Available In:
Contemporary fax.dot (Template)
Close File
Close File
Description
The font of the underlying paragraph style +
Close
6

Click close to try out the styles in your own document

More about styles

If you haven't already realized it, styles are very important to a word processor like Word. Styles form the key to producing professional documents with total consistency of formatting. Their use ensures efficient control over your documents.

However, there are some additional things to know about styles which can make their use even more efficient. They are presented here as a collection of tips and notes — bear them in mind when you use Word.

Tip:

Format all text in a document with styles – that way if you want to change the document's appearance you only have to change a handful of styles, not the various text elements.

Tip:

When you create a new document, base it on a template – templates are complete with their own styles which you can use immediately. If there's a particular style of document you want, design it, then save it as a template. Each time you create a new document based on that template it'll be exactly as you want it. (Templates are covered later.)

Tip:

While we've said all along how you should enter all your text first, then apply styles to it there is a more elegant way which calls on Word styles' ability to change to another style when a paragraph ends. In both the New Style or the Modify Style dialog boxes there is a drop-down list box called Style for Following Paragraph. In here is a list of all available styles. Choose one. Then as your style which has a specified style to follow ends, the next style comes into force.

This is useful, say, for headings and subheadings (which are nearly always of a single paragraph and are followed by, say, normal style). As you finish typing the heading text and press ↵ or Enter, the next paragraph is automatically stylized with the next style.

Tip:

You can arrange your document window to display which style is applied to a paragraph (see below) by adjusting the **Style Area Width** box in the **View** tab of the **Options** dialog box (choose **Tools→Options**, or type Alt + T then O, then click **View** if it's not already at the front of the dialog box). Specify a width greater than 0 to display the style area in your document.

Take note:

If you delete a style (using, say, the **Delete** button on the **Style** dialog box) the Normal style is applied to all text which was formatted with the style.

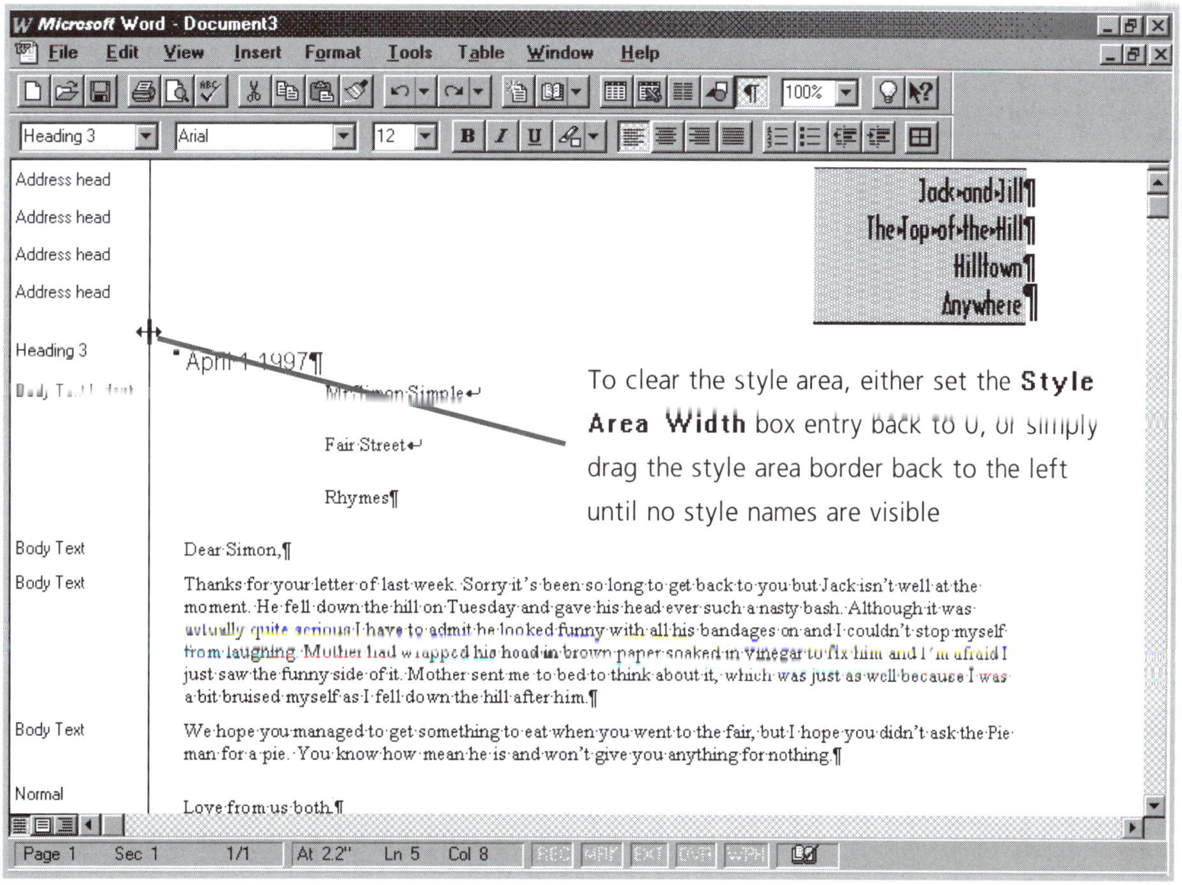

Microsoft Word - Document3

File Edit View Insert Format Tools Table Window Help

Heading 3 | Arial | 12 | 100%

Style area	Document
Address head	Jack and Jill
Address head	The Top of the Hill
Address head	Hilltown
Address head	Anywhere
Heading 3	April 1 1997
Body Text Indent	Mr Simon Simple / Fair Street / Rhymes
Body Text	Dear Simon,
Body Text	Thanks for your letter of last week. Sorry it's been so long to get back to you but Jack isn't well at the moment. He fell down the hill on Tuesday and gave his head ever such a nasty bash. Although it was actually quite serious I have to admit he looked funny with all his bandages on and I couldn't stop myself from laughing. Mother had wrapped his head in brown paper soaked in vinegar to fix him and I'm afraid I just saw the funny side of it. Mother sent me to bed to think about it, which was just as well because I was a bit bruised myself as I fell down the hill after him.
Body Text	We hope you managed to get something to eat when you went to the fair, but I hope you didn't ask the Pie man for a pie. You know how mean he is and won't give you anything for nothing.
Normal	Love from us both.

Page 1 Sec 1 1/1 At 2.2" Ln 5 Col 8

To clear the style area, either set the **Style Area Width** box entry back to 0, or simply drag the style area border back to the left until no style names are visible

More about styles (contd)

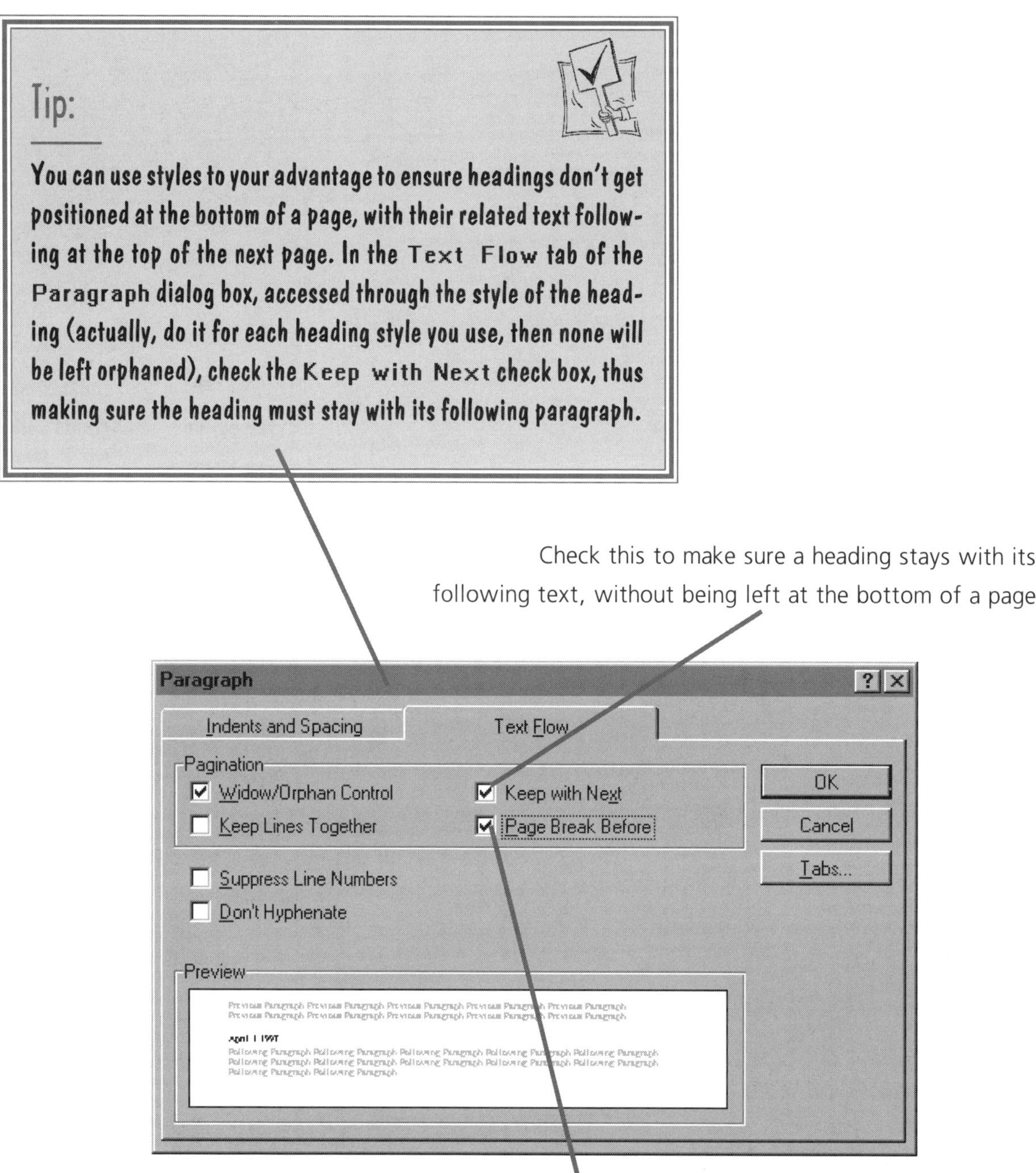
Tip:
You can use styles to your advantage to ensure headings don't get positioned at the bottom of a page, with their related text following at the top of the next page. In the Text Flow tab of the Paragraph dialog box, accessed through the style of the heading (actually, do it for each heading style you use, then none will be left orphaned), check the Keep with Next check box, thus making sure the heading must stay with its following paragraph.
Check this to make sure a heading stays with its following text, without being left at the bottom of a page
Paragraph
Indents and Spacing
Text Flow
Pagination
Widow/Orphan Control
Keep with Next
Keep Lines Together
Page Break Before
OK
Cancel
Tabs...
Suppress Line Numbers
Don't Hyphenate
Preview

Check this to create a page break before a major heading — in other words the major heading will always start at the top of a page

Take note:

If you change a font, or any other formatting parameter, in a style which another style is based on, the other style's font (or other parameter) changes, too – unless you have already specified a different parameter in the second style.

Tip:

You can use the above to advantage when you set up the styles in your document – to specify the style which will follow another style. For example, if you specify that a heading is followed by body text then, every time you type a heading and press Enter or ↵ (as long as Word knows that the heading *is* a heading – see next paragraph), the next paragraph will be in the body text style.

To enter styles as you go along, you *can* select the style from the style list box in the Formatting toolbar, but it's a lot easier to assign the style a keyboard shortcut which you can enter whenever you want to change style.

Tip:

If you can't be bothered to arrange styles to best suit your documents, at least use Word's AutoFormat command. This does a similar job, automatically – properly defined styles are always better, on the other hand.

Take note:

Styles are probably the most important feature of a word processor like Word. If you manage the styles in your documents properly, taking care in how they are formatted, how they are based, what text flow is associated with them, and so on, your documents will be much better for it. Not only do they look *better*, but it is also much easier to make large formatting changes to suit the way you want your documents to look. For example, if all styles are based on each other in a hierarchical way, a single change of font or size will change the whole document.

About templates

In places throughout the book, the term *template* has been used, without any clear explanation. Now it's time to say exactly *what* a template is.

Effectively, a template is a skeleton document. It has all the bones of any document, in terms of document parameters — just not all the flesh in terms of text you enter.

Word uses templates to store all document parameters. Character and paragraph formats, tables, styles, sections, AutoText entries, graphical items, and so on — and even text — can all be stored in a template.

Then, when you create a new document, you can base it on the chosen template and up pops a new document looking exactly as you want it — all you need to do is enter any final details and *hey, presto!*, a complete document. You could use a template, for example, when you create a letter. In the template might be a letterhead, complete with a company logo, and styles which specify fonts and formats for use in the letter. Another example could be a template set up for your monthly sales figures — the document is complete; you just add the figures. See the next page for details of creating your own template.

A default installation of Word includes a number of built-in templates as standard. When you first start up Word, the first document on-screen is even based on a template (the Normal template, actually). When you create a *new* document, on the other hand, you are given an option to choose which of the built-in templates you want to use for the document.

Basic steps:

1. Choose **File→New**, or type Alt+F then N, or type Ctrl+N. This calls up the **New** dialog box.
2. Click a tab to see the templates associated with it.
3. Click a template.
4. Click **Template** if you want to create a new template based on the template chosen.
5. Click **OK** to create the document based on that template.

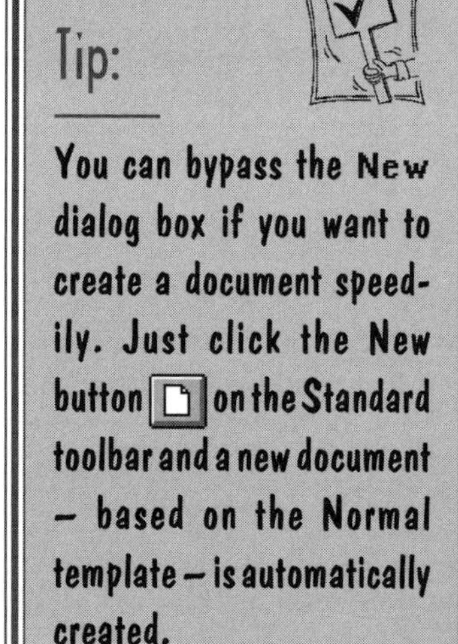

Tip:

You can bypass the New dialog box if you want to create a document speedily. Just click the New button on the Standard toolbar and a new document – based on the Normal template – is automatically created.

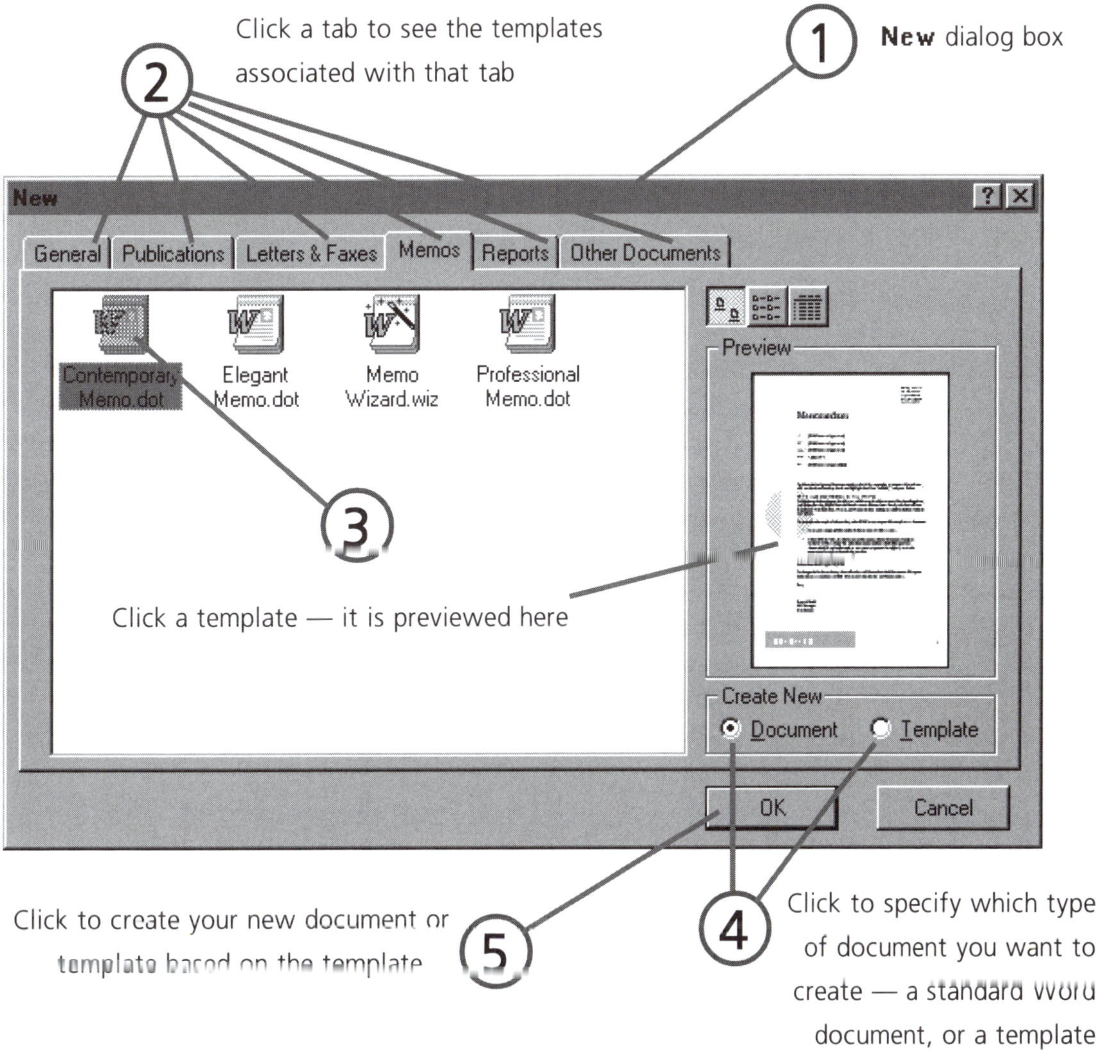

1 **New** dialog box

2 Click a tab to see the templates associated with that tab

3 Click a template — it is previewed here

4 Click to specify which type of document you want to create — a standard Word document, or a template

5 Click to create your new document or template based on the template

Take note:

The Normal template is a special case template – it holds all the document parameters you use most in Word. All the toolbars, their buttons, their positions, the menus and shortcut keys, and everything else you have as default items, are stored in the Normal template. If you use another template to create other documents, on the other hand, all these features are still available in those other documents.

Creating a template

Basic steps:

It's easy to create your own template. If there's a document type you find you're using quite a lot, it's worth making a template of it, then whenever you want to create another document with the same style just create the document from the template.

Once you've got the document looking just the way you want it (remember, you only need the bare bones of it), follow the steps here.

1 Choose **File↳Save As**, or type Alt+F then A. This calls up the **Save As** dialog box.

2 Click the **Save File as Type** drop-down list box to see the drop-down list of types you can save the document as.

3 Select **Document Template.**

4 Enter a name for your template — something easy to remember.

5 Click **Save.**

Save As
dialog box
1

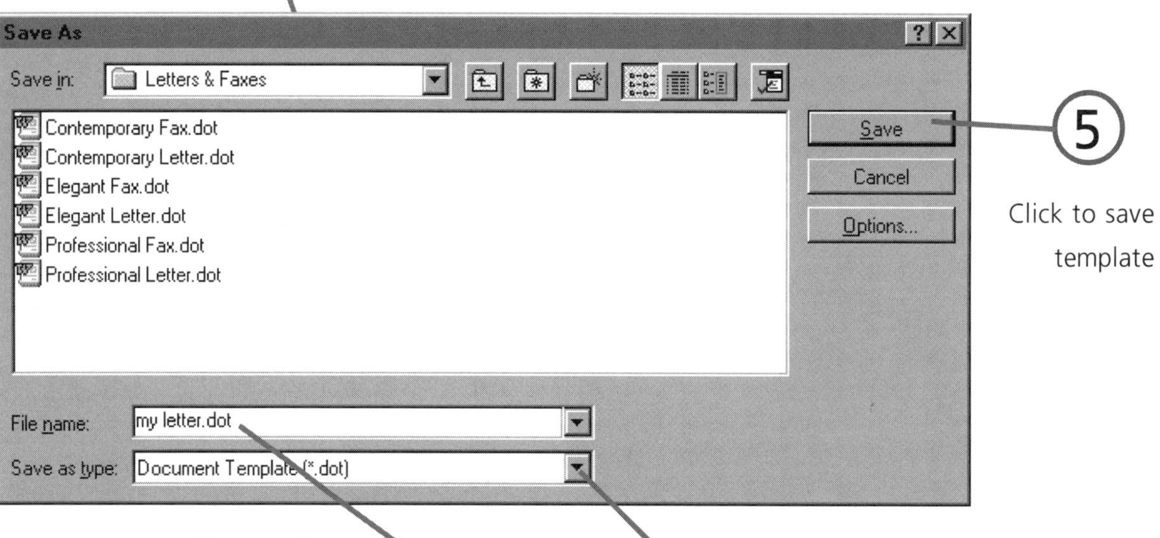
Save As
Save in:
Letters & Faxes
Contemporary Fax.dot
Contemporary Letter.dot
Elegant Fax.dot
Elegant Letter.dot
Professional Fax.dot
Professional Letter.dot
Save
Cancel
Options...
File name:
my letter.dot
Save as type:
Document Template (*.dot)

5 Click to save template

4 Enter a name you'll remember. Note the *.dot* extension, meaning Word will save it as a template

2 & 3 In the drop-down list select the **Document Template** option

Here's an example of a template for a letterhead. It combines a heading with a border (the underlining) and a simple graphic

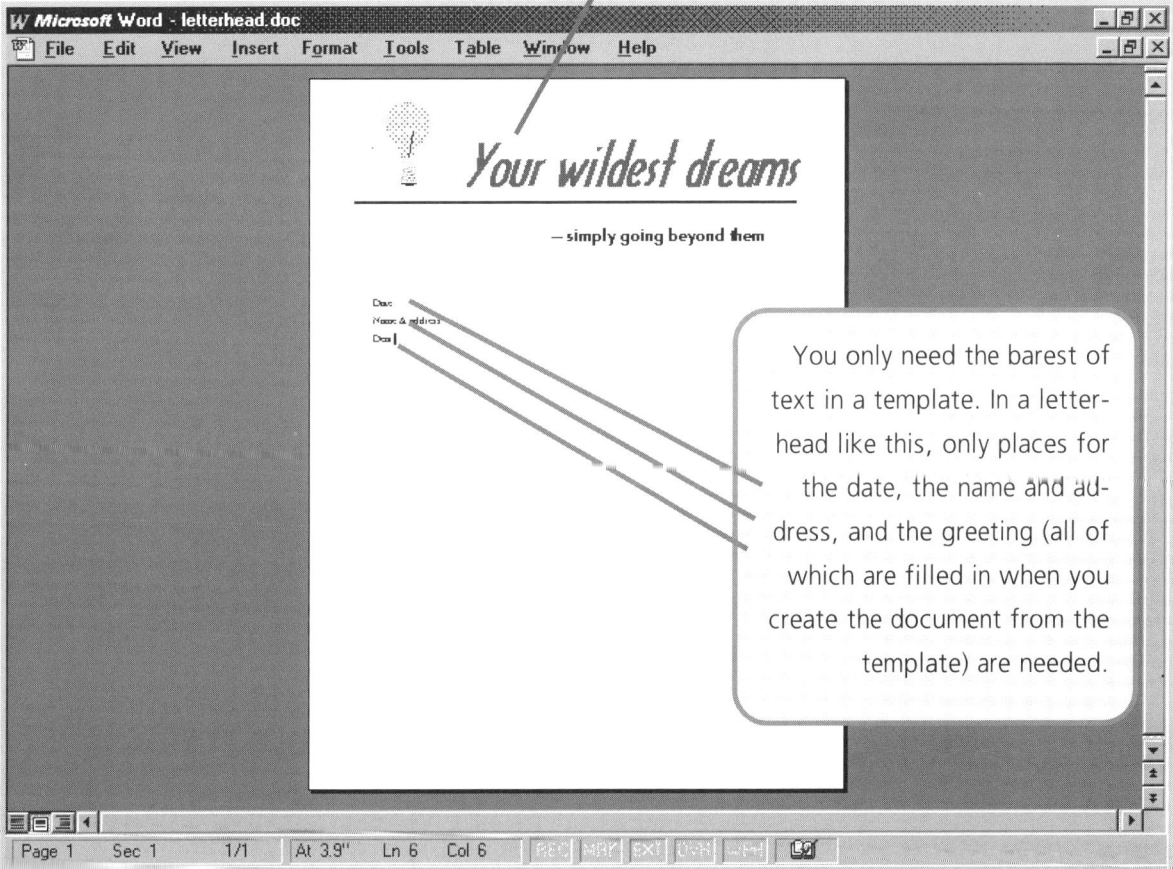

Microsoft Word - letterhead.doc

File Edit View Insert Format Tools Table Window Help

Your wildest dreams

– simply going beyond them

You only need the barest of text in a template. In a letterhead like this, only places for the date, the name and address, and the greeting (all of which are filled in when you create the document from the template) are needed.

Page 1 Sec 1 1/1 At 3.9" Ln 6 Col 6

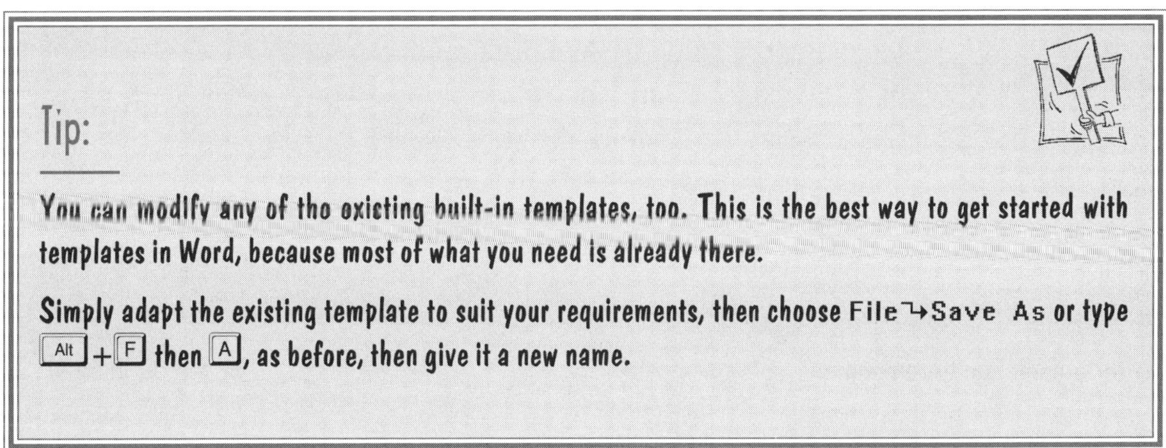

Tip:

You can modify any of the existing built-in templates, too. This is the best way to get started with templates in Word, because most of what you need is already there.

Simply adapt the existing template to suit your requirements, then choose File→Save As or type Alt+F then A, as before, then give it a new name.

Summary for Section 6

- Use styles containing all formatting parameters you need in a document.
- Set up styles which are based on other styles. Use a hierarchy of styles to create your document.
- There are two kinds of styles — paragraph and character styles.
- To create styles (1) apply formats to a sample of text then create the style from those formats, (2) adapt an existing style, or (3) copy styles from other documents (or templates).
- Use keyboard shortcuts to help you apply styles.
- Make sure headings (1) stay with the following paragraph — to prevent a heading being left at the bottom of the page — and (2) have a following style — to make sure your body style, say, is automatically applied when you press Enter or ↵. Use styles to do this.
- Use templates to speed up how you create good-looking documents. Templates hold skeleton information about a document — styles, graphics, some text — you only need to fill in the meat on the bones.
- If you find yourself using the same type of document over and over again, set up a template comprising the fundamental aspects of your document. Then, when you go to create a document following that type, create it from your template.

7 Technical thingamajigs

Print preview 138
Printing 140
Print options 141
Starting Word at turn-on 142
Shortcut keys 144
Toolbars 146
Summary for Section 7 140

Print preview

Basic steps:

Before you print a document, it's best to stand back and take a look at it. Print previewing does this job for you, giving you an overall view of the document, while letting you edit the document if you need to, before you go ahead and waste your paper.

Print preview brings with it its own toolbar, with some new buttons.

1 Choose **File→Print Preview**, or type [Alt]+[F] then [V], or simply (best) click the Print Preview button on the Standard toolbar. The display changes to print preview, fitting complete pages of your document into the print preview window.

2 Use buttons on the Print Preview toolbar to adjust the display.

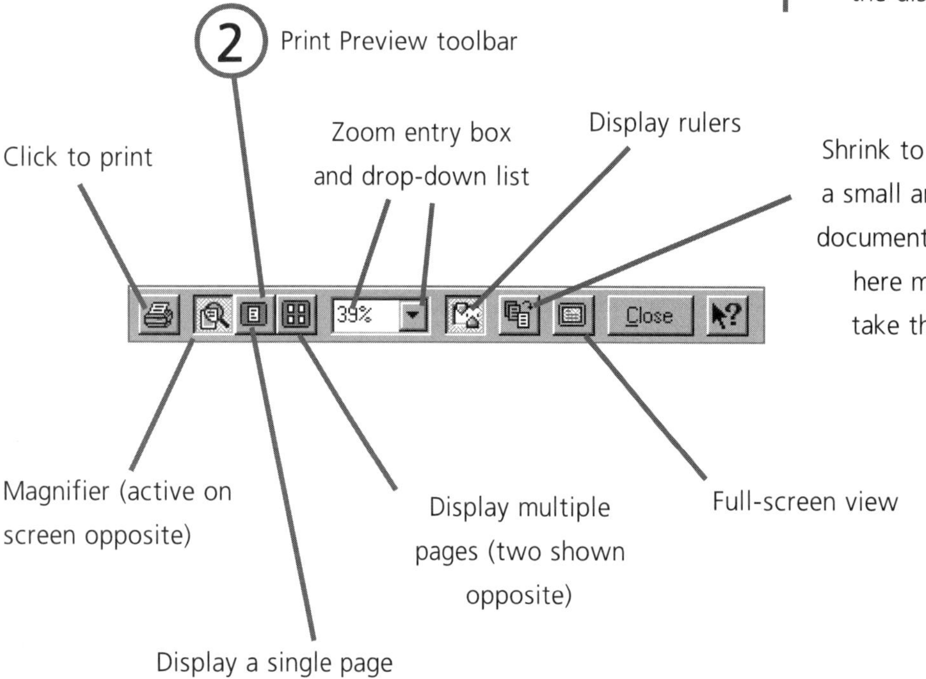
2
Print Preview toolbar
Click to print
Zoom entry box and drop-down list
Display rulers
Shrink to Fit — if there's only a small amount of text on the document's last page, clicking here might (if you're lucky) take the text back to fit on one page less
39%
Close
Magnifier (active on screen opposite)
Display multiple pages (two shown opposite)
Full-screen view
Display a single page

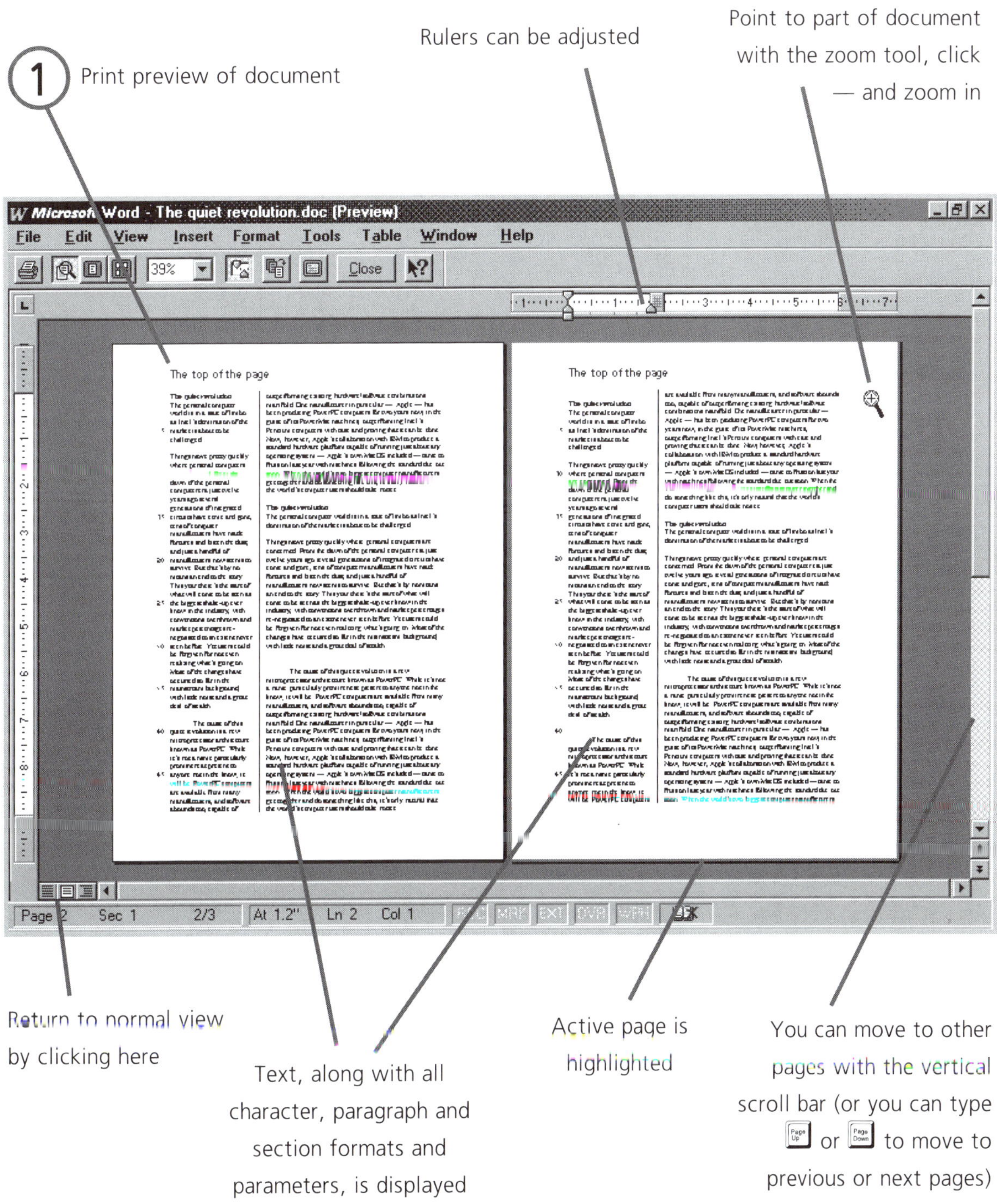
1
Print preview of document
Rulers can be adjusted
Point to part of document with the zoom tool, click — and zoom in
Microsoft Word - The quiet revolution.doc (Preview)
File Edit View Insert Format Tools Table Window Help
39%
Close
The top of the page
The top of the page
Page 2 Sec 1 2/3 At 1.2" Ln 2 Col 1
Return to normal view by clicking here
Text, along with all character, paragraph and section formats and parameters, is displayed
Active page is highlighted
You can move to other pages with the vertical scroll bar (or you can type Page Up or Page Down to move to previous or next pages)

Printing

Basic steps:

While printing from a PC can cause many headaches, use of the Windows environment coupled with Word itself makes life a lot easier. We assume that your computer is properly connected to a printer, and that both are on and working. After that, there are only a few things you need to know.

1 Choose **File→Print**, or type [Alt]+[F] then [P], or type [Ctrl]+[P]. This calls up the **Print** dialog box.

2 As the default dialog box stands, if you click **OK**, one copy of the text in the active document will be printed to the printer shown — you can adjust controls and entries to change this.

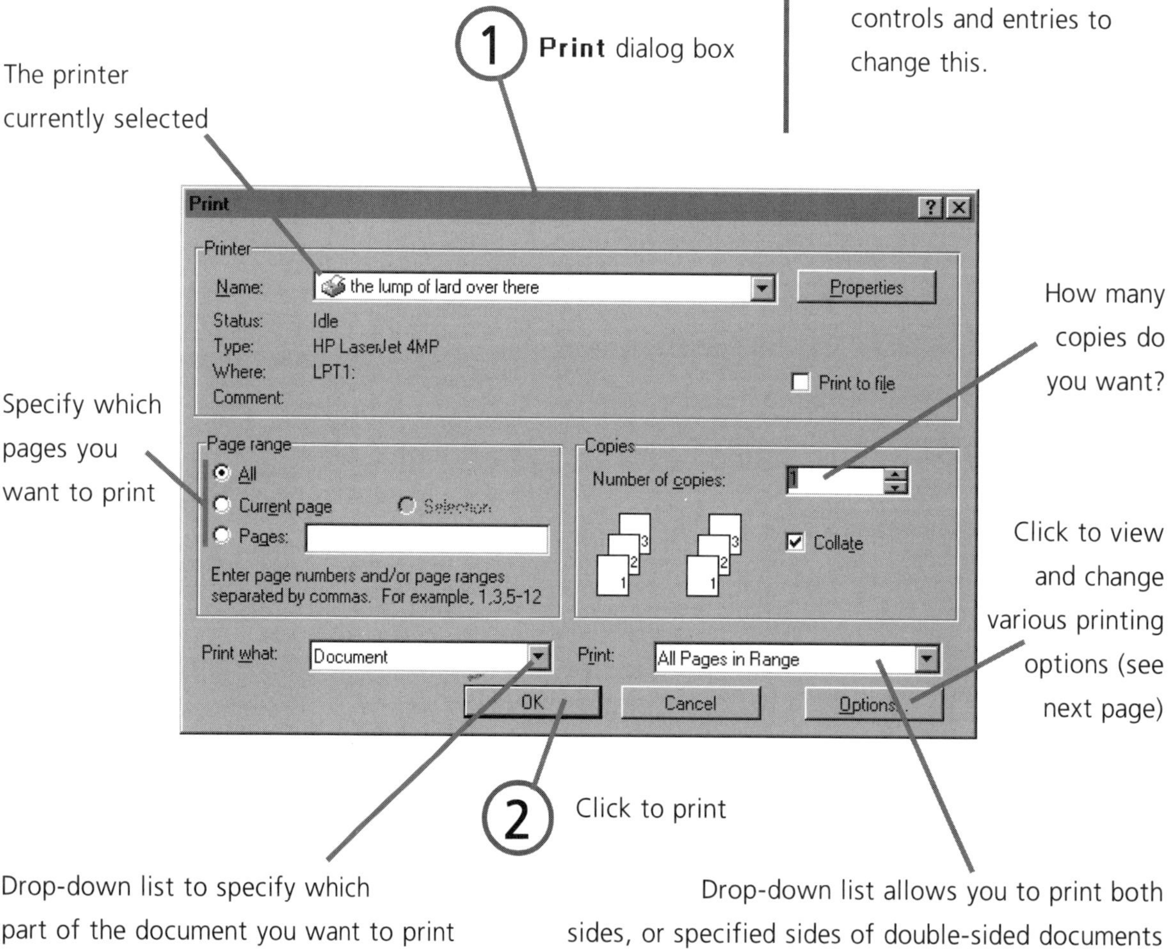

1 **Print** dialog box

The printer currently selected

Print

Printer

Name: the lump of lard over there

Properties

Status: Idle

Type: HP LaserJet 4MP

Where: LPT1:

Comment:

Print to file

How many copies do you want?

Specify which pages you want to print

Page range

All

Current page

Selection

Pages:

Enter page numbers and/or page ranges separated by commas. For example, 1,3,5-12

Copies

Number of copies: 1

Collate

Click to view and change various printing options (see next page)

Print what: Document

Print: All Pages in Range

OK

Cancel

Options...

2 Click to print

Drop-down list to specify which part of the document you want to print

Drop-down list allows you to print both sides, or specified sides of double-sided documents

Print options

Basic steps:

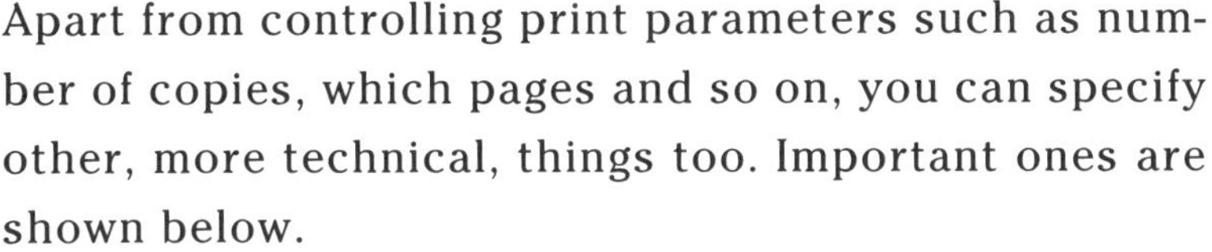

Apart from controlling print parameters such as number of copies, which pages and so on, you can specify other, more technical, things too. Important ones are shown below.

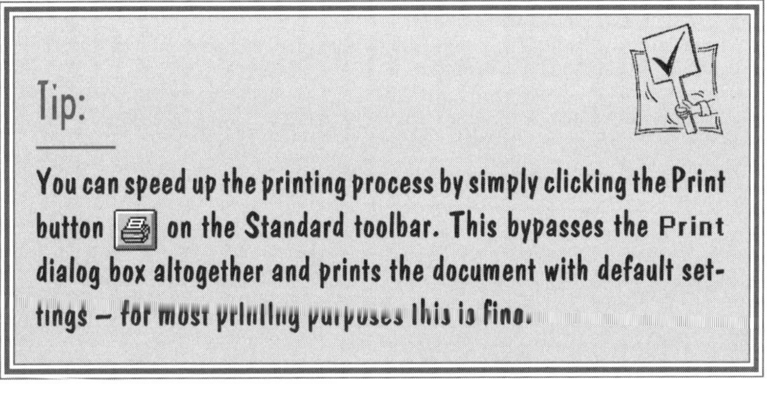

Tip:

You can speed up the printing process by simply clicking the Print button on the Standard toolbar. This bypasses the Print dialog box altogether and prints the document with default settings – for most printing purposes this is fine.

1 From the **Print** dialog box, click **Options**. This calls up the **Options** dialog box.

2 Click the **Print** tab, if it's not already in front.

(1) **Options** dialog box

(2) **Print** tab

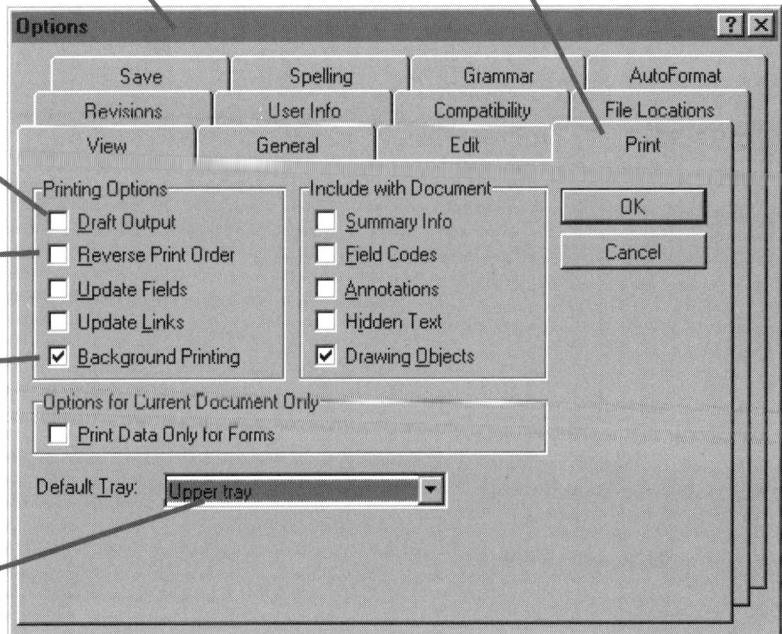

Uses draft mode of printer to print rapid copies. Not all features of your documents may be printed

Prints pages of your documents in reverse order

Prints in background (allowing you to get on with your work while printing takes place)

Select which tray of your printer paper comes from

Starting Word at turn-on

Basic steps:

If you use Word just about every time you turn on your computer, you can set it up to start Word (or any other program for that matter) automatically.

1. Choose Start ↳**Settings**↳**Taskbar**, this calls up the **Taskbar Properties** dialog box.
2. Click the **Start Menu Programs** tab.
3. Click **Advanced**. This calls up an Explorer window for the Start Menu.

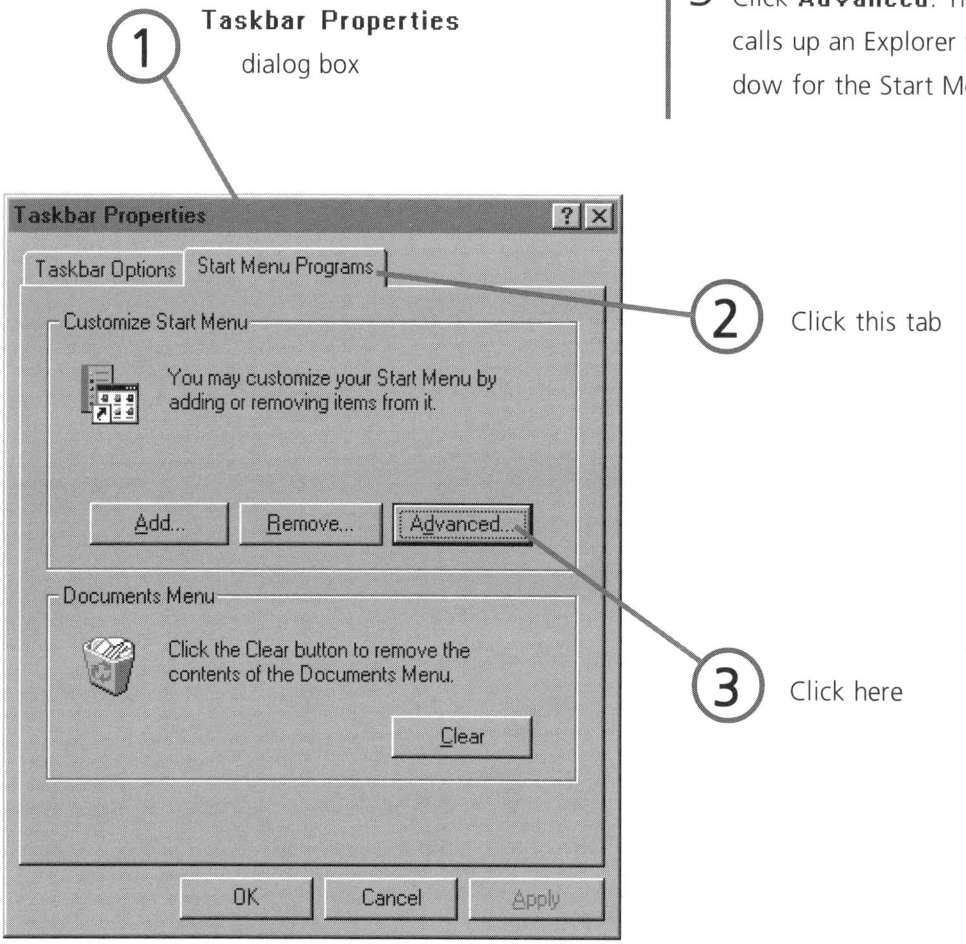

1 **Taskbar Properties** dialog box

2 Click this tab

3 Click here

4 Open the **Programs** folder in the left half of the window. If Microsoft Word is in this folder, go to step 5. If MSOffice is in the **Programs** folder, open the **MSOffice** folder.

5 Hold down Ctrl and drag the Microsoft Word icon from the right half of the window to the **StartUp** folder in the left half.

Tip:

Holding down Ctrl while dragging *copies* the Word icon to the StartUp folder. Dragging without holding Ctrl would merely move it! Now, whenever you restart your computer Word will automatically start up. If you ever want this *not* to happen, simply delete the icon.

Open the **Programs** folder — you may need to open the **MSOffice** folder too, depending on how Word is installed on your computer

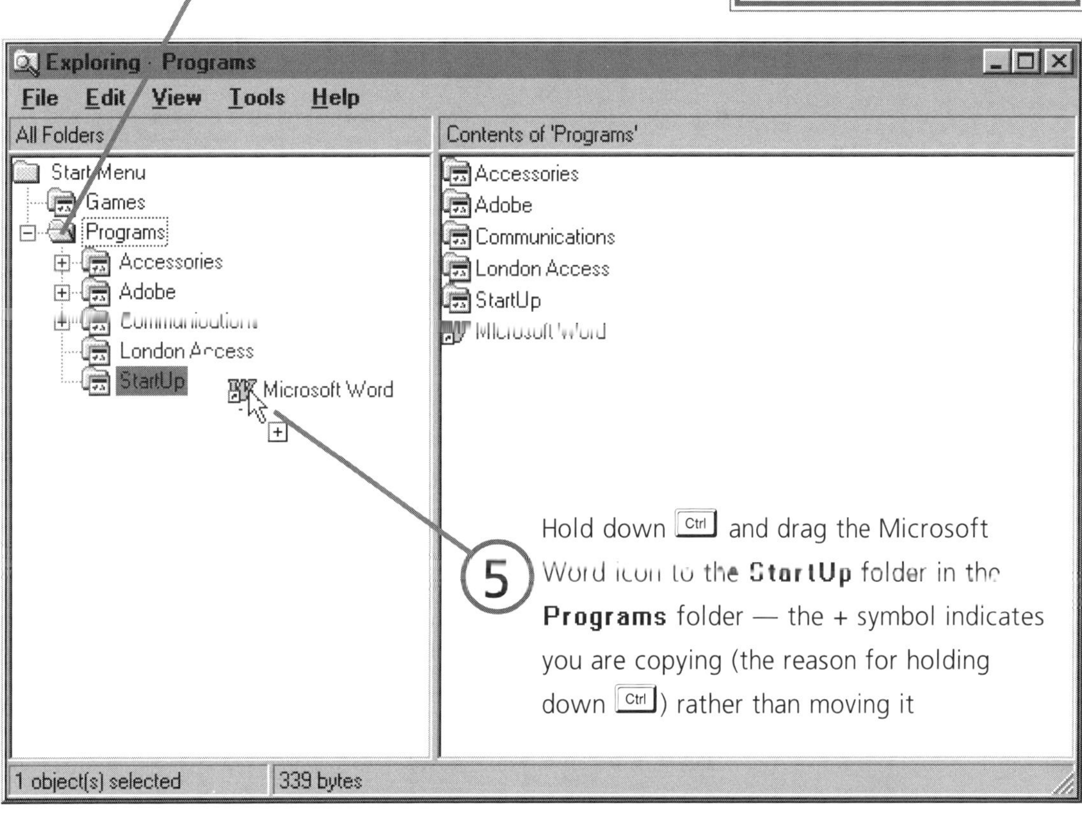

4
Exploring - Programs
File Edit View Tools Help
All Folders
Contents of 'Programs'
Start Menu
Games
Programs
Accessories
Adobe
Communications
London Access
StartUp
Microsoft Word
5
1 object(s) selected
339 bytes

Hold down Ctrl and drag the Microsoft Word icon to the **StartUp** folder in the **Programs** folder — the + symbol indicates you are copying (the reason for holding down Ctrl) rather than moving it

Shortcut keys

Basic steps:

A great many things you do in Word, you do a great many times. Some of these things can be called upon with the click of a button on a toolbar, or a shortcut key command. Although buttons are a boon over choosing a command through the ordinary menu method, undoubtedly shortcut keys are the quickest.

At first sight, you might think not all commands are available as shortcuts. However, you can assign your own shortcut key commands to *any* command available in Word.

1. Choose **Tools↳Customize**, or type Alt+T then C, to call up the **Customize** dialog box.
2. Click the **Keyboard** tab if it's not already in front.

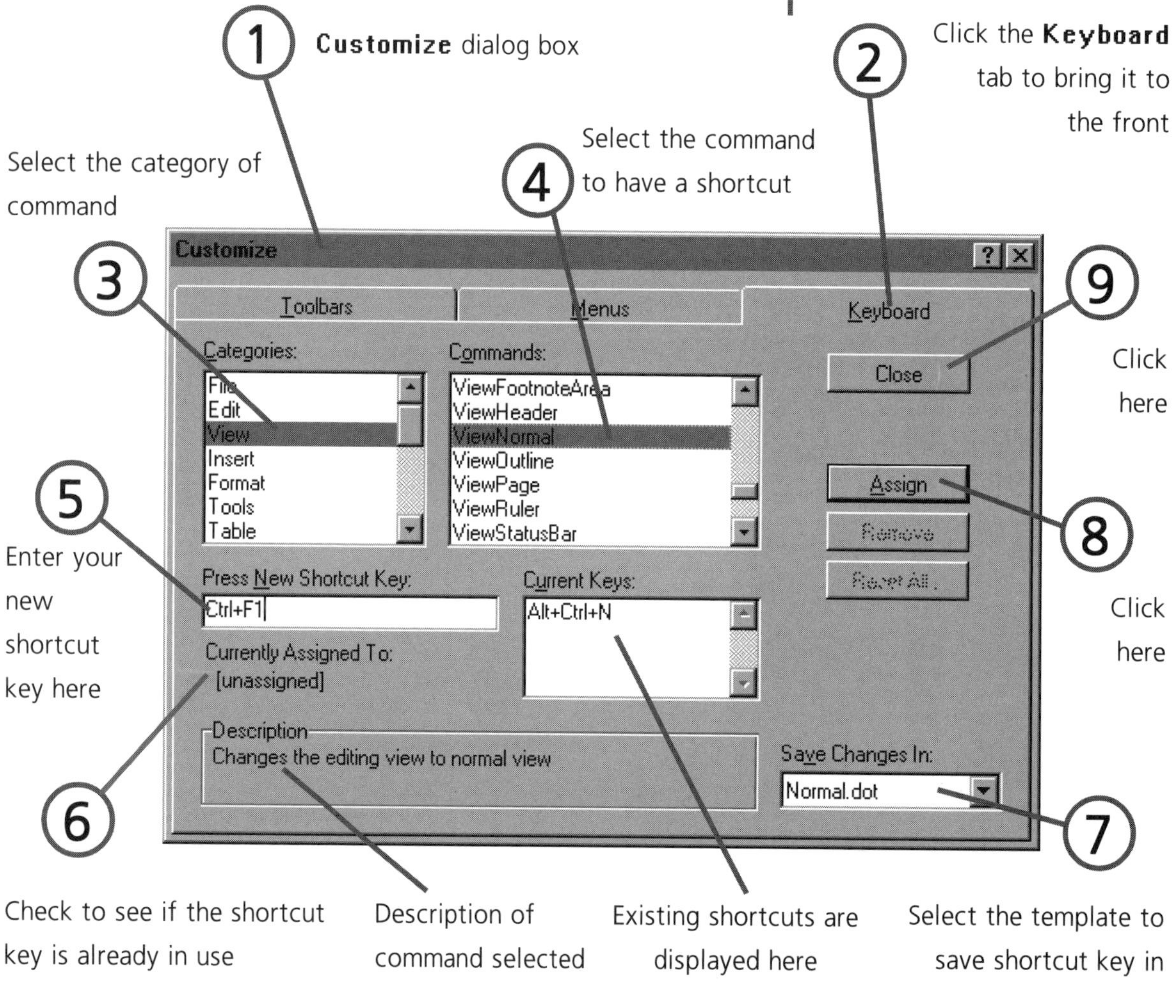

1 **Customize** dialog box

2 Click the **Keyboard** tab to bring it to the front

3 Select the category of command

4 Select the command to have a shortcut

5 Enter your new shortcut key here

6 Check to see if the shortcut key is already in use

7 Select the template to save shortcut key in

8 Click here

9 Click here

Description of command selected

Existing shortcuts are displayed here

Customize

Toolbars | Menus | Keyboard

Categories: File, Edit, View, Insert, Format, Tools, Table

Commands: ViewFootnoteArea, ViewHeader, ViewNormal, ViewOutline, ViewPage, ViewRuler, ViewStatusBar

Close

Assign

Remove

Reset All...

Press New Shortcut Key: Ctrl+F1

Current Keys: Alt+Ctrl+N

Currently Assigned To: [unassigned]

Description
Changes the editing view to normal view

Save Changes In: Normal.dot

3 In the **Categories** scrollable list, select the category of the command you want to assign a keyboard shortcut to.

4 In the **Commands** scrollable list, locate the command.

5 In the **Press New Shortcut Key** field, enter your desired shortcut. Do this by literally pressing the keys you want as the shortcut.

6 View the **Currently Assigned To** field directly below the **Press New Shortcut Key** entry field — Word tells you whether the key is already in use or not. If the shortcut key you want is unassigned you can use it now. If it's assigned already, you are about to override its previous use. Choose another shortcut key if you want, or go to step 7.

7 Locate the template to save your shortcut.

8 Click **Assign.**

9 Click **Close**.

Tip:

You can remove a shortcut key, too, by locating the command in the Customize dialog box, selecting the shortcut key in the Current Keys field, then clicking Remove.

Tip:

If you save a shortcut key in the default template (Normal.dot) it will be available in *all* new documents you create. If you save it in a *specific* template, on the other hand, it will be available only in new documents you create using that specific template.

Tip:

You can revert back to Word's default shortcut key arrangement by clicking the Reset All button on the Customize dialog box. Bear in mind though, that this reverts *all* shortcut key changes you have made.

Toolbars

Basic steps:

While Word has a large number of toolbars, they may not always be to a user's liking. They might have the wrong buttons for your particular tasks, or they might not have the buttons you want at all.

You can customize toolbars (by adding, deleting, changing, and moving around buttons), and you can create your own toolbars (designing buttons from scratch if you want). You can also choose from a wide range of built-in buttons to assign to commands in Word.

ADAPTING A TOOLBAR

1 Choose **Tools→Customize**, or type Alt+T then C, to call up the **Customize** dialog box.

2 Click the **Toolbars** tab if it's not already in front.

3 Drag a button onto the toolbar of your choice to add it (or drag a button *off* a toolbar to delete it).

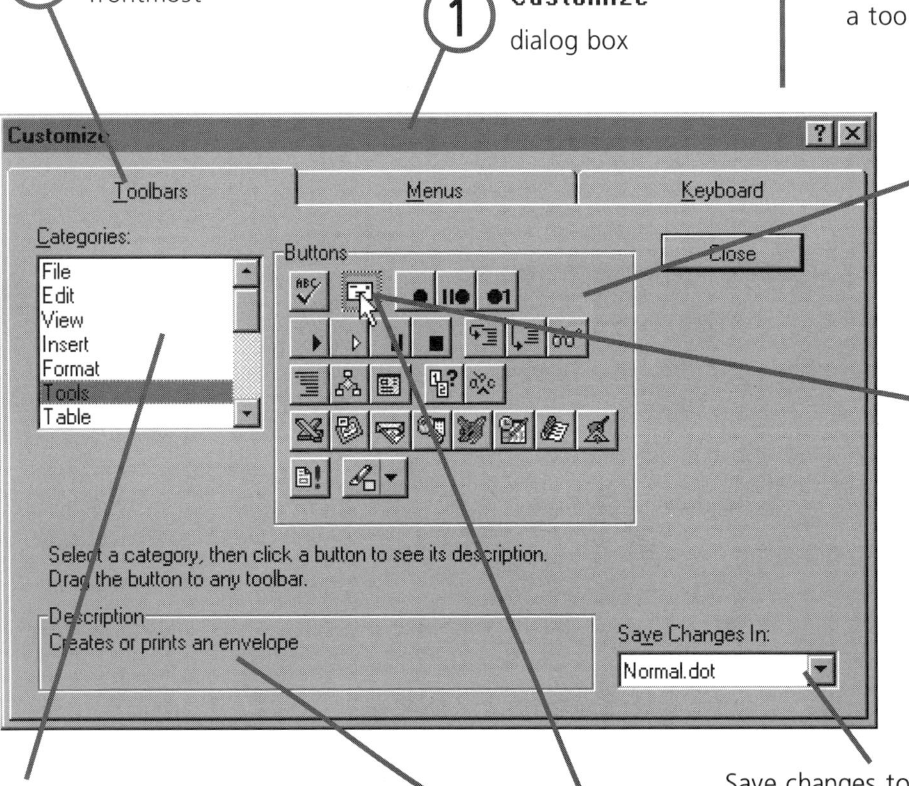

2 Click if not already frontmost
1 **Customize** dialog box
Customize
Toolbars
Menus
Keyboard
Categories:
File
Edit
View
Insert
Format
Tools
Table
Buttons
Close
Select a category, then click a button to see its description.
Drag the button to any toolbar.
Description
Creates or prints an envelope
Save Changes In:
Normal.dot
Built-in buttons available for commands in the chosen category
Drag the chosen button to the toolbar of your choice
Categories of commands
Click a button above and you see a description of its command here
Save changes to a template (default is *Normal.dot* — which means changes affect all your Word documents)

CREATING A TOOLBAR

1 Choose **View ↳ Toolbars**, or type Alt + V then T, to call up the **Toolbars** dialog box.

2 Click **New**, to call up the **New Toolbar** dialog box.

3 Give the new toolbar a name.

4 Click **OK** — the new toolbar is displayed as a floating toolbar on the screen and the **Customize** dialog box is called up with the **Toolbars** tab already frontmost (see below).

5 Drag buttons and adapt your new toolbar as before.

Tip:

You can move (or delete) a toolbar button without the Customize dialog box. Just hold down Alt and drag the button to its new location (or drag it off the toolbar altogether to delete it). If you hold down Alt + Ctrl while you drag, the button is copied.

Drag selected buttons to your toolbar

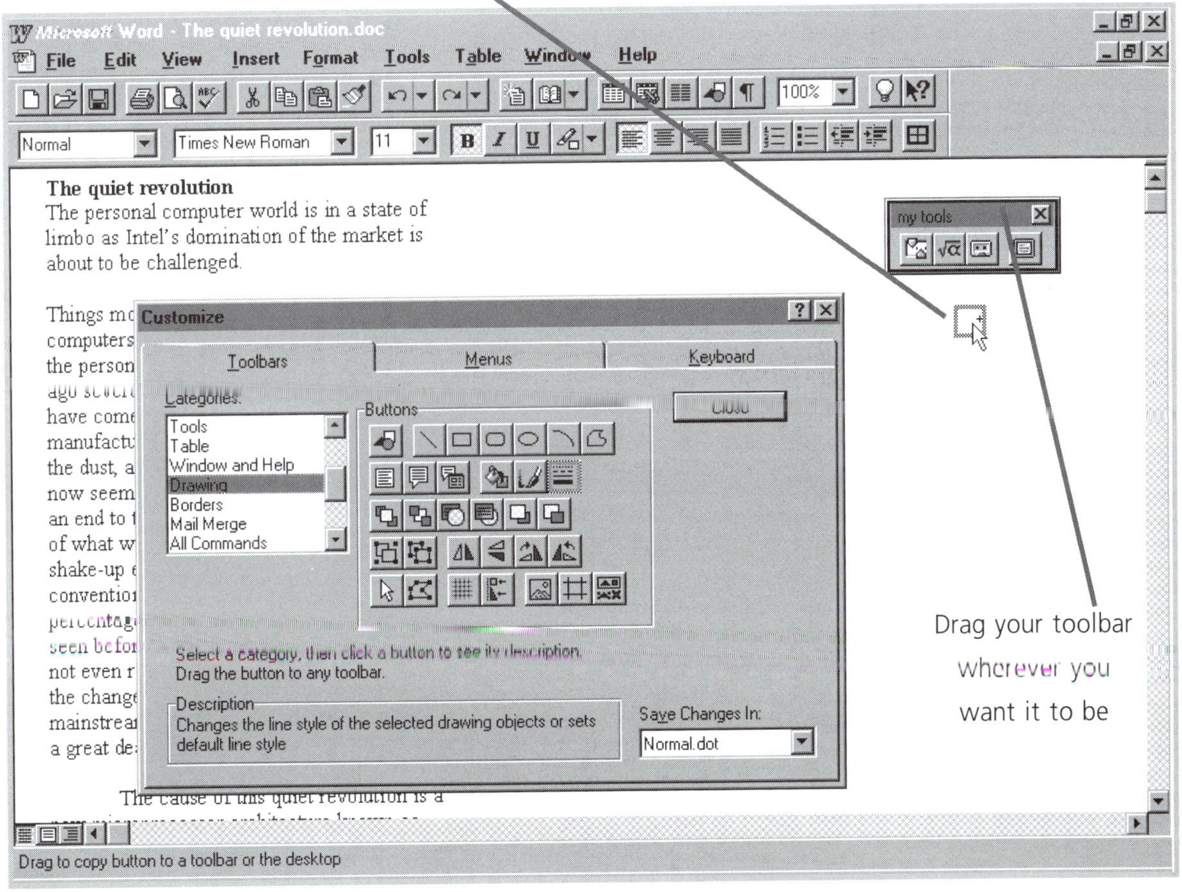

Drag your toolbar wherever you want it to be

Summary for Section 7

- Before printing, preview your work in Print Preview. This way you save some paper finding out where your overall problems are.

- Use the **Print** dialog box to adjust controls regarding the pages you print, the number of copies you want, and so on.

- Use the **Options** dialog box with the **Print** tab frontmost to adjust finer details of printing.

- Use the Print button to print without any dialog boxes.

- Start up Word automatically each time you turn on your computer by copying Word's icon to the **StartUp** folder in the Explorer window for the Start menu's **Programs** folder.

- Assign your own shortcut keys to commands you use a lot through the **Customize** dialog box, with the **Keyboard** tab frontmost.

- Adapt existing toolbars, and create your own toolbars, through the **Customize** dialog box, with the **Toolbars** tab frontmost.

Index

A

AutoCorrect 100
AutoFormat 46
AutoText 102

B

Borders 17, 66
  toolbar 66
Borders and shading 66
Buttons 12, 15

C

Character
  formatting 46, 48
Character styles 121
Clipboard 38
Columns 74, 86
Commands
  assigning shortcut keys 144
Counting
  words, lines, paragraphs 113
Creating a new document 23
Cut, copy, and paste 38

D

Dingbats 42
Document 23
  based on template 128
  creating 128
  setting up 76
  window 3
Drag-and-drop editing 40

E

Edit menu 4
Editing
  drag-and-drop 40
  text 30
Entering
  symbols 42
Exiting 25

F

File menu 4
Finding
  formats 92
  text 92
Fonts
  formatting toolbar 49
  size 49
  TrueType 49
Format menu 5
Formats
  character 48
Formatting 46
  automatic 46
  character formatting 46
  creating styles 122
  painting 53
  paragraph 54
  paragraph formatting 46
  removing 52
  section 74
  styles 118
  tables 112
  toolbar 121
Formatting codes
  Word's lack of 56
Full screen view 19

G

Graphics 17
  borders and shading 115
  editing 115
  filters 115
  importing 114
  resizing 115
Gutter 78

H

Headers and footers 74, 79, 80
  toolbar 82
Help
  for WordPerfect users 11, 29
  menu 5
  on-line Word system 6

I

Indenting
  keyboard shortcuts 59
  paragraph dialog box 57
  paragraph formats
    paragraph dialog box 57
  toolbar buttons 15, 56
Insert menu 5
Insertion point 3, 51, 55, 75

K

Keyboard shortcuts
  assigning your own 125

L

Leaders 65
Line count 113
Line numbering 74, 84

M

Margins 17, 74, 77
Mathematical symbols 42
Menu bar 3, 4
Menus 4
Minimize 25
Mistakes 36

N

Normal template 133
Normal view 16

O

On-line help 6
Opening 22
Orphan 58
Outline view 18, 104
Outlining 104
  procedure for 106
  symbols 105
  toolbar 105

P

Page count 113
Page layout view 17, 79
Painting a format 53
Paragraph
  formats 54
  formatting 46
  styles 46
Paragraph count 113
Paragraph dialog box
  indenting 57
Paragraph formats 54
  indenting 56
Paragraph formatting 46
Print preview 137, 138
  toolbar 138
Printing 137, 138, 140
  options 141

R

Replacing
  formats 94
  text 94
Ruler
  indent stops 56

S

Saving 21
Section 74
  end 74
  formatting 74
Selecting text 32
Setting up a document 76
Shading 66
Shortcut keys 144
  assigning commands 144
Spelling
  checking 96
  spelling button 96
  underline highlighting 96
    turning off 99
Starting up
  at turn-on 142
Status bar 3, 29
Styles 118
  character 121
  copying 126
  creating 122, 124
  deleting 129
  modifying 124
  paragraph 121
Symbols 42

T

Table menu 5
Tables 108
  AutoFormat 112
  converting into text 111
  converting text into 111
  creating from toolbar 109
  dragging boundaries 110
  dragging gridlines 110
  formatting 112
  moving around 109
  simple, using tabs 62
Tabs 60, 64
Templates 23, 128, 132
  creating 134
  modifying built-in 135
  normal 133
Text
  editing 30
  selecting 32
Text flow
  orphan 58
  widow 58
Toolbars 3, 12, 14
  creating, modifying 146
Tools menu 5
ToolTips 6
TrueType 49
Typographical symbols 42

U

Undo 37

V

View menu 4

W

Widow 58
Window menu 5
Word count 113
WordPerfect users help 11, 29

Z

Zooming 20